Manipulating Data

SELECT Retrieves rows from tables.

INSERT Puts rows in tables.

UPDATE Changes data values.

DELETE Removes rows from tables.

COMMIT WORK Makes changes permanent.

ROLLBACK Disregards changes.

OPEN Readies a cursor* for use.

FETCH Retrieves rows from cursors.*

CLOSE Empties a cursor* of data.

CASE Expressions Specify conditional values.

CAST Expressions Convert datatypes.

Datetime Value Functions Reference current date or time.

Numeric Value Functions Perform arithmetic operations.

Predicates Define sophisticated tests of data for operations.

Row and Table Value Constructors Specify rows and tables.

String Value Functions Operate on character or bit strings.

Subqueries Queries* used within other statements.

Establishing Security and Data Controls

CREATE ASSERTION Defines a general rule for data.

DROP ASSERTION Eliminates a general rule for data.

SET CONSTRAINTS MODE Controls when constraints* are checked.

SET SESSION AUTHORIZATION Specifies the current session user.

SET TRANSACTION Prevents or allows changing of data.

GRANT Gives users or applications privileges on objects.*

REVOKE Takes away privileges on objects.*

Constraints Details on restricting data.

NOTE See glossary.

SQL

INSTANT REFERENCE

SQL

INSTANT REFERENCE

Martin Gruber

San Francisco • Paris • Düsseldorf • Soest • London

SYBEX®

Associate Publisher: Richard Mills
Contracts and Licensing Manager: Kristine O'Callaghan
Acquisitions & Developmental Editor: Denise Santoro-Lincoln
Editor: Bronwyn Shone Erickson
Technical Editor: Keith Hare
Book Designers: Patrick Dintino and Maureen Forys
Electronic Publishing Specialist: Maureen Forys, Happenstance Type-O-Rama
Associate Production Editor: Jennifer Durning
Proofreaders: Dave Nash and Suzanne Stein
Indexer: Ted Laux
Cover Designer: Design Site
Cover Illustrator/Photographer: Sergie Loobkoff, Design Site

Library of Congress Card Number: 99-64122

ISBN: 0-7821-2539-5

Manufactured in the United States of America

10 9 8 7 6 5 4 3 2 1

Table of Contents

Introduction

This book provides a reference on SQL, the industry standard language for interfacing to relational databases. Relational database systems are the most widely used database systems in the world today. These systems have solved many of the problems that had plagued the earlier nonrelational products. Earlier products required programmers and database administrators to become engaged with the details of how the data was stored and structured in the database, which made applications complex to develop and nightmarish to modify. Relational systems allow you to work with the data at a higher level. All operations on the data are handled by a program called a DBMS (database management system), which responds only to statements expressed in a high-level language. Although some products also supply their own proprietary languages, the industry standard language supported by all significant relational products is SQL. Therefore anyone who plans to make use of relational databases will be using SQL.

The SQL Standard: Something Old, Something New

SQL was developed by IBM in the 1970s. The first company to implement it commercially was Oracle. These two companies were followed by several others, each of which introduced variations into the language. In the interest of keeping SQL one language rather than several, the industry decided to standardize it.

SQL has been an official standard, promulgated by the International Institute for Standardization (ISO) and its American affiliate, the American National Standards Institute (ANSI), since 1986. The early SQL standards (SQL86 and SQL89) mostly ratified the common ground between various existing products and left the rest of the decisions up to the implementers who built these products. However, as computer systems became more integrated and the marketplace began calling for applications and skill sets that could apply to multiple databases, there was a push for a more complete SQL standard. Also, there had been some new ideas for features to add to the language, and it seemed best to implement these in a standardized way. This led to SQL92, which is the standard commercially implemented as of this writing (2000).

SQL92 both introduced many new features and standardized features that vendors previously had implemented in their own fashion. The most important thing about this standard, though, is its relative completeness. The intention of the ISO is that you can learn SQL92 and, with only a little additional knowledge about particular systems, operate on databases on all conforming systems in the same way, and you can integrate the data in all of them. As a result, the standard itself is both more complex and more important than it had been.

The SQL92 standard builds on the previous standards, SQL86 and SQL89, so that, with minor exceptions, everything specified in the previous standards applies also to SQL92. This book clearly indicates what is part of the older standards and what is part of SQL92. Therefore, you can use this book regardless of which standard your system conforms to.

The newest SQL standard is SQL99. This is an enormously complex work, and it is not yet clear how much industry support it will attract. It frankly seems unlikely that anyone will implement SQL99 in its entirety. However, SQL99 is designed to allow for this. Rather than having a series of conformance levels, each incorporating its predecessors, SQL99 has a basic functionality called "Core SQL" and various optional enhancement levels. Core is the prerequisite for all of the enhanced levels, but the enhanced levels are (generally) independent of one another. This means a product that implements Core can pick and choose which enhanced levels it might also wish to support.

Part IV, Chapter 1 of this book provides an overview of SQL99, and Part IV, Chapter 2 delves into more detail on Core SQL. These parts of the book are written in a narrative rather than reference form because they introduce new concepts and because they describe functionality that is not yet available on the market in the form the standard specifies. The gist of SQL99 definitely reflects where the language is going, and products are likely to follow its approach in a general sense, particularly in regard to object-oriented and procedural extensions to SQL. Nonetheless, it is not yet clear (as of the year 2000) how many companies will undertake implementing it as such. There was also official U.S. government certification for SQL92 conformance, which is not the case for SQL99, so this may lead to companies claiming conformance while actually taking liberties with the details.

Who Can Use This Book?

Given that it documents a standard rather than a specific product, this book is invaluable for anybody using SQL in a database system that conforms to the old or new standards at any level. This includes virtually all SQL products. Those who use SQL are primarily applications developers, Web site or Intranet developers, database administrators, database designers, systems designers, systems analysts, and relatively sophisticated end users. People in this last group may wish to use SQL interactively to store and retrieve database information, although this is often done through an application, partly to make it easier for users who do not know SQL.

How This Book Is Organized

This book has four parts:

- Part I explains how relational databases work and outlines the SQL language, highlighting special features of the 92 standard. If you already know SQL, it is still a good idea to look over the section on SQL92 features.

- Part II is the Statement Reference. For each statement (commands in SQL are traditionally called "statements," both in the standard and in the literature), you'll find the syntax, an explanation of usage (at the Full SQL92 conformance level), notes on differences at lower or earlier conformance levels, and cross-references to related entries. Examples are included as needed.

- Part III covers Common Elements. This is material that is common to several statements or contexts and is too detailed to specify thoroughly everywhere it is used.

- Part IV, Chapter 1 is an overview of SQL99. The SQL99 specification is over four thousand pages in length, so this is necessarily an overview rather than a detailed reference. Regardless of whether the product you are using directly supports SQL99, SQL99 embodies the industry consensus regarding the future development of the language, and some of its features already have commercial support, but not in a fully standardized way. Therefore, it is helpful to understand SQL99 conceptually, even if you do not have an implementation of it in front of you. SQL99 does introduce changes into the basic way SQL works, including such things as object-orientation and procedural extensions, and these things have been or are being implemented regardless of whether a given product strictly follows the standard.

- Part IV, Chapter 2 covers Core SQL. Products that support SQL99 at all must support Core SQL, so this is the portion of SQL99 that is likely to find widespread support first. However, it does involve some new concepts beyond how SQL has been used traditionally. Therefore, this part also takes a narrative form.

The appendices cover more global issues, including embedded SQL, dynamic SQL, the module language, linguistic elements and conventions, and error codes. There is also a glossary.

The inside covers of the book include a Contents Grouped by Subject chart, designed to make it easier to locate statements whose names you may not know.

Essentially, we assume you probably will read some or all of Part I, refer to Parts II and III (the core of the book) as needed, and study Part IV where it is relevant to the product(s) you use.

Part I

Introduction to SQL

The following is a complete reference to the SQL92 standard, which is the version implemented commercially as of this publication (2000). It also includes some coverage of common variations on the standard. The reference has the following structure:

- Part I: Introduction to SQL. This is the part you're reading now.

- Part II: SQL Statement Reference. This is an alphabetical reference covering every SQL statement in the standard.

- Part III: Common Elements. This is an alphabetical reference covering elements that are common to many of the SQL statements in Part II.

- Part IV: SQL99.

  - Chapter 1: SQL99—An Overview.

  - Chapter 2: Core SQL99.

- Appendix A: Mapping SQL to Other Languages.

- Appendix B: Specification of the Module Language.

- Appendix C: Specification of Dynamic SQL.

- Appendix D: SQL Linguistic Definitions and Conventions.

- Appendix E: Upgrade Path from SQL92 to Core SQL99.

- Appendix F: Error Codes.

- Appendix G: Glossary.

- Index.

The rest of this introduction provides an overview of relational databases and the SQL language and an overview of the notable features of the standard.

SQL: An Overview

This part of the book provides a general context for the specific information that follows. It begins with an overview of SQL and relational database principles for the uninitiated. The initiated may want to skip ahead to the "Notable Features of Standard SQL" section, which outlines the major features of the 92 standard. There are a considerable number of these. Note that a detailed tutorial in SQL is beyond the scope of this book, which is intended merely as a reference. For a tutorial in SQL, see *Mastering SQL* by the same author and publisher.

The Fundamentals of SQL and Relational Databases

SQL (pronounced "sequel"; the letters originally stood for Structured Query Language, but by now the acronym is mostly used as the name) was developed in the 1970s by IBM. It has become the standard language used to interface to relational database management systems (DBMSs) such as IBM's own DB2 and SQL/DS products, Oracle, Microsoft SQL Server and Access, Sybase Adaptive Server Enterprise, Sybase SQL Anywhere, Computer Associates' Ingres, Informix, MySQL, mSQL, First SQL, and others. It is safe to say that if you are going to use relational databases in the near future, you will be working with SQL.

Typically, a relational database product includes more than just the DBMS. The DBMS—sometimes called the "back end," the database "engine," or even simply the "server," though the last term is also used in a more general sense. It stores the data and retrieves or updates it in response to SQL statements. In a client/server environment, the DBMS typically resides on the server. In an Internet or Intranet environment, it will typically be accessed by the Web server, constituting a three-tiered architecture (the tiers being the browser, the Web server, and the database). There may be any number of additional layers in addition to those three.

Also, relational products usually provide various "front end" or "middleware" tools that make it easier to communicate with the back end and provide you with facilities to use the data that you have retrieved. Among the tools you may encounter are forms, report generators, fourth-generation languages (4GLs), graphical query languages, user-interface generators, multimedia presentation software, hypertext authoring systems, CAD/CAM systems, spreadsheets, and good, old-fashioned, direct-to-user interfaces. All of these use SQL to request the DBMS to perform various actions. The DBMS is in charge of storing, organizing, and retrieving the data, ensuring its integrity, protecting security, and keeping simultaneous users of the data from interfering with each other. Our focus here is on how the front end must interface to the back end, rather than on the nature of the front-end tools or on the details of how the back end is actually implemented.

Forms of SQL

Technically, SQL is a data sub-language, which means it is only used to interface to the database; it does not, in itself, have the features necessary to produce complete programs. It is used in three ways:

1. Interactive or stand-alone SQL is employed by users to directly extract information from or enter it into the database. For example, a user could ask the database to produce a list of account activity for the current month. The output would simply be sent to the screen or possibly redirected to a file or printer.

2. Static SQL is fixed SQL code, written in advance rather than generated at runtime, used in applications. By fixed SQL code, we mean that the statements themselves do not vary, although they can contain variables or parameters that pass values to or from an application. There are two versions of Static SQL. In Embedded SQL, SQL code is incorporated into the source code of another language. Most of the application is written in a languages such as C++ or Java, but when the database needs to be addressed, it is done in SQL. This is the version that uses variables to pass values around. The other version of Static SQL is the module language. In this approach, modules of SQL are

linked with modules of code in other languages. The modules of SQL code pass values to and from parameters, similarly to how parameters are passed through subprogram calls in most procedural languages. This was the approach the original SQL standard advocated; Embedded SQL was not officially part of the standard until later.

3. Dynamic SQL is SQL code generated by an application at runtime. It is used instead of the static approach when the SQL code that would be needed cannot be determined at the time the application is written—it depends on choices that the user makes. This form of SQL often can be generated by tools such as graphical query languages in response to user activity.

The requirements of the three forms are different, and this is reflected in the language constructs each uses. Both Static and Dynamic SQL supplement stand-alone SQL with features that are applicable only to their situations. This book treats all three forms together, noting those items that apply only to a particular form. The bulk of the language is the same for all three forms.

A Relational Database Primer

Relational databases (and the SQL standard) are based on a few simple rules or principles:

1. All data values are drawn from simple datatypes. Unlike other languages you may be familiar with, SQL has historically had no arrays, pointers, vectors, or other complex datatypes. This situation changes in SQL99.

2. All data in a relational database is represented in the form of two-dimensional tables (*relations* in the mathematical jargon). A table contains zero or more rows (*tuples* in jargon) and one or more columns (*attributes*). All rows in a table have the same sequence of columns filled with values, but with a different series of values in those columns. Table I.1 illustrates a simple table.

3. Once you've entered data into a database, you can compare values from different columns, usually in different tables, and merge rows where matches are found. This enables you to correlate and perform some fairly sophisticated processing of your data across the entire database.

4. All operations are defined by logic, not by the position of a row within a table. That is, you ask for all rows where (x = 3) and not for the first, third, and fifth rows, for example. The rows of a relational database table are in arbitrary order—the order in which they appear will not necessarily reflect the order in which they were entered or that in which they are stored.

5. Because you can't identify rows by position, you need to have one or more columns that are unique within the table to identify each row. These columns are called the table's *primary key*. In Table I.1, the first column serves this purpose.

TABLE I.1: Clients—A Simple Relational Database Table

ID_NUM	NAME	CITY	STATE
1809	Stoklas	San Francisco	CA
1996	Abril	New York	NY
1777	Vencera	Portland	OR

Now let's see what these rules mean in practice.

One of the strengths of the relational approach is that you can deal with the data as information and (ideally) not worry about the details of how it is represented or physically maintained in the database itself. Having to deal with these kinds of implementation details made the older hierarchical and network database systems cumbersome and difficult to manage. If you are used to those systems, however, you will have to learn to change your approach a bit to deal with the relational world.

NOTE The terms "record" for row and "field" for column are still sometimes used but are holdovers from older systems and actually refer to how information is organized on disk. Although many relational systems are implemented using record and field disk organization, they need not be, so this is not the best terminology to use.

Designing a Database

One virtue of the relational approach is simplicity. All data is represented, and all output emerges, in the same simple form: tables. Problems do arise when complex situations have to be modeled this way, but perfect solutions are rather scarce in this world.

What happens when a column can logically have multiple values for the same row? Let's suppose we need to add a telephone number column to the table. Well, most people have at least two phone numbers—home and work—and they may have more—fax, cell phone, beeper, vacation home, voicemail, and so on. One of the basic premises of the relational model is that column values are atomic—one value per column in each row, period. Put more than one value in and they will be treated as one value by the DBMS anyway.

The solution is to build another table (called, say, Client_Phone), with one column for the phone number, one for a description of the type of number (home, fax, voicemail, and so on), and one indicating when the person normally can be reached at that number. Of course, we also have to relate the phone number to the person we will find on the other end—the person represented in our first table—so we must find a way to relate the two tables to one another.

We do this by putting the primary key—our unique identifying column from the Clients table—in the Client_Phone table, too. Since this number is unique for every client, we always know which client a given number matches. (For clarity's sake, we could also include the name in Client_Phone, but this would be redundant and take up more disk space. Since the number links the two tables, we can always determine the proper name.) The id_num column in Client_Phone is called a *foreign key*, and we say that it references the primary key of Clients. (In this book, keys referenced by foreign keys are called *parent keys*.) Table I.2 illustrates this relationship. If all the foreign key values in Client_Phone reference values that actually are present in Clients, the system has *referential integrity*. If they do not, we're in trouble, because it would mean that there are phone numbers in the database for clients who are nonexistent or who cannot be identified.

TABLE I.2: The Client_Phone table

ID_NUM	PHONE	TYPE	AVAIL
1809	415 555 8956	home	after 6 PM
1809	510 555 6220	work	9–5 MF
1996	212 555 0199	work	app. 10–7
1996	212 555 7878	beeper	any
1777	503 555 2279	fax	any
1777	503 555 9188	home	after 7 PM

We also need a primary key for the Client_Phone table—every table should have a primary key. We can't use id_num because it is not unique (it will be repeated for each phone number of the same client). What about the phone number itself? This is better, but it is possible that we will get two clients in the same household or office. If this were to happen, we probably still would want to track their phone numbers separately. Otherwise, this situation could require a lot of special handling that it probably wouldn't get.

A primary or a foreign key need not be a single column. We can combine the id_num and phone columns. This combination should always be unique because, if we list the same number for the same person twice, we've really made the same entry twice and should delete one anyway. So the combination of id_num and phone is the logical primary key of the Client_Phone table. A key of more than one column is variously referred to by different products as a multicolumn, composite, or concatenated key.

To summarize, each table has a group of one or more columns that must, as a group, have a different set of values for each row. This value, or group of values together, makes up the primary key and serves to identify the row. A table may also have a group of one or more columns that indicate a relationship to another table. This group is called a foreign key, and the group of columns in the other table to which it relates is called its parent key. A parent key must be a unique identifier, so that you can tell to which row of the parent key table a foreign key is referring. The foreign key will have the same number and type of columns as the parent key, although it may use different names. The foreign key values do not have to be, and generally are not, unique in their own table, only in the table of the parent key. A system has referential integrity if all foreign key values are present in the referenced parent key.

> **NOTE** A parent key must be a unique identifier. This means it must be either a primary key or a unique key. A unique key is a group of one or more columns that must be distinct for logical reasons, although not for the sake of database structure. For example, if your database stores insurance ID numbers for employees, but uses social security numbers as the primary key in a table, the insurance ID numbers might be a unique key. Generally, parent keys are primary keys. Since every table should have a primary key, there should always be one that you can use. Since primary keys, like foreign keys, are a fundamental part of the database structure, they are also a more logical choice than unique keys, which are distinct for reasons external to the database structure.

This process of breaking down complex situations so they can be represented with simple tables is called *normalization*. By normalizing a database, you remove redundancy and repeating groups of data, and you ensure that every column depends on, and only on, the key.

Joining Tables

Now, how do we put the two tables back together to match the phone numbers with the information about the clients who have them? The two tables remain separate entities in the database, but when we extract the information contained in them, we can link each foreign key value to its parent key and to whatever other columns we might want to see from either table. An operation that extracts information from the database is called a *query*, and one that extracts it from more than one table at the same time by relating columns in one table to columns in the other(s) is called a *join*. A join of a foreign key to its parent key is usually—although not in the official standard, which uses this term somewhat differently (See Part II: SELECT)—called a *natural join*, because it is built into the structure of the database. It reunites what we put asunder in separate tables for the sake of the relational structure. There are other kinds of joins that are explained under SELECT in Part II.

A group of related tables that model some real-world situation is called a *schema*. A description of the schema's contents—how many tables there are, how many columns in each, and so on—is contained in a special group of tables called the INFORMATION_ SCHEMA in the official SQL standard. In some products, this is called the data dictionary or catalog, although the term "catalog" is used somewhat differently in the standard. The information in the INFORMATION _SCHEMA is called the *metadata*—the data about the data. Putting it in tables means that all requests for information about the database operate the same as requests for information from the database and produce their output in the same structure: tables. This uniformity is called *closure* and is considered one of the strengths of the relational approach.

A schema is owned by a *user*. (Technically, it is owned by an *Authorization ID*, which generally means a user, although there are exceptions, as noted under "Application-Owned Privileges," later in this section. For simplicity's sake, this discussion will use the term "user.") The user fills the schema with *objects*. The definition of "object" used in the relational world is different from that used in the world of object-oriented programming, which unfortu- nately can be expected to generate no end of confusion as the two worlds converge. An object in the relational sense is simply any- thing in the schema that has a name and a persistent identity. The objects that we have seen so far have been tables, but there are other kinds as well. A user can grant other users access to the tables he or she owns, by using the GRANT statement. There are various types of access, called *privileges*, that will allow the users to apply various statements to the objects. See Part III for an explanation of the possible privileges.

See Also   Part II: GRANT.

Basics of the SQL Language

SQL differs from conventional programming languages in several ways. First, it is nonprocedural. A language like C gives the com- puter step-by-step instructions for carrying out a task. SQL merely specifies what is to be done and lets the DBMS worry about how to do it. This is in keeping with the relational philosophy. The DBMS is a "black box"—how things are done inside it need not concern you; you only have to worry about getting the correct answer from the database or making the desired changes to it. By shielding the user from the implementation, SQL simplifies operations and offers greater flexibility to database implementers. With SQL99, some procedural constructs are introduced into SQL, however.

For example, if we want to extract all data from our Clients table for customers in Prague, we would use the SELECT statement to form a query as follows:

```
SELECT *
FROM Clients
WHERE city = 'Prague';
```

The first line means simply "select all columns," and the FROM clause indicates the table from which to select them. But the WHERE clause is a bit more interesting. We are not just asking for a particular row but rather for all rows that meet this criterion. It doesn't matter if there are zero or fifty thousand rows for Prague in the Clients table; they all will be produced by this statement. If we are just looking for one specific row in a table, the way to do it is to look for the primary key value. (This is one reason primary keys are so important.) SQL statements generally work on arbitrarily large sets of data at once. This is called *set-at-a-time operation*; most languages employ *item-at-a-time operation*.

Another important feature of SQL is its three-valued logic (3VL). In most languages a Boolean expression can be either TRUE or FALSE. SQL, however, allows NULL values to be entered into the database. A NULL is a marker used to fill a place in a column where data is missing for any reason. (The value might be not applicable, like the hair color of a bird; missing, like the hair color of a bald man; or unknown, like the hair color of a man wearing a hat.) When NULLs are used in comparisons, the Boolean result is neither TRUE nor FALSE, but UNKNOWN. This is probably the most controversial aspect of the SQL language. A number of subtleties involved in 3VL are discussed in the "Predicates" entry.

Traditionally, SQL statements are categorized by function. These categories are a useful conceptual tool and may have practical importance in some situations. The 92 standard indicates a number of specialized categories, but there are three that are generally under-stood and traditionally used in discussions about databases. These three are defined below:

- Data Definition Language (DDL) comprises all the statements used to define schemata and the objects within them. The most important statements in DDL are those used to create the various objects, such as CREATE SCHEMA, CREATE TABLE, CREATE VIEW, CREATE ASSERTION, and CREATE DOMAIN.

- Data Manipulation Language (DML) comprises all the state-ments that store, alter, or retrieve the data in the tables. The essential statements here are SELECT, INSERT, UPDATE, and DELETE. SELECT is the statement used to form queries; it is perhaps the most complex single statement in SQL. The other statements affect the data in the tables.

- Data Control Language (DCL) comprises all the statements that control what users may or may not do with the objects in the database. (Often, and in the 92 standard, this is regarded as part of DDL.) The basic statements here are GRANT and REVOKE.

For reference, the other categories supported in the 92 standard are transaction statements, connection statements, session state-ments, dynamic statements, and diagnostics statements.

The main practical import of the categories is that the standard does not require that you be able to mix DDL and DML statements in the same transaction (a group of statements that succeed or fail as a unit) See COMMIT WORK in Part II. Most products do allow it, but if yours does not, it helps to understand these categories.

Embedded SQL

In Embedded SQL, you enter SQL statements into the source code of an application written in a conventional programming language, which is called the *host language*. An early SQL standard unofficially supported Pascal, COBOL, Fortran, and PL/I. SQL92 added C (which applies also to C++), Ada, and MUMPS to the list and makes the support official. Implementations are, however, free to choose which languages they wish to support. Actually, most products that use Embedded SQL have been supporting C for a while. This section pro-vides an overview of how Embedded SQL works. In most respects, it is the same in all supported languages.

Values are passed from the output of SQL statements to variables that can be referenced by the host code. Values are passed to SQL statements from the host code in the same way. All host variables that will be referenced in SQL statements have to be declared in a SQL DECLARE SECTION. As we mentioned, SQL allows NULLs to be entered into a table when data is missing. These behave differently in comparisons than any known values. NULLs are, of course, not used in most other languages, so Embedded SQL provides a way to process NULLs by using *indicator variables*. These are numeric variables used in conjunction with other variables to indicate whether they are NULL. If the indicator is negative, the corresponding variable is NULL; otherwise it is not. The indicator can be used to control program flow and to force appropriate results from comparisons. In addition to the variables used to pass values, you must DECLARE either SQLSTATE or SQLCODE (or both). These pass messages about the results of the last SQL statement—essentially error, warning, or success status codes. SQLCODE is from the old standard and is still supported, but it has been deprecated, meaning that it may not be supported in the future. It is being retained to protect the durability of existing application code. SQLSTATE is the preferred way to handle this now, as it standardizes many error codes, whereas SQLCODE's error codes were all implementation-dependent.

Overview of the SQL Standards

Although SQL was first commercially implemented by Oracle in 1979, there was no official standard until 1986, when one was published jointly by ANSI (the American National Standards Institute) and the ISO (International Organization for Standardization). The 86 standard was revised in 1989 to introduce features that enforce referential integrity.

NOTE Because ANSI is a part of ISO, this book will refer to both organizations simply as ISO.

By the time the 86 standard appeared, a number of products on the market already used SQL, and ISO attempted to draft a standard to which they could all conform relatively painlessly. ISO did this in part by leaving a great many things up to the various implementers and defining a fairly minimal standard. Certain essential functions, such as the destruction of objects and the revocation of privileges, were omitted from the standard entirely. Now, with the heterogeneous computing world becoming increasingly interconnected, developers and users want to be able to interface to various database engines transparently. As a result, there is a demand for standardization of features previously left to the implementer's discretion. In addition, several years of experience and research have produced some new ideas that many would like to see implemented in a uniform way. To address these needs, ISO developed SQL92.

SQL99 constitutes a further building on SQL92. It takes SQL further than it has gone, for example, by making it usable as a complete applications programming language and by providing an approach to integrating the relational and object-oriented methodologies.

The general pattern with all of the standards is as follows:

- SQL86 is the beginning.

- SQL89 is a superset of SQL86. In other words, everything in SQL86 is also in SQL89.

- SQL92 is a superset of SQL89 with minor exceptions. There are three levels to SQL92: Entry, Intermediate, and Full. Each of these is a superset of its predecessor. As of this publication (2000), most products support Entry SQL92 with some features drawn from the more advanced parts. Entry SQL92 is a superset of SQL89.

- SQL99 is a superset of Entry SQL92. It includes some features from Intermediate and Full conformance but does not have either of those levels as a prerequisite. SQL99 consists of Core SQL and several optional enhanced levels of conformance. The enhanced levels are all supersets of Core SQL but not of one another (with one exception).

Since SQL92 is essentially a superset of the 89 standard, you will be able to refer to the 92 standard if the product you use conforms to the 89 standard or is at some intermediate stage. The entries in Part II and III of this book indicate which portions of a statement match which levels of ISO conformance.

Naturally, the products you use are free to extend the standard with their own features. To make it easier for application programmers to locate and deal with these extensions, the standard requires the use of a *flagger*, a program that examines the source code and flags (marks) all SQL statements that do not conform to the standard. Unflagged statements behave as described in this reference. For the flagged statements, of course, you should refer to your system documentation. Occasionally, the flagger may indicate a statement that is phrased in standard SQL but that behaves differently than the standard specifies. This is acceptable, so long as the statement is flagged. In any case, the standard is more complete than before, so that nonstandard features are no longer as necessary for basic functionality as they were.

Notable Features of Standard SQL

This section describes the major features of the SQL standard as covered in this book. It provides an overview of those features that may be peculiar to this version of SQL or that may have been previously commercially implemented in a non-standard way. It does assume basic knowledge of SQL. To see which SQL statements specifically pertain to which general functions of the language, see "Contents Grouped by Subject" on the inside cover.

Users, Schemas, and Sessions

Here is an overview of the SQL environment as defined in the standard. This aspect is little changed by SQL99.

First, there is the organization of the data itself. Data is contained in tables, tables are group into schemata, and schemata are grouped into catalogs. The catalogs can be further grouped into *clusters*.

NOTE Some database products have been using these terms slightly differently than defined in the standard, and your system documentation may reflect this.

From the viewpoint of a particular SQL session, a cluster is the world. It contains all of the tables that session can access, and all interrelated tables must be in the same cluster.

Clarifying the context of SQL requires identifying who or what issues SQL statements. In the standard, an entity that produces SQL statements is technically called a *SQL agent*. A SQL agent is associated with an Authorization ID, which is an identifier that has a group of privileges permitting certain actions. For the most part, this reference will simplify by just using the term "Authorization ID." The Authorization ID could be a user directly executing SQL, or it could be an application. It is the Authorization ID that establishes a connection to a DBMS. Once the connection is made, a session is begun. Optionally, implementations may allow SQL agents to switch to some other connection and session possibly as a different Authorization ID. (Hence, SQL Agent and Authorization ID are not strictly synonymous, but only the latter concept is relevant to the execution of SQL itself, generally speaking. Almost all of how connection switching is actually done is still implementation-defined.) At any one time, there will be a current session that is active and perhaps some others that are dormant. The Authorization ID under which the statements are run is that of the user or, if the module language is being used, that of the module.

Schema Definition Statements

A *schema* is a named set of database objects that are under the control of a single Authorization ID and can be treated as a whole for certain purposes. Previously, the SQL standard defined procedures for creating and dropping tables and other objects, but it simply equated schemata with Authorization IDs. To accommodate users who may want to create more than one schema, the new standard includes statements for creating and dropping schemata as well as tables and other objects. It also allows schemata to be grouped into catalogs and these into clusters.

See Also   Part II: CREATE SCHEMA, DROP SCHEMA, SET SCHEMA.

Temporary Tables

We have in this book kept the discussion of base tables primarily confined to permanent base tables. These are base tables that store data whose content remains intact from session to session. Since such data is the whole point of a database, permanent base tables are by far the most important kind. However, you can also create temporary base tables, whose data is not retained from one session to the next. These are primarily useful for intermediate results and other kinds of working storage.

Temporary tables fall into two categories: created and declared.

Created temporary tables are objects with a persistent identity in the database from session to session. Although the data is not held between sessions, the empty tables are there for you when you begin each session, so you do not have to create them afresh each time. Created temporary tables come in two flavors: local and global. The difference between these is the scope. For more on created temporary tables, see CREATE TABLE, which is the statement used to create them, in Part II.

Declared temporary tables are objects that exist only in applications (or modules) and do not have a persistent identity in the database. You include the code to create these in applications. Once the application exits, the DBMS never heard of the declared temporary table. For the sake of completeness, these tables are usually called *declared local temporary tables*, though there is no global variety.

See Also Part II: CREATE TABLE, DECLARE LOCAL TEMPORARY TABLE, DROP TABLE.

Built-in Join Operators

The ability to perform joins is part of the SELECT statement, but previously there were no mechanisms built into SQL to automatically generate joins of various types. Specifying multiple tables (or the same table more than once) in the FROM clause of a query implied a join, but beyond that you were on your own to write the rest of the statement to get the type of join you wanted. Well, the new standard has built-in operators that produce joins of the following types:

CROSS	This is a straight Cartesian product—all possible combinations of rows, one from each table joined.

Natural	In principle, this is a join of a foreign key to the key it references, which we call its parent key. In the standard, the term is used a bit more loosely to mean an equi-join of two or more tables over all columns that have the same name. (An *equi-join*, the most common type, is any join based on column values being equal, as opposed, for example, to one being greater than another.) In other words, the standard assumes you follow the convention of naming foreign key columns after their parents. If not, you can still get a natural join, as that term is generally understood, by using one of the remaining forms.
INNER	This is an equi-join of tables A and B such that every row represented from each had a match in the other.
LEFT (OUTER)	This includes all rows from table A, matched or not, plus the matching values from B if applicable. Unmatched rows are padded out with NULLs. As with all the types that use it, the word *OUTER* is optional and indicates that unmatched rows are included along with the matched.
RIGHT (OUTER)	Predictably, the reverse of left. In other words, all the rows from table B are presented in conjunction with any matches from A.
FULL (OUTER)	A combination of left and right. All rows from both tables are shown, merged where matches were found.

UNION	A union join is the opposite of an inner join—it includes only those rows from each table for which no match was found. If you took a full outer join and subtracted everything contained in a similarly constructed inner join, the union join would be what was left. (Don't confuse a union join with the UNION operator used to merge the output of multiple queries.)

All of these types of joins are supported with special operators in the FROM clauses of queries. You can find examples of each in Part II, under SELECT.

See Also   Part II: SELECT.

Read-Only, Scrollable, Insensitive, and Dynamic Cursors

A *cursor* is an object used to store the output of a query for processing in an application. In SQL89, a cursor that was updatable in principle—that is, one that didn't violate any of a series of rules that prohibited update statements—was updatable in fact. In SQL92, you have the option of declaring it read-only. Besides enhancing security, read-only cursors can improve performance by reducing the need to lock the data.

Sensitivity has to do with the reflection in the cursor of external changes to the data. Since a cursor translates SQL's set-at-a-time operation into the item-at-a-time operation of conventional languages, it spreads what would otherwise be a simultaneous occurrence over time. In other words, a cursor can be opened and then read (FETCHed) gradually. This creates the possibility that the cursor's data could be changed while it still is being read. What happens if another statement changes some data yet to be read in an opened cursor? In the early standards, the answer was "God only knows." Possibly, this is not the ideal answer. In SQL92, on the other hand, you can declare the cursor to be *insensitive*, in which case the rest of the world will be gleefully ignored by the cursor. Only read-only cursors can be insensitive. Currently, you cannot, in the standard, declare a cursor sensitive, meaning that external changes to the data will be reflected in the cursor. (You still have the option of leaving the cursor indeterminate. What happens when you do this is implementation-dependent. It is not unreasonable, however, to hope that the implementation at least will behave consistently in this matter and tell you what to expect in the system documentation.)

You can also *scroll* cursors now. Although the rows of a table are, in principle, unordered, once these rows are placed in a cursor they will have some order, whether arbitrary or imposed. Previously, you had to operate on these rows one at a time, beginning with the first and proceeding straight through to the end. Now you can jump around, go back to where you were, and so on. A cursor that permits this is called a *scroll cursor*; such a cursor must be read-only.

See Also   Part II: CLOSE, DECLARE CURSOR, FETCH, OPEN. For additional information specifically on the use of cursors in Dynamic SQL, see ALLOCATE CURSOR, EXECUTE, EXECUTE IMMEDIATE, PREPARE.

Client/Server Orientation

Standard SQL is designed around the concepts of client/server or of multi-tiered architectures. It enables you to manage connections, recognizing that a very common database configuration is one in which front-end software on one computer, called the *client*, attempts to extract information from a back-end DBMS located on another computer, called the *server*. Many of the new features regarding standardized connection procedures, locking schemes, and error diagnostics were motivated by the desire to enable clients to communicate with a variety of DBMSs, possibly on a variety of servers, in the same way.

What Is a Client/Server Architecture?

In a client/server architecture, multiple computers are connected over a network. The computers are grouped into clients and servers. Users directly interact with clients to perform most of the front-end user interface functions. Servers perform various intensive tasks in response to requests from clients. A DBMS typically resides on a server and responds to SQL requests from the clients. SQL is well suited to such an arrangement because as a declarative language it is very concise, and the network therefore does not get bogged down passing detailed instructions back and forth between the client and server. Nonetheless, the language is sufficiently precise for the server to perform the required task autonomously without further client input. Particularly for queries, this is an improvement over the older file server approach, where the server may transmit an entire table to the client and leave it to extract the data that it needs.

Client/server architectures do, however, introduce the issue of connections. A client must be connected to a server in order to communicate with it. Since the standard has to be neutral with regard to the particularities—which platforms and networks are being used, for example—much is necessarily left up to the implementation here. But the 92 standard does define what a SQL connection is and provide some ground rules for how one behaves. The standard is tailored to the realities of client-server computing, in which clients may want to interface to multiple servers and servers normally interface to multiple clients.

This is not to say that the standard can be applied only to client/server architectures, however. SQL92, like its predecessors, is a functional specification. Any configuration—stand-alone PC, traditional minicomputer, or mainframe computer—that functions as specified is acceptable.

How Do the Internet and Intranets Fit into This?

The Web and Intranets that utilize the HTTP protocol are sometimes viewed as simple client/server architectures. In this analysis, the Web browser is commonly regarded as a "client" of a Web server, such as Apache or iPlanet. When a DBMS is involved, however, it is usually as another layer behind the Web server. This is called a *three-tiered architecture*. There may, in fact, be any number of additional layers, particularly between web server and DBMS. These situations are generally termed *n-tiered architectures*. In these situations, the Web server is a server to the browser but a client to the DBMS. Since "client" and "server" refer to functions of a software module rather than its fundamental nature, there is nothing wrong with this approach. Since this is a database-centric book, we will be viewing Web servers and middleware chiefly as clients.

See Also   Part II: CONNECT, DISCONNECT, SET CONNECTION.

Enhanced Transaction Management

A *transaction* is a group of successive SQL statements that succeed or fail as a unit—a failure in the transaction causes the whole sequence to be canceled, or *rolled back*. The DBMS automatically begins a transaction whenever you issue a statement that calls for one and no other transaction is active. Transactions are ended by a COMMIT WORK statement (to save the changes) or a ROLLBACK statement (to disregard them) or by a system crash or disconnect. If a transaction cannot be committed, it will be rolled back; ROLLBACK can never fail.

SQL92 provides features that make transactions considerably more sophisticated. However, these features are part of Intermediate, rather than Entry, SQL92 conformance. These features are useful enough that many of them are, in fact, implemented, but variations abound. Among the special features of transactions in SQL92 are the following:

- Transactions can be specified as read-only. This means that statements within the transaction that attempt to change the content or structure of the database will produce an error. This will tend to improve performance of concurrent operations as it reduces the need to lock the data.

- You can defer constraint checking until the end of the transaction, and you can choose which constraints you wish to defer. Constraints control the data that may be placed in the database. See the discussions under SET CONSTRAINTS MODE in Part II and Constraints in Part III.

- Transactions can specify the isolation levels of the locks placed on the data. See the discussion under SET TRANSACTION in Part II.

- Transactions can specify the size of the diagnostics area for statements within the transaction. See the discussion in Appendix F.

See Also Part II: COMMIT WORK, ROLLBACK, SET CONSTRAINTS MODE, SET TRANSACTION.

Application-Owned Privileges (Definer's Rights)

Actions performed on a database are associated with an Authorization ID, a name that's unique within the database. This allows the privileges linked to a particular Authorization ID to determine which actions may be taken by a user. For example, an Authorization ID could have the privilege to retrieve data from a table or to use a translation on a character set. Generally, an Authorization ID is associated directly with a user and defines possible actions whether the user is employing stand-alone SQL or running an application that interfaces to the database. It is often useful with applications to grant privileges to the application itself instead of to the user, so that users can execute the statements in the application without having the same privileges in other contexts. Applications, especially if they use Static SQL, can greatly control what users do with their privileges and thus offer a good deal of security.

Application-owned privileges are sometimes said to embody *definer's rights*, whereas a module that makes users execute it under their own privileges is enforcing *invoker's rights*. There are other terms as well, since some products have had application-owned privileges for a while as a nonstandard feature.

See Also   Part III: Authorization IDs, User Value Functions.

See Also   Appendix B.

Standardized Connection Procedure

In earlier standards, SQL statements were associated with Authorization IDs, but how a particular Authorization ID was associated with a particular statement was up to the implementation. Authorization IDs had privileges to perform certain statements and, if they created objects such as tables, had control over those objects. They were generally understood to be users, although the standard did not actually say this. And in fact, users, from the standpoint of a DBMS or an operating system, may not have a one-to-one correspondence to each other or to real-world users. In some commercial environments, a single Authorization ID could be shared by several real-world users, or users could have multiple Authorization IDs. This is particularly common with a DBMS for which a

Web server is a client. Also, the way an Authorization ID was identified by the DBMS—the connection procedure—was left up to the implementers.

The SQL92 standard standardizes much of this and makes it explicit that users, directly or through applications, establish connections to the DBMS. Thus, it is possible for a given user to have several concurrent connections, only one of which will be active at a time. Users explicitly switch between connections using the SET CONNECTION statement.

See Also   Part II: CONNECT, DISCONNECT, SET CONNECTION.

Standardized System Tables

A catalog in the standard is a collection of schemata. It contains an INFORMATION_SCHEMA, which is a set of tables that describes the contents of the schemata—what columns are in the various tables, what views are defined, what privileges are associated with which Authorization IDs, and so on. It is these tables themselves that are called the "catalog" in some commercial products. The standardized INFORMATION_SCHEMA specified by SQL92 allows both users and applications to use the same SQL statements to get information about any schema under any DBMS that they may be using.

Standardized Error Codes and Diagnostics

Two standard error variables are supported. In the old approach, information about the result of a SQL operation was transmitted through a numeric variable called SQLCODE. This variable would be set automatically after the execution of each SQL statement to indicate what happened when the statement was executed. There were three possibilities:

- A value of 0 indicated successful completion.

- A value of 100 indicated that the statement executed properly but had no effect or produced no output. For example, a query that produced no data or an attempt to delete a row that wasn't there would produce a SQLCODE value of 100.

- Any negative number indicated an error.

Of course, the idea was for the specific negative number to indicate the specific error, but the mapping was left up to the implementation, so now they are all different. For the sake of the upward-compatibility of existing products and maintainability of existing applications, SQLCODE is still supported, but it has been deprecated, which means that it is not recommended now and may not be supported in the future.

The new approach is to use another variable called SQLSTATE. This is a five-character text string with standard values for various error classes. It also provides for implementation-defined error conditions. In fact, errors are classified at two levels of detail: class and subclass. Often, an error message will use a standard class and a proprietary subclass, so that the standard tells you the general nature of the error and the subclass gives you more specific information. There are no standard subclasses, but if the class describes the error adequately, the subclass may be omitted (set to '000').

The standard also now provides a diagnostics area with multiple error messages and codes produced by the execution of a single statement. You access this using the GET DIAGNOSTICS statement. For a detailed description of the diagnostics area, see Appendix F.

See Also   Part II: GET DIAGNOSTICS. Appendix E.

Domains

Relational theorists such as E. F. Codd, the father of relational database theory, have long promoted the use of *domains*, to account for the fact that data may need to be typed more precisely than can be achieved with a standard set of datatypes. For example, telephone numbers are not the same type of data as social security numbers even though both are numbers. Although they could be of the same datatype, it makes no sense to directly compare them; they are in different domains.

SQL92 supports domains, but they are not quite what Codd had in mind, because they do not restrict possible comparisons. As we will discuss in Part IV Chapter 2, the distinct UDTs of SQL99 are closer to Codd's conception of domains and complement SQL92 domains rather well. A domain in SQL92 is effectively a standard datatype accompanied by some combination of standard refinements. It gives you a convenient way to bundle the refinements. You create these domains as objects in a schema and then declare columns of tables to be of domains rather than datatypes. A domain definition contains a datatype, but it may also contain clauses that specify a default value, one or more constraints (rules that restrict the values allowed in particular columns), and a collation (a sorting order for character sets) to apply to the domain. Domains once defined can still be altered or even dropped.

Domains are a convenient way to reproduce customized packages of constraints, default values, and collating sequences uniformly across a schema. They will be particularly useful to apply the same constraint to several tables, for example, to perform check-digit validation on ID codes. They could also come in handy in large and complex schemata or in schemata that use complex data requiring many constraints, as in some engineering applications.

See Also Part II: ALTER DOMAIN, CREATE DOMAIN, DROP DOMAIN. Part III: Constraints, Datatypes.

Assertions and Deferability of Constraints

Constraints are rules that you establish to restrict the values that can be placed in your columns. In basic SQL, constraints are contained in the definitions of base tables and are of two kinds: column constraints and table constraints. The former are part of a column definition and check their rules whenever a statement attempts to insert or change a value in that column. The latter are part of the table definition and therefore can accommodate rules that involve checking multiple columns of the table. In both kinds, the constraints can be either of certain predefined kinds—NOT NULL, for example, or UNIQUE—or can be CHECK constraints that allow the table creator to create value expressions using the column values. If the expression is FALSE, the constraint is not satisfied, and the statement is rejected.

An extension of this concept is *assertions*—constraints that exist in the schema as independent objects, not in a table. This means that they can refer to multiple tables in their predicates. They can also be used to ensure that a table is never empty, which cannot be done within the table itself. Assertions allow you to design general principles that your data must meet, for example, to design validity checks. Assertions can be created and dropped. You can also put constraints in domains, as discussed under "Domains" elsewhere in this chapter.

SQL92 constraints are named, either explicitly or automatically by the DBMS. This enables them to be deferred (explained shortly) or dropped from tables or domains. You drop constraints using the ALTER TABLE, ALTER DOMAIN, and DROP ASSERTION statements.

You have the option of deferring the checking of constraints (for the rest of this discussion, "constraints" can be taken to mean constraints in tables, constraints in domains, or constraints in assertions, unless otherwise specified) until the end of the transaction. This gets rather sophisticated. Basically, a constraint can be checked at any of the following times:

1. After every statement that affects the table(s) to which it refers

2. At the end of every transaction that contains one or more statements that affect the table(s) to which it refers

3. At any time between 1 and 2 when the user or application decides it should be checked and therefore forces the issue

When you define a constraint, you specify whether it must be checked immediately after each statement or may be deferred until the end of the transaction. If you choose the latter, you can also specify whether it will default to being checked immediately or default to being deferred. Then, during your transaction, you can change this default by setting a *constraints mode*, which explicitly controls whether your deferrable constraints are checked immediately after each statement or deferred until the end of the transaction (your non-deferrable constraints, by definition, must be checked immediately). You can set the constraints mode for all constraints at once or for specified ones. If you set your constraints mode at any time to immediate, the constraints you indicate will be checked immediately. Use this technique when you want the third type of checking listed above. The statement to force or defer the checking of constraints is SET CONSTRAINTS MODE.

There are certain things you can do only if you can defer constraints. For example, you may want to have two tables each with a foreign key referencing the other. Suppose additionally that the foreign keys both have the NOT NULL constraint, so that neither table can have a foreign key value entered until a matching parent key value exists in the other, and neither can accept any rows without having some foreign key values. Whichever table you attempt to insert into first will get an integrity violation, because the parent key in the other table will not yet exist. This is an example of *circularity*. The solution is to defer the checking of the FOREIGN KEY constraint until after you have been able to insert rows into both tables.

Keep in mind, however, that if you could a constraint violation at the end of a transaction, you could lose all of the work accomplished in that transaction. Unless you are very concerned with performance and can save a bit of time by performing all of your checks at once, you probably should check your constraints as soon as possible, rather than putting it off until the end of a long transaction. If you use SET CONSTRAINTS MODE to force checking of constraints before you terminate the transaction, you're better off. If any constraint is currently violated, setting the constraints mode to immediate will fail. This lets you know there is a problem without rolling back the transaction.

See Also   Part II: CREATE ASSERTION, CREATE TABLE, DROP ASSERTION, SET TRANSACTION. Part III: Constraints.

International Language Support

One of the things that truly qualifies SQL92 as a worldwide standard is its support for customized character sets. No longer is SQL anchored to English. The standard enables implementers and users great flexibility in defining their own character sets. For example, characters need not be one-byte long as English-language letters usually are; they can even vary in length. They should be sortable. This means that a collating sequence, or "collation," exists to impose an order on the characters. An expression like *character 1 < character 2* is then evaluated as "character 1 precedes character 2 in the collating sequence." Normally, collations should correspond to alphabetical ordering. In any case, collations can be overridden, even for standard character sets. You can also define your own translations from one character set to another. The character sets, collations, and translations are all defined as objects in the schema, and users must have the USAGE privilege on them to use them.

See Also   Part II: CREATE CHARACTER SET, CREATE COLLATION, CREATE TRANSLATION, DROP CHARACTER SET, DROP COLLATION, DROP TRANSLATION. Part III: CAST Expressions, Collations, Datatypes.

Date, Time, and Interval Datatypes

Dates and times have special features that make it difficult to handle them properly as simply character strings or numbers. Hence, they have their own datatypes. There is also an interval datatype for doing math with date and time values. These types work as follows:

- A date value consists of a year, a month, and a day.

- A time value consists of hours, minutes, seconds, and decimal fractions of a second.

- A timestamp is a combination of date and time.

With time and timestamp, you also have the option of specifying decimal fractions of seconds. Timestamp, in fact, defaults to four decimal places, e.g., 11:09:48.5839. Time itself defaults to no decimal. Either time or timestamp can also have a time zone indication that shows how far the indicated time is offset from Universal Coordinated Time (UCT).

The standard also supports two types of intervals: year-month and day-time. Intervals are used to represent the differences between various days and times; they enable you to perform date and time arithmetic. For example, if you subtract the time 2:00 from the time 5:30, you get the interval 3:30, for three hours and thirty minutes. Likewise, you could take the date value of July 2003, add an interval month value of three, and get the date value of October 2003. Note that, although intervals are either year-month or day-time, not all of the components of the year or time have to be expressed. Interval arithmetic will work with what you give it. The reason for the two types is that we cannot say in general how many days are in a month. It depends on the month. This means we would not know, when incrementing the day values in a theoretical month-day interval, when we could switch and increment the month value. It is undetermined.

See Also Part III: Datatypes.

Binary Datatypes

SQL92 supports binary data. This is different from the BLOBs (Binary Large Objects) of SQL99 in that SQL92 provides no special features, such as SQL99 locators, for managing binary data. In SQL92, binary data is treated simply as string data. For more on

SQL99 BLOBs, see Part IV Chapter 2. For more on SQL92 binary datatypes, see Datatypes in Part III.

There are two types of binary data in SQL92: fixed-length and varying-length. Although you will frequently need to use varying-length data, using the fixed-length type improves performance and reduces storage space. One place where you may be able to use fixed-length is with digitized images. If all of the images are of the same size and resolution (which is likely), and no image compression is used (which is possible), they should all be of the same size.

See Also   Part III: Datatypes.

Datatype Conversions

SQL is a strongly typed language. Although all datatypes are, of course, ultimately represented in the DBMS as binary numbers, operations cannot freely mix them or operate on them as binaries or as numbers, as is possible in some computer languages. This has advantages and disadvantages. Often it is useful to convert from one datatype to another, but problems can arise if this process is not controlled. The standard allows you to convert datatypes by using the CAST expression. This enables you to instruct the DBMS to convert an integer to a character string or a character string to binary data, for example. This is especially handy for joins and unions, where all columns being joined or merged have to be of similar datatypes.

See Also   Part III: CAST Expressions, Datatypes.

Built-In Value Functions

SQL provides system values in the form of built-in string variables whose values are automatically set by the system to reflect the Authorization IDs being used to identify the current user and the currently applicable privileges. There are three types: SESSION_USER, CURRENT_USER, and SYSTEM_USER.

CURRENT_USER, also known as USER, refers to the Authorization ID used to determine which actions currently can be performed. This will be the Authorization ID either of the user or of a possibly emulated module. The latter would be the case whenever a module that has an Authorization ID of its own is being executed (see "Application-Owned Privileges" elsewhere in this chapter). Otherwise, CURRENT_USER identifies the user. In any case, the Authorization ID associated with the user will be contained in the variable SESSION_USER. (Note that although SESSION_USER is set automatically, implementations do have the option of allowing user override with the SET SESSION AUTHORIZATION statement.)

SYSTEM_USER is the current user as identified by the operating system. Most often, this would be the same as SESSION_USER, but how operating system users correspond to Authorization IDs is implementation-defined, so the two may differ. Refer to your system documentation for details on this.

There are also built-in functions for DATE and TIME values. These are as follows: CURRENT_DATE, which provides (surprise!) the current date, CURRENT_TIME, which does the same for time, and CURRENT_TIMESTAMP, which is a combination of the other two.

See Also   Part II: SET SESSION AUTHORIZATION. Part III: Authorization IDs, Privileges, Value Expressions.

New Operators for Strings

The standard provides a concatenation operator and several functions that operate on text strings. We can divide these into two categories. First, there are those that operate on strings and produce strings as output: the CONCATENATE operator (written ||), SUBSTRING, UPPER, LOWER, TRIM, TRANSLATE, and CONVERT. Then there are those that operate on strings but produce numeric output: POSITION, CHAR_LENGTH, OCTET_LENGTH, and BIT_LENGTH.

Of the first group, only CONCATENATE is *dyadic*, meaning it operates on two strings at once. It simply appends the second string to the first, so that `'Mary ' || 'Schmary'` becomes `'Mary Schmary'`. SUBSTRING takes a string, a starting position within it, and a number of characters to extract and produces a new string, so that `SUBSTRING ('Astarte' FROM 2 FOR 4)` returns `'star'`. UPPER and LOWER convert a string to all upper or all lowercase, respectively; either of these operations is called a *fold*. TRIM is used to remove leading or trailing blanks from strings. You can specify leading, trailing, or both.

TRANSLATE and CONVERT address SQL's use of various and customized character sets. TRANSLATE converts from one character set to another. CONVERT keeps the character set the same but switches to a different definition of how the character set is represented.

POSITION finds the starting position of one string within another, so that POSITION ('star' IN 'Astarte') returns 2. If there is no match for the substring, POSITION returns 0. The other three functions all give you the length of a string, either in the number of characters, the number of octets (8-bit sequences, commonly called bytes), or the number of bits.

See Also Part II: CREATE CHARACTER SET, CREATE COLLATION, and CREATE TRANSLATION. Part III: Collations, String Value Functions.

Row and Table Value Constructors

Predicates in SQL compare values in terms of operators like = or in terms of SQL's own operators and return a value of TRUE, FALSE, or (in the presence of NULLs) UNKNOWN, based on the result of the comparison. Previously, SQL predicates could compare single values to single values or could, in some situations, compare single values to a column of values derived from a subquery (a query used to derive values for use within another query). In SQL92, SQL can deal with sets of values that correspond to entire rows or entire tables. This functionality is part of Full SQL92 conformance, which, as of this writing (2000), is claimed by few if any vendors. Nonetheless, the feature is useful enough that some products support it as an extension to their standard conformance level.

For example, previously you could have a predicate that said

```
WHERE c1 = 3
```

or one that said

```
WHERE c1 = 3 AND c2 = 5
```

In SQL92, you could express the latter as

```
WHERE (c1, c2) = (3, 5)
```

This functionality is more than just a convenience, however. It enables you to do things you could not do before, such as comparing a row produced by a subquery to an enumerated row of values. You can even use subquery operators such as ANY or ALL with such subqueries. If an inequality is used instead of =, the expression is evaluated as a sort with the first value having the highest priority and each subsequent value the next highest. In other words,

```
(1, 7, 8) < (2, 0, 1)
```

is TRUE because 1 < 2 and once a pair of unequal values is found, the rest of the values don't matter.

A table value constructor consists of a set of row value constructors, preceded by the word VALUES and separated by commas. This syntax enables table value constructors to neatly extend the standard syntax for INSERT.

See Also   Part II: INSERT. Part III: Predicates, Row and Table Value Constructors.

Referential Integrity Refinements

In SQL89, foreign keys consisted of one or more columns in a table (*table A*) that referenced one or more columns in another table (*table B*). This meant that, for every row of *table A* where the foreign key was not NULL, there had to be a row in *table B* with the same values in its referenced columns—the parent key. The parent key in *table B* had to have either the UNIQUE or the PRIMARY KEY constraint, so that it would be assured of having unique values.

In SQL92, things have grown more complex. First, matches of a foreign key to its parent can be either partial or full. The distinction comes when you have a composite (multicolumn) foreign key that is partially NULL. A partial match is a match of values that are not NULL in the foreign key; a full match is a match of all values. You specify in the FOREIGN KEY constraint which type of match is enforced.

Also, the standard supports referential triggered actions, known in some existing products as update effects and delete effects. These specify what happens when you change a parent key value that is referenced by one or more foreign key values. You can specify this effect independently for ON UPDATE and for ON DELETE, and for each there are four possibilities:

SET NULL   This sets to NULL all foreign keys that reference a parent key being deleted or changed.

SET DEFAULT   This sets all columns in the referencing foreign keys to the value defined as a default in the default value clause that applies to them. If there is no such value, the default is NULL.

CASCADE   A change in the parent key value automatically produces the same change in the foreign key value(s).

NO ACTION   The foreign key value does not change. If this would produce an integrity violation, the statement is disallowed. Keep in mind, however, that you can defer checking for an integrity violation until the end of the transaction, so there is time to change the foreign key value to a new one that would still be valid. For more information on deferring the check of the integrity constraint, refer to the discussion of "Assertions and Deferability of Constraints" in this chapter.

If none of the four is specified, NO ACTION is the default.

See Also   Part II: CREATE TABLE. Part III: Constraints.

Conditional Expressions

CASE (conditional) expressions are similar to the case statements found in many programming languages. They are not statements, however, but expressions. Rather than directing actions, they have values and can be used practically anywhere a value expression can. The expressions list one or more predicates and give a value for each. The predicates are tested in the order listed. As soon as one is found that is TRUE, the CASE expression returns the value corresponding to that predicate to the SQL statement in which it is contained. There may be an ELSE clause at the end of the CASE expression that determines the value of the clause if none of the predicates are TRUE. If there is no ELSE clause, ELSE NULL is implied.

Two other new expressions are actually just shorthand for certain types of CASE expressions: NULLIF and COALESCE. NULLIF relates two values. If the two are the same, the condition is TRUE and NULLIF returns the value NULL. Otherwise, NULLIF returns the first of the values. COALESCE lists a series of values. It traverses the list until it finds the first one that is not NULL. It then assumes this value. If no non-NULL value is found, it assumes the NULL value. Both NULLIF and COALESCE can be expressed, albeit less succinctly, with CASE.

See Also   Part III: CASE Expressions.

Automatic Flagging of Variations on the Standard

This feature is very useful for knowing when you can simply follow the standard and this book and when you have to resort to reading the system documentation. It also helps you to write SQL code that will work the same on all engines. Basically, the flagger is a program that reviews the SQL source code in applications or modules and determines whether each statement conforms to SQL92, is an implementer extension or variation, or is in error. It then flags (marks) the statement appropriately. Of course, if the statement contains syntactic errors, the flagger may not be able to tell whether the intended statement is standard or an implementation extension. The flagger will flag at a certain level of standard conformance: Entry, Intermediate, or Full. Features that conform to a higher level of conformance than specified will be flagged as extensions. In addition to extensions, the flagger will also indicate variations—statements that are acceptable to the standard in syntax but behave somewhat differently in the implementer's version. ISO accepts these if flagged, so that the implementer's existing products can be upwardly compatible.

Modules and Compilation Units

Although this is not actually a new feature of SQL92, it is an aspect of how the SQL standard works that seems to get more complicated as time goes on, so it is worth explaining here. The standard supports multiple "binding styles": one is the module language where modules of SQL code are called, and the other is Embedded SQL, where SQL code is directly interspersed in the source code of another language. Dynamic SQL is an extension of Embedded SQL in this regard. The standard is actually written in terms of the (infrequently used) module language and then specifies ways for Embedded SQL to emulate its behavior. Hence, things like scope, application-owned privileges, and the like are frequently specified in terms of modules. When Embedded SQL code is pre-compiled, it does indeed generate modules called *compilation units*, but the mapping of these to the module language modules is implementation-defined and not necessarily one-to-one. The upshot is that the meaning of things like scope and application-owned privileges is largely left up to the implementation. The implementation, should, however, have well-defined compilation units that have a well-defined mapping to modules. For details, however, you will have to resort to your system documentation.

Part II

SQL Statement Reference

This is an alphabetical reference to the statements recognized by the SQL92 standard. Although SQL99 is published, as of this publication (2000) it is SQL92 that you will find in the marketplace. We cover SQL99 elsewhere in this book, though at a lesser level of detail than this reference provides. Elements common to multiple statements, such as datatypes, predicates, and value expressions are covered in the next part. If you are unsure of the name of the statement you need, see the Contents Grouped by Subject chart inside the front cover of this book or the Index. To understand the context in which these statements are used, consult Part I of the book.

Each entry presents the following information: the purpose of the statement, its syntax and usage rules, its requirements for various levels of standard conformance, and cross-references to related subjects. References that appear in UPPERCASE letters are to statement entries in Part II; those in Mixed Case are to entries for other SQL elements in Part III.

The SQL92 standard is designed so that implementers can bring their products into conformance gradually. The standard defines three levels of conformance, each incorporating its predecessor: Entry, Intermediate, and Full. The entire standard, save for minor incompatibilities noted in Appendix F, builds on the previous SQL86 and SQL89 standards, so these can be considered prior levels of conformance. Unless otherwise noted, any feature required for some level of conformance is also required for any higher level, so that all Entry features are also required for the Intermediate level, and all SQL86 features are also part of SQL89 and SQL92.

SQL99 is an exception; it builds directly on Entry-level SQL92. Keep in mind that conformance to the standard is, in any case, optional. ISO does not enforce or officially certify conformance. The National Institute of Standards and Technology (NIST) used to certify SQL conformance but has abandoned this role. It is not clear at this writing whether anyone else will take it up.

Each entry describes the features of the statement as required for Full ISO SQL92 conformance. Following each description is an outline of the conformance levels, showing what features are not required by products claiming lesser levels of conformance to the 92 standard or claiming conformance to an earlier standard. The conformance levels are shown here:

Intermediate	Not required for Intermediate-level conformance to the ANSI/ISO SQL92 standard.
Entry	Not required for Entry-level conformance to the ANSI/ISO SQL92 standard.
SQL89	Not required for conformance to the 1989 ANSI/ISO SQL standard.
SQL86	Required for conformance to the 1986 ANSI/ISO SQL standard.
Non	Not required by any ANSI/ISO official standard, but commonly used.

Except for Non, each of these levels implies conformance to all of its predecessors unless otherwise noted, so that any SQL code that conforms to Entry 92 also conforms to SQL89, and code that conforms to Full 92 also conforms both to Intermediate and Entry. The syntax diagrams use conventions that mostly follow the BNF (Backus Naur Form) standard, but we have introduced some variations to enhance readability. The conventions we use are as follows:

- The symbol ::= means "is defined as". It is used to further clarify parts of a statement's syntax diagram.

- Keywords appear in all uppercase letters. These reserved words are literals that are actually written as part of the statement.

- Placeholders for specific values, such as *domain name* in the CREATE DOMAIN statement, appear in *italic* type. These placeholders identify the type of value that should be used in a real statement; they are not literals to be written as part of the statement. The Usage discussion explains their possible values and any restrictions on them. This is not a standard BNF convention.

- Optional portions of a statement appear in square brackets ([and]).

- A vertical bar (|) indicates that whatever precedes it may optionally be replaced by whatever follows it.

- Braces ({ and }) indicate that everything within them is to be regarded as a whole for the purpose of evaluating other symbols (e.g., vertical bars or ellipses).

- Ellipses (…) indicate that the preceding portion of the statement may be repeated any number of times.

- Ellipses with an interposed comma (.,..) indicate that the preceding portion may be repeated any number of times, with the individual occurrences separated by commas. The final occurrence should not be followed by a comma.

NOTE Ellipses with an interposed comma, as described above, are not a standard BNF convention; we use them for simplicity and clarity in representing the many SQL statements that use this construct. Without them, the diagrams would be considerably more complex.

- Parentheses (()) used in syntax diagrams are literals. They indicate that parentheses are to be used in forming the statement. They do not specify a way of reading the diagram as braces or square brackets do.

Carriage returns or line feeds in SQL are treated the same as blanks—they simply delimit the elements of statements. In other words, they are white space. Carriage returns and spacing are used in our syntax diagrams for readability only; you need not duplicate them in your SQL code.

It is worth pointing out here the distinction between two terms that will frequently turn up in discussion of the standard: *implementation-dependent* and *implementation-defined*. The two are not quite the same. The former means that the implementation can simply do what it likes; the latter also allows the implementation to do as it sees fit but requires that it commit itself—the implementation's behavior must be both documented and consistent.

> **NOTE** The terminology we use here is not always the official ISO terminology. The official terminology can get quite labyrinthine, so we have simplified things somewhat. For this reason, we sometimes use different terms than the ISO or even use the same terms somewhat differently. For example, "predicate" in the standard is an expression using =, BETWEEN, EXISTS, or similar operators that can be TRUE, FALSE, or UNKNOWN. A "search condition" is some combination of predicates using AND, OR, NOT, and parentheses and also can be TRUE, FALSE, or UNKNOWN. In this book, we have effectively defined "predicate" recursively to incorporate both of these terms into a single term.

ALLOCATE CURSOR
(Dynamic SQL Only) Associates a Cursor with a Prepared Statement

Syntax
```
ALLOCATE extended cursor name
[INSENSITIVE] [SCROLL]
CURSOR FOR extended statement name;
```

Usage
The ALLOCATE CURSOR statement is used in Dynamic SQL to associate a cursor with a SQL statement previously readied by a PREPARE statement. It differs from the dynamic version of DECLARE CURSOR in that the cursor name is a host-language variable. This means you can use an ALLOCATE CURSOR statement to create an indefinite number of cursors by executing it repeatedly with different values for the name parameter.

The extended statement is the name of an object previously created with a PREPARE statement, which must be a properly formed SELECT statement, suitable for use in a cursor. ALLOCATE CURSOR must conform to the rules for cursors specified under DECLARE

CURSOR. INSENSITIVE means that the content of the cursor will not be changed if the data changes while it is in use. SCROLL enables you to retrieve the rows of the cursor in any order you want, but it may only be used with read-only cursors. Both of these are explained in more detail under DECLARE CURSOR. If applicable, an updatability clause may be appended to the SELECT statement in order to restrict the cursor's updatability and thus limit its lock usage. If so, it is included in the SELECT string given to the PREPARE statement, rather than as part of this statement. Again, see DECLARE CURSOR.

The extended cursor name is a simple target specification, that is, a host-language variable that cannot have an indicator variable appended. At the time the ALLOCATE CURSOR statement is executed, the variable must have a value, and that value must be different from the names of all existing allocated cursors in the same module or compilation unit. To destroy (deallocate) the cursor, close it using the CLOSE statement and then simply deallocate the prepared statement on which it is based, using the DEALLOCATE PREPARE statement.

Example

In the following example, the content of the host variable cursor-name will be set to the name of the allocated scrollable cursor. We assume that cursorname is of a text string type, although the specific type will depend upon the host language. The current value of cursorname will become the name used to refer to the cursor in other SQL statements. Statement5 is a prepared SELECT statement. It is assumed that the application numbers statements as they are prepared.

```
ALLOCATE :cursorname SCROLL CURSOR
FOR :statement5;
```

Conformance Levels

Intermediate The implementation is not required to support the ALLOCATE CURSOR statement at this level.

See Also Part II: DECLARE CURSOR, PREPARE. Appendices A and C.

ALLOCATE DESCRIPTOR
(Dynamic SQL Only) Creates a Descriptor Area

Syntax

```
ALLOCATE DESCRIPTOR descriptor name
  [ WITH MAX num occurrences ];
```

Usage

A descriptor area is an area used in Dynamic SQL to store information about the parameters of a dynamically generated SQL statement. There can be one descriptor area for input variables and another for output. Host language variables provide an alternative to descriptor areas for either or both of these purposes. Descriptor areas are used because the statements in Dynamic SQL are generated spontaneously at runtime, with dynamic parameters represented by simple question marks. The ALLOCATE DESCRIPTOR statement creates a descriptor area with the given name and the number of allocated descriptor items specified by *num occurrences*. The actual descriptor area can have this number of items or fewer. If the WITH MAX clause is not used, some implementation-dependent default greater than zero will apply. For a detailed explanation of the content of descriptor areas, see Descriptor Areas in Part III.

Example

The following statement allocates a 17-item descriptor area called descrip_stat5.

```
ALLOCATE DESCRIPTOR 'descrip_stat5'
  WITH MAX 17;
```

Conformance Levels

Intermediate   The name of the descriptor and the number specified in the WITH MAX clause may be restricted to being literals rather than variables. This is not true for Full conformance.

Entry   There is a discrepancy in the standard in that it does not state that descriptor areas are not required for Entry-level conformance, but it does state that Dynamic SQL generally is not so required. Since descriptors are used only in Dynamic SQL, we assume the intent is that descriptors are not required at this level.

SQL89   Dynamic SQL and descriptors areas were
                   not part of the standard.

See Also   Part II: DEALLOCATE DESCRIPTOR, DESCRIBE, GET
DESCRIPTOR, SET DESCRIPTOR. Part III: Descriptor Areas.

ALTER DOMAIN
Changes the Definition of a Domain

Syntax
```
ALTER DOMAIN domain name
  { SET DEFAULT default   }
| { DROP DEFAULT  }
| { ADD constraint clause }
| { DROP CONSTRAINT constraint name };
```

Usage
ALTER DOMAIN changes the definition of a domain by adding
or dropping a default or constraint. Domains are alternatives to
datatypes on which columns can be based. For more on domains,
see CREATE DOMAIN. ALTER DOMAIN can be issued only by the
owner of the schema that contains the domain. Any changes you
specify with it instantly affect all columns based on the domain.

SET DEFAULT defines a default value that will be applied to all
columns based on the domain unless overridden by a default
defined on the particular column (see Part II: CREATE TABLE).
The new default applies to rows added to the tables after this
statement is issued; default values already present in the data are
unaffected. For example, if you change a default city from London to Tokyo, rows in columns based on this domain that previously had London set by default will not have their values
changed, but new rows will have Tokyo.

DROP DEFAULT removes the existing default. In the absence of
an existing default, it will produce an error.

ADD places a new constraint on the domain. This constraint
will use the keyword VALUE wherever it references the column
value to be checked. In other words, VALUE replaces a specific column reference, as any number of columns could be based on this
domain.

DROP CONSTRAINT eliminates a constraint. If the constraint was not assigned a name when created, it will have some name assigned by the DBMS (for any level of SQL92 conformance). Any such generated name will be listed in the INFORMATION_SCHEMA. The standard does not allow multiple changes in the same ALTER DOMAIN statement. In other words, you cannot drop a default and add a constraint at the same time.

Example

The following statement restricts the range of values that can be entered into the domain id_nums to those between 0 and 10000 inclusive (the domain, of course, is assumed to have a numeric datatype).

```
ALTER DOMAIN id_nums ADD range_check
CHECK(VALUE BETWEEN 0 AND 10000);
```

This constraint is not deferrable.

Conformance Levels

Intermediate   ALTER DOMAIN is not required at this level.

Entry   No support for domains is required at this level.

See Also Part II: CREATE DOMAIN, DROP DOMAIN. Part III: Constraints, and Appendix G.

ALTER TABLE
Changes the Definition of an Existing Base Table

Syntax

```
ALTER TABLE table name
{ ADD [COLUMN] column definition }
| { ALTER [COLUMN] column name alter action}
| { DROP [COLUMN] column name RESTRICT | CASCADE }
| { ADD table constraint definition }
| { DROP CONSTRAINT constraint name
RESTRICT | CASCADE };


alter action ::=
{ SET DEFAULT default option } | { DROP DEFAULT }
```

Usage

The table affected cannot be a view or a declared local temporary table. (See CREATE VIEW and DECLARE LOCAL TEMPORARY TABLE, respectively, in this chapter.) The ALTER TABLE statement must be issued by the owner of the schema in which the table is located.

ADD COLUMN places a new column in the table, which will be its new last column. The optional word COLUMN is allowed for clarity; it is not needed and has no effect. The DBMS can distinguish ADD COLUMN from ADD used for table constraints because the latter use begins with a keyword while the former begins with a column name, which cannot be a keyword. The new column is defined just as it would have been in a CREATE TABLE statement. It may include constraints, a default, and a collating sequence.

If the table is not empty at the time the new column is added, the column will be initially set to the default value for every row in the table. This implies that there must be a default value for the added column. The default will be that defined for the column or, if none such, that defined for the domain or, if none such, NULL. If the column has the NOT NULL constraint, and the table is not empty when the column is added, either the column or its domain, if any, must have a default value. Users with privileges on the table will also have them on the new column, unless those privileges are column-specific (see Part II: GRANT).

ALTER COLUMN is used to create or drop a default value for the column. Again, the word COLUMN is optional. The default value, of course, should match the datatype of the column or of its domain, whichever is applicable. The default may include user value functions. (See Value Expressions in Part III for more information.)

DROP COLUMN is used to eliminate a column from the table. Any data currently in the column is destroyed. Naturally, there are restrictions. First, the column to be dropped may not be the only one in the table. (If this is what you want to do, use DROP TABLE.)

If you specify RESTRICT, the statement will fail if the column is currently referenced in any views, constraints, or assertions, except for constraints that are contained in the table and reference only the specified column. Sometimes, references to a column can be hidden; for example, a view that includes SELECT * (SELECT all columns) will include the column even without naming it. So may one that uses the NATURAL JOIN operation (see SELECT).

If you specify CASCADE, such referencing objects will be dropped, and all column-specific privileges on the column will be revoked from all users.

> **WARNING** Warning: With CASCADE, views referencing the column will not be modified—they will be dropped.

ADD *table constraint definition* will add a new table constraint to the table, and DROP will drop an existing one. If RESTRICT is specified for DROP, the column must not currently be used as the parent key to any foreign key. If CASCADE is specified, any such foreign keys will have their REFERENCES or FOREIGN KEY constraint dropped as well. If the foreign key is also a parent (possible but unusual), any foreign keys that reference it will also lose their constraints.

Example

This statement adds a column called country to the Clients table. The column is a fixed-length text string with a ten-character maximum length and a default value of USA.

```
ALTER TABLE  Clients ADD country CHAR(10) DEFAULT = 'USA';
```

Conformance Levels

Intermediate   ALTER TABLE is required for Intermediate or Full SQL92 conformance. It has been supported by many products for some time but not in a fully standardized fashion.

See Also Part II: CREATE TABLE, DROP TABLE, CREATE DOMAIN. Part III: Constraints, Datatypes.

CLOSE

(Static or Dynamic SQL) Closes a Currently Open Cursor

Syntax

```
CLOSE cursor name;
```

Usage

If the cursor is not currently open, the CLOSE statement will produce an error. It does not matter whether any or all of the rows have been fetched. Once the cursor is closed, its content is lost. If it is reopened, the query contained will be executed again with possibly different results (if the data has been changed in the interim). For more on cursors, see DECLARE CURSOR.

Conformance Levels

SQL86   CLOSE is required by the original 86 standard.

See Also   Part II: ALLOCATE CURSOR, DEALLOCATE CURSOR, DECLARE CURSOR, FETCH, OPEN.

COMMIT WORK

Makes Current Changes Permanent

Syntax

```
COMMIT [WORK];
```

Usage

The COMMIT WORK statement terminates a transaction (a group of statements executed together) and attempts to make permanent the changes dictated by statements within the transaction . This attempt can fail because, for example, of a system crash or a constraint violation. If the transaction cannot be committed, it will be rolled back (aborted). In the more advanced conformance levels, WORK is an optional word provided for clarity; it has no effect.

If your system is configured so that transaction management is under the control of the operating system, this statement produces an error.

Before the COMMIT is performed, all constraints that were deferred are checked. After the execution of all statements in the transaction, the database must be in a state that satisfies all constraints. Otherwise, the transaction is rolled back. For more on deferring constraints, see Constraints in Part III.

When the transaction is committed, all open cursors are closed, and any temporary tables whose definitions specify ON COMMIT DELETE ROWS are emptied of data.

Conformance Levels

Intermediate   Deferability of constraints is not required by the standard.

Entry   The keyword WORK is not optional.

See Also   See Also Part II: CLOSE, ROLLBACK, SET TRANSACTION. Part III: Constraints.

CONNECT
Establishes a Connection to the DBMS

Syntax
```
CONNECT TO { SQL environment spec
    [ AS connection name ]
    [ USER user name] }
    | DEFAULT ;
```

Usage

Since some connection procedure is necessary in most SQL environments, most products already have their own approach to this problem. The standard technique indicated here won't be required until Full SQL92 conformance is reached, although many products may try to implement it even if they do not claim such conformance.

If there is already an active connection between the user and the DBMS, the previous connection becomes dormant, and the new one is current.

DEFAULT indicates implementation-defined values for *SQL environment spec*, *connection name*, and *user name*. Likewise, omitting the AS or USER clauses implies that the implementation has some technique for naming the connection and for ascertaining the Authorization ID under which the statement should be run. The Authorization ID may be obtained from the operating system, for example, or it and a password may be prompted for. Other than meeting the basic conventions (outlined in Appendix D), restrictions as to format and possible values of all of these are implementation-defined. It is also up to the implementation to determine from the *SQL environment spec* which server to connect to, what protocol to use, and so on.

If the CONNECT statement is issued by a SQL module or compilation unit emulation thereof, this module may have its own Authorization ID. If so, it is implementation-defined whether the user name must be that Authorization ID or could instead be the user's own ID. In any other case, the username would be the Authorization ID normally identifying the user. For more on modules, see Appendix B.

If the user already has a connection with the indicated connection name, the statement will produce an error. This includes the DEFAULT. If the statement produces an error, the current connection, if any, will remain the current connection.

Example

The following statement initiates a connection to the environment called Marketing_Dept under the Authorization ID (for SESSION_USER) Carrie:

```
CONNECT TO Marketing_Dept USER Carrie ;
```

Conformance Levels

Full	Only required at this level.
Non	Some form of connection initiation is supported by all major products, but it may not precisely follow the standard.

See Also   Part II: DISCONNECT, SET CONNECTION. Part III: Authorization IDs.

CREATE ASSERTION

Defines an Assertion

Syntax

```
CREATE ASSERTION constraint name
CHECK ( predicate )
[ constraint attributes ];
```

Usage

An assertion is a schema object whose content is a CHECK constraint, which is to say a predicate preceded by the keyword

CHECK. The constraint is violated if the predicate is FALSE. The rules, behavior, and syntax of CHECK constraints are described in Part III: Constraints. An assertion is not part of a table definition but exists independently of any particular table and can refer in its predicate to any tables in the schema. It can be used to ensure that tables are not empty, which cannot be done from within the tables because constraints within tables are checked only when table values are inserted, updated, or deleted. The assertion must conform to the following principles:

- The name must be supplied. With other types of constraints, you have the option of letting the DBMS name the constraint for you (although it is usually not a good idea). For assertions, you do not have this option.

- If the assertion is created as part of a CREATE SCHEMA sequence, and the assertion's name is qualified by a schema name, the latter must be the name of the schema being created.

- The predicate cannot reference a temporary table. Temporary tables are explained under CREATE TABLE.

- The predicate cannot use target specifications (the variables used to output data to the host language in Static SQL) or dynamic parameter specifications (which serve a similar function in Dynamic SQL).

- The predicate may not use datetime value functions or user value functions (CURRENT_USER and so on).

- The assertion is named as a constraint. Therefore, its name must be different from the name of every other constraint in the schema.

- The predicate cannot contain a query that is possibly non-deterministic (possibly non-deterministic queries are defined in Part II: SELECT).

- For every column specifically referenced in the predicate, the creator of the assertion must have the REFERENCES privilege on that column or the CREATE ASSERTION statement will fail.

- For every table referenced without regard to column names (for example, if an assertion containing the aggregate function COUNT (*) were used on the table to impose a maximum size), you must have the REFERENCES privilege on at least one column of that table.

- The assertion fails if it is FALSE at the time the constraint is checked. A value of UNKNOWN, which can be caused by NULLs, will not cause a failure (see Part III: Predicates for an explanation of NULLs and UNKNOWNs).

- The constraint attributes clause allows you to define whether the constraint can be deferred and whether it is deferred by default. If no constraint attributes are included, the constraint will not be deferrable and will be effectively checked after every relevant statement (see Constraints in Part III).

If the text of the constraint is too long to fit in the allocated space in the INFORMATION SCHEMA (the set of tables that describe the content of the database), you will get a warning message, but the statement will not fail. The text will be truncated in the INFORMATION_SCHEMA, but will still execute as though it were present in full.

Example

The following statement defines an assertion on the Salespeople table that ensures that either the salary or commission columns must have a value (both may have values). The constraint will be deferrable but checked immediately by default.

```
CREATE ASSERTION Check_on_pay
CHECK (Salespeople.salary IS NOT NULL
OR Salespeople.commission IS NOT NULL)
DEFERRABLE INITIALLY IMMEDIATE;
```

Conformance Levels

Intermediate   Support for assertions is not required at this level.

See Also   Part II: CREATE SCHEMA, DROP ASSERTION, SET CONSTRAINTS MODE. Part III: Constraints, Datetime Value Functions, Predicates, Value Expressions (for User Value Functions), Appendix D.

CREATE CHARACTER SET
Defines a Character Set

Syntax

```
CREATE CHARACTER SET character set name [ AS ]
GET character set source
[ COLLATE collation name
/ COLLATION FROM collation source ];
```

Usage

The CREATE CHARACTER SET statement defines a character set for text strings. As part of its internationalization, SQL92 provides this facility primarily to enable the use of languages other than English. This statement can also be used to change the default collation of a character set by defining a new version of it with a different collation.

Each SQL implementation comes with one or more character sets already defined. These will either follow national or international standards or be defined by the implementer. One of these sets is the SQL TEXT character set that is used to express the SQL language itself. This statement enables you to create new character sets by changing the existing definitions and supplying new names.

A character set consists of a *repertoire*, an *encoding*, a *form-of-use*, and a *collation*. A repertoire is a set of characters, an encoding is a way of representing them internally in the database (i.e., as binary numbers), a form-of-use is a data format used by the encoding, and a collation is a way of sorting them. The form-of-use is associated with the repertoire and generally need only be considered separately if you want to change it (see Part III: String Value Functions). This statement combines the repertoire of some existing character set with a collation to define a new character set. A character set is an object in the schema. It has an owner, and other users must be granted the USAGE privilege on it to access it.

A character set follows the ordinary rules for schema objects. That is to say, it must be created by the schema owner, its name must be unique within the schema, and if it is part of a CREATE SCHEMA sequence, it will be part of the schema being created and cannot specify another with a qualified name. The creator of the character set will be able to grant the USAGE privilege on it to others. If the CREATE CHARACTER SET statement is contained in a module or compilation unit, the current Authorization ID, whether that of the user or the module, must be that of the schema owner.

The GET clause identifies the character set that provides the repertoire. To use a character set as the source of your repertoire, you must have the USAGE privilege on that character set. In this case, you would simply be creating a new character set with the same repertoire but a different collation than the old. For example, you might use this to make ASCII and EBCDIC collate the same way, which of course they normally do not. You would own and control access over this new character set.

Lastly, you define the default collation for this character set. If a CREATE CHARACTER SET statement is part of a CREATE SCHEMA sequence, you may use a COLLATE clause to explicitly specify a collation. Otherwise, you must use COLLATION FROM and apply some predefined collation or other collation source as defined under CREATE COLLATION.

Example

The following statement defines a new character set based on the ASCII repertoire but with the reverse collating sequence, so that 'a' > 'b'.

```
CREATE CHARACTER SET Backwards_ASCII
GET ASCII COLLATION FROM DESC(ASCII);
```

Conformance Levels

Intermediate	At this level, being able to simultaneously define a character set and collation in a CREATE SCHEMA sequence is not required.
Entry	Entry-level conformance does not require support for the CREATE CHARACTER SET statement.

See Also Part II: CREATE SCHEMA, DROP CHARACTER SET. Part III: Collations. Appendix D.

CREATE COLLATION
Defines a Collating Sequence

Syntax

```
CREATE COLLATION collation name
FOR character set specification
FROM collation source
[ NO PAD | PAD SPACE ]

collation source ::=
collation name
| DESC ( collation name )
| DEFAULT
| EXTERNAL ('external collation name')
| { TRANSLATION translation name
  [ THEN COLLATION collation name ] };
```

Usage

Text strings in SQL are normally sortable. This means that they fall in some intrinsic sequence, such as alphabetical order. You can apply relational operators such as less than and greater than to such strings, and the expression will be evaluated in terms of the collating sequence. For example, 'a' < 'b' means "'a' precedes 'b' in the collating sequence, and 'c' > 'b' means "'c' follows 'b' in the collating sequence". Strings of more than one character are sorted by comparing the first character of each, then the second, and so on until a difference between the two strings is found. That difference determines the sorting order.

A collation is a named schema object that defines a collating sequence. As with other schema objects, all collations in a schema must have distinct names. If they are part of a CREATE SCHEMA sequence, and a schema name is prefixed to their own, it must be the name of the schema being created.

The Authorization ID issuing the CREATE COLLATION statement must have the USAGE privilege on all collations and translations referenced within it. This Authorization ID will own and have the USAGE privilege on the created collation but will have the

GRANT OPTION on this privilege only if it also has the GRANT OPTION on all the contained collations and translations.

If the *collation source* is a collation name, that collation is duplicated. It may be a collation from a different schema, so you can transfer customized collations between schemas this way. You can also define a new version of a collation with a different pad attribute (explained below). Naturally, if the collation is drawn from a schema other than the current default, the name must be preceded by the schema name and a dot.

If the *collation source* specifies DESC (descending) followed by a collation name, the new collation will be the reverse of the old.

If the *collation source* specifies DEFAULT, the collation will be the order in which the characters are represented in the repertoire. This is implementaion-defined.

If the *collation source* specifies EXTERNAL, the nature of the collation and any restrictions upon it are implementation-defined.

If the *collation source* specifies TRANSLATION, an already-existing translation will be applied to the character set. The source character set of the translation must be the same as that of the collation being here defined. If the THEN COLLATION clause is used, its character set must match the target of the translation. For more on translations, see CREATE TRANSLATION.

Example

The following statement defines a collation based on the Cursive character set. The collation will follow the order in which the characters are represented in the repertoire.

```
CREATE COLLATION Normal_cursive
  FOR Cursive
  FROM DEFAULT;
```

Conformance Levels

Intermediate   Support for the CREATE COLLATION statement is not required.

See Also Part II: CREATE CHARACTER SET, CREATE SCHEMA, CREATE TRANSLATION. Part III: Collations. Appendix D.

CREATE DOMAIN
Defines a Domain

Syntax

```
CREATE DOMAIN domain name [ AS ] datatype
[ DEFAULT default value    ]
[ constraint definition... ]
[ COLLATE collation name   ];

constraint definition ::=
[ constraint name definition ]
check constraint
[ [NOT] DEFERRABLE ]
[ {INITIALLY IMMEDIATE}
| {INITIALLY DEFERRED}]
```

Usage

The CREATE DOMAIN statement creates a domain, an object in the schema that serves as an alternative to a datatype in defining columns. A domain specifies a datatype and additionally offers options for defining a default value, a collation, and one or more constraints. Ideally, it denotes a logical category of values.

AS is provided for clarity; it is not necessary and has no effect. You can create a domain without specifying any of the optional clauses. You might do this to group columns into comparisons that make sense. For example, it makes no sense to compare social security numbers and telephone numbers even though both may be the same datatype—they are in different domains. Domains can also be a useful way to standardize complex packages of constraints or an unusual collation.

Only the Authorization ID that owns the schema can create, and thus own, the domain. This Authorization ID must have the REFERENCES privilege on every column referenced in the domain and the USAGE privilege on every domain, character set, translation, or collation so referenced. This Authorization ID will have the USAGE privilege on the domain. If the Authorization ID was granted all of the privileges listed above with GRANT OPTION specified, it will be able to pass along the USAGE privilege on the domain itself.

If the CREATE DOMAIN statement is part of a CREATE SCHEMA sequence, and the domain name is prefixed with a schema name, the domain must be part of the schema being created. Also, if a character string datatype is used with no character set or no collation specified, the schema defaults apply. (Collations can only be specified for character string datatypes.)

The optional arguments follow the same rules as the same arguments used in other contexts. See Part II: CREATE TABLE and Part III: Constraints and Collations.

All constraints must be expressed as CHECK constraints. As is ordinarily the case with constraints, the naming and attributes are optional. The attributes determine the deferability of the constraint, as described in Part III: Constraints. If the attributes are omitted, the constraint cannot be deferred. If the name is omitted, and your system conforms at least to Entry SQL92, the DBMS will assign a name, which you can determine by querying the INFORMATION_SCHEMA (see Appendix D).

Note also that domains cannot be circular. That is, a domain may contain constraints that reference columns; and these columns may be based on domains that have constraints of their own that reference columns in turn. But at no point in this chain should the domain we started with come up again. All domains referenced directly or indirectly in the constraints of a domain are said to be in usage by those constraints. No domain may be in usage by its own constraints.

Example

The following statement creates a domain called id_nums, which is to be filled with positive integers. The default value will be NULL.

```
CREATE DOMAIN id_nums AS integer CHECK(VALUE > 0);
```

Conformance Levels

Intermediate	At this level, the user cannot name the constraints or specify a collation. The constraints are named, but by the DBMS rather than the user.
Entry	Domains are not required at this level.

See Also   Part II: ALTER DOMAIN, CREATE TABLE, DROP DOMAIN. Part III: Constraints.

CREATE SCHEMA
Defines a Schema

Syntax

```
CREATE SCHEMA schema name clause
[ DEFAULT CHARACTER SET character set ]
[ { CREATE DOMAIN statement
| CREATE TABLE statement
| CREATE VIEW statement
| GRANT statement
| CREATE ASSERTION statement
| CREATE CHARACTER SET statement
| CREATE COLLATION statement
| CREATE TRANSLATION statement
  [ character set ] } ]...;

schema name clause ::=
schema name
| AUTHORIZATION authorization ID
| schema name AUTHORIZATION authorization ID
```

Usage

The CREATE SCHEMA statement creates a schema, a named group
of related objects. It may contain several other statements to create objects in the schema, such as tables, character sets, and
domains, and to grant privileges on them. All of these objects are
effectively materialized at the same time. Therefore, some circular
references are possible that would not be normally, such as having
two tables each with a foreign key referencing the other table as
parent. Objects and privileges may also be added later to the schema.

The creator of a schema owns it and largely controls the usage of
the objects in it. The right to create schemas is itself implementation-
defined. The schema is part of a group of one or more schemas called
a *catalog*. Its name must be unique within the catalog.

The schema name clause specifies the name of the schema. This
may be a full name, in the form

```
cluster.catalog.schema
```

If the cluster and catalog are not specified, defaults may apply in
an implementation-defined manner.

If no AUTHORIZATION clause is used, there are two possibilities:

- If the CREATE SCHEMA statement is part of a module or compilation unit (see Appendix B Specification of the Module Language), and the module has its own Authorization ID, the schema will be under the Authorization ID of the module. This means that use will be controlled by any user executing the module (see Appendix B).

- Otherwise, the schema will be under the Authorization ID of the SQL session user who creates it. For more on SQL session users, see User Value Functions in Part III.

If no *schema name* is given in the CREATE SCHEMA statement, but just the AUTHORIZATION clause, the Authorization ID is used as the *schema name*. The implicit assumption is that one Authorization ID will create only one schema, at least within the current catalog. This was the approach of the SQL86 standard, and SQL92 supports it, in large part for compatibility.

If both the Authorization ID and the schema name are indicated, the first indicates the owner and the second the schema. In any case, the schema name must be unique within its catalog.

The DEFAULT CHARACTER SET clause determines the character set that will be used for all columns and domains with CHARACTER STRING datatypes if none other is specified. If it is omitted, there will be some implementation-defined default.

If the AUTHORIZATION clause is used and the CREATE SCHEMA statement is part of a module, then the CREATE SCHEMA statement and any other statements that are part of it (for example, CREATE TABLE, CREATE DOMAIN, or any of the statements listed in the syntax diagram above) will operate under the indicated Authorization ID. After the CREATE SCHEMA statement and all of its contained statements have executed, the rest of the statements in the module will revert to the Authorization ID and the schema that were in effect before the CREATE SCHEMA statement.

Example

The following statement creates a schema called Joes_Schema, populated with a single domain and a single table and performing a single GRANT.

```
CREATE SCHEMA Joes_Schema   AUTHORIZATION Joe
DEFAULT CHARACTER SET ASCII
```

```
CREATE DOMAIN id_nums AS integer CHECK(VALUE > 0)
CREATE GLOBAL TEMPORARY TABLE Fluctuations
( item_num    id_nums NOT NULL PRIMARY KEY,
item_name     CHAR10 NOT NULL,
start_price   DEC(4,2),
max_price     DEC(4,2),
min_price     DEC(4,2),
avg_price     DEC(4,2),
end_price     DEC(4,2)
ON COMMIT PRESERVE ROWS )
GRANT SELECT ON Fluctuations TO Sarah;
```

Conformance Levels

Intermediate   Intermediate-level conformance need not allow assertions, collations, or translations as parts of a CREATE SCHEMA sequence.

Entry   Entry-level conformance does not require support for domains or character sets. It also does not mandate being able to name the schema—your only option may be to omit the name clause so that the schema is named after the Authorization ID of its creator (as specified in SQL89).

See Also   Part II: CREATE ASSERTION, CREATE CHARACTER SET, CREATE COLLATION, CREATE DOMAIN, CREATE TABLE, CREATE TRANSLATION, CREATE VIEW, DROP SCHEMA, GRANT, REVOKE. Part III: Authorization IDs,Collations. Appendix D.

CREATE TABLE
Creates a Permanent or Temporary Base Table

Syntax

```
CREATE [ {GLOBAL | LOCAL} TEMPORARY ] TABLE table name
( {column definition
| [table constraint ] }.,...
[ ON COMMIT { DELETE | PRESERVE } ROWS ] );

column definition ::=
```

```
column name {domain name
  {domain name | datatype[(size)]    }
  [ column constraint...]
  [ default value  ]
  [ collate clause ]
```

Usage

If TEMPORARY is specified, the table is temporary, and either GLOBAL or LOCAL must be specified; otherwise the table is a permanent base table and neither GLOBAL nor LOCAL apply. The distinction between permanent and temporary base tables will be clarified later in this entry. The ON COMMIT clause can only be used for temporary tables. If the table is temporary, and the ON COMMIT clause is omitted, then ON COMMIT DELETE ROWS is implied.

The table will contain one or more column definitions and zero or more *table constraints*, all separated by commas. The order of the columns in the CREATE TABLE statement determines their order in the table. A column definition must include:

- The name of the column. The column must be named as outlined in Appendix D.

- Either a datatype or a domain that will apply to all column values.

The table creator must have the USAGE privilege on a domain to define a column on it. Some datatypes will accept size arguments indicating, for example, the length of a fixed-length character string or the scale and precision of a decimal number. The meaning and format of these vary with the datatype, but there will be defaults in any case. See Datatypes in Part III for more information on these arguments.

In addition to the elements shown above, there are a number of optional elements that can be included in column definitions. These elements, discussed below, may be specified in any order.

Default Values and Collations   One such element is a default value for the column. If a default is given for a column specified on a domain that already has its own default, the default of the column overrides that of the domain. If the NOT NULL constraint (described below) is specified for a column, then either a default value must be defined or every INSERT or UPDATE command on the column must leave it with a specified value.

You may also specify a collating sequence for the column, if that column has a character string datatype or is defined on a domain with such a datatype. This sequence overrides the ordinary collating sequence of the character set or of the domain. See Collations in Part III for more detail.

Column and Table Constraints   You may also place one or more constraints on the table. Constraints following the definition of a column apply to that column; those standing alone as table constraints may reference any one or more columns in the table. Starting with SQL92 (any level), constraints are named, although the names may be generated internally, rather than defined by the table creator. The following description of the types of constraints is an overview; see Constraints in Part III for more detailed information on collating sequences. The possible constraints are:

NOT NULL   In the standard, this can only be a column constraint. This forbids NULLs from being entered into a column.

UNIQUE   This mandates that every column value, or combination of column values if a table constraint, be unique.

PRIMARY KEY   This has the same effect as UNIQUE, except that none of the columns in a PRIMARY KEY constraint may contain NULLs, while those in a UNIQUE constraint may. (Note that this is not true for Entry-level SQL92 conformance, as noted under the conformance levels. In fact, Entry-compliant implementations may allow NULLs in UNIQUE as an extension to the standard.) Also, the PRIMARY KEY constraint behaves a bit differently with foreign keys (explained later in this entry). This constraint may be used only once in a given table.

CHECK	This is followed by a predicate, in parentheses, that uses column values in some expression whose value can be TRUE, FALSE, or (in the presence of NULLs) UNKNOWN. The constraint is violated only when the predicate is FALSE. See Part III: Predicates.
FOREIGN KEY | REFERENCES	FOREIGN KEY is the table constraint version; REFERENCES is for column constraints. For a table constraint, the words FOREIGN KEY are followed by a parenthesized list of the column names in this table that will do the referencing. After that, the two versions are the same: the keyword REFERENCES followed by the name of the table containing the parent key and a parenthesized list of the column(s) that are to be referenced. This constraint identifies the columns as a foreign key referencing a parent key in the same or (usually) another table. The parent key must have the PRIMARY KEY or the UNIQUE constraint. If the former, the column name(s) can be omitted from the FOREIGN KEY or REFERENCES constraint. Note that you can specify what happens when a parent key is changed or deleted, and you can specify full or partial matches of foreign to parent keys, which behave differently when NULLs are present. See Part III: Constraints for details.

You can define constraints so that they are not checked until the end of the current transaction. This is very useful when, for example, you want to update a table that references itself as a parent key. This operation usually creates intermediate states where referential integrity has to be violated. By default, constraints are not deferrable. See Part III: SET CONSTRAINTS MODE or Constraints for more information.

Temporary Tables

Temporary tables are tables whose data is destroyed at the end of every SQL session, if not earlier. They are used for intermediate results or working storage. There are three kinds: global temporary tables, created local temporary tables, and declared local temporary tables. The first two are created with the CREATE TABLE statement by specifying GLOBAL TEMPORARY or LOCAL TEMPORARY, respectively. Declared local temporary tables are created with the DECLARE LOCAL TEMPORARY TABLE statement. The difference between the first two types, which we will call created temporary tables, and the third, the declared tables, is that the created tables have definitions that are permanent parts of the schema, even though their data is not. Declared tables are created at runtime by a SQL module or a program that uses SQL; outside that module or program, their names and definitions are not stored in the database.

The difference between the global and local tables created by this statement is their visibility. Although neither can be seen by other SQL sessions (and thus by other users), the data in global temporary tables can be accessed by any program or module within the session. Created local tables, on the other hand, cannot share data between modules or compilation units. For further discussion of modules and compilation units, see Appendix B.

To summarize, temporary tables are base tables. The data they contain is their own, not (as with views) an indirect representation of the data in other tables. They typically are created and filled with data by applications or modules. But this data is not saved in the database. It is automatically destroyed at the end of a SQL session, and when the table is to be used again, new data must be inserted into it. Global temporary tables have definitions stored permanently (that is, until dropped like any other table with a DROP TABLE statement) in the schema. Their data can be accessed by any statement within the same SQL session. Created local temporary tables also have definitions that are permanent parts of the database schema, but their data can be accessed only by the SQL module or program that called them. Declared local temporary tables, created with the DECLARE LOCAL TEMPORARY TABLE statement, do not even have definitions that are part of the database schema. Their definitions are part of the code in a module or Embedded SQL program, and they are defined when that code is executed. Table II.1 summarizes the characteristics of the various types of base tables. Since declared tables are created with a different statement, we will omit them from the remainder of this discussion.

TABLE II.1: Characteristics of Base Tables

Table Type	Visibility of Data	Definition Persistence	Data Persistence
Permanent	Universal (subject to privileges)	Permanent	Permanent
Global Temporary	Session	Permanent	Session
Created Local	Module or C.U.	Permanent	Session
Declared Local	Module or C.U.	Module or C.U.	Session

The ON COMMIT clause specifies what happens at the end of the transaction. DELETE ROWS will empty the table, while PRESERVE ROWS will retain the data for the next transaction in the session. If the transaction rolls back (is aborted), the table is returned to its state at the end of the previous transaction, with the rows either deleted or preserved. If the aborted transaction was the first in the session, the table is emptied. As we mentioned, DELETE is the default, so be sure to specify PRESERVE if you will ever want to retain the data across transaction boundaries. You can always empty the table, but you cannot preserve the data in a table that specifies ON COMMIT DELETE ROWS.

Ownership and Access Control

Like all database objects, a table resides in a schema and is created by the owner of that schema. If the table name is qualified by a schema name in the CREATE TABLE command, it identifies the containing schema. If the table name is not so qualified, it will be part of the current default schema. (See Appendix D for details.) As with all schema objects, if the table is part of a CREATE SCHEMA sequence, then the schema being created will be the containing schema. In any case, the table name must be unique within its schema.

Tables and other database objects are created and owned by Authorization IDs, which means users in most contexts (the exception is with modules, see Appendix B). The owner of an object controls the privileges others have on it. In a sense, then, all privilege flows from the right to create objects. Who has this right? In SQL89, it was undefined. In SQL92, tables are grouped into schemas and can only be created by the owner of the schema (which can be a module) in which they reside. Who has the right, then, to create a schema? That is still undefined.

There are, of course, very good reasons why it is impractical to standardize this point, but since it must be addressed, implementers have taken their own approaches. One that is used in some major products is to define a privilege called, for example, "resource" that gives the user the right to create objects. This is granted by some user with the DBA privilege—a superuser privilege. Users without the resource privilege will at least have the connect privilege—the right to log on.

Example

The following statement creates a global temporary table whose rows will be preserved between transactions. The primary key is based on the id_nums domain; the other columns are based on standard datatypes.

```
CREATE GLOBAL TEMPORARY TABLE Fluctuations
( item_num id_nums NOT NULL PRIMARY KEY,
item_name CHAR10 NOT NULL,
start_price   DEC,
max_price DEC,
min_price DEC,
avg_price DEC,
end_price DEC
ON COMMIT PRESERVE ROWS );
```

Conformance Levels

Intermediate — Implementations at this level are not required to support temporary tables and collation definitions. Certain special features of foreign keys, namely partial matches and update effects (see Part III: Constraints), do not come into play at this level. Also, at this level you may have to name the columns of a multicolumn FOREIGN KEY constraint in the same order that the parents they match were named in the UNIQUE or PRIMARY KEY constraint that applies to them. Note: If your system has conformed to the new standardized INFORMATION_SCHEMA (and perhaps even if it has not), you can find the order there. In the standard INFORMATION_SCHEMA, you would look in the view KEY_COLUMN_USAGE. At this level you may not be able to name constraints. If that is the case, internal names must be generated.

Entry	If UNIQUE or PRIMARY KEY is specified, NOT NULL should be specified too (this was the old standard's approach, and it remains permissible until the Intermediate level of SQL92 conformance).
SQL89	Naming of constraints, either by the user or the system, is not supported at this level.
SQL86	Use of the FOREIGN KEY and REFERENCES constraints is not supported at this level; they were added to the standard in SQL89.

See Also   Part II: ALTER TABLE, COMMIT WORK, CREATE SCHEMA, CREATE VIEW, DECLARE LOCAL TEMPORARY TABLE, DROP TABLE, ROLLBACK. Part III: Constraints, Datatypes. Appendix B.

CREATE TRANSLATION
Translates Text Strings from One Character String to Another

Syntax
```
CREATE TRANSLATION translation name
FOR source character set
TO target character set
FROM translation name
| { EXTERNAL ('translation name') }
| IDENTITY ;
```

Usage
The CREATE TRANSLATION statement defines a translation from one character set to another. Once defined, the translation can be applied by using the TRANSLATE statement. A translation is

an object in the schema and follows the conventional rules for such objects.

The translations that a given product supports are implementation-defined. This statement effectively allows you to define new translations based on the existing ones.

Example

The following statement imposes an external translation on the ASCII character set. The resulting character set is called Czech. The external translation is called Convert1, and the translation defined here is called Convert2. Effectively, this makes an imported translation part of the schema.

```
CREATE TRANSLATION Convert2 FOR ASCII TO CZECH
FROM EXTERNAL ('Convert1');
```

Conformance Levels

Intermediate   Not required at the Intermediate level or below.

See Also   Part II: CREATE CHARACTER SET, CREATE COLLATION. Part III: Collations, Datatypes Appendix D.

CREATE VIEW
Defines a View

Syntax

```
CREATE VIEW table name [(column list)]
(AS SELECT statement
[WITH [CASCADED | LOCAL] CHECK OPTION] );
```

Usage

The CREATE VIEW statement creates a view, also known as a virtual or derived table. A view is an object that is treated as a table but whose definition contains a query, which is to say a valid SELECT statement (see SELECT). Views are referenced in SQL statements just like base tables are. When the view is referenced in a statement, the query is executed and its output becomes the content of the view for the duration of that statement. In some cases, views can be updated, in which case the changes are transferred to the underlying data in the base table(s) referenced by the query. Views are not the same as temporary tables, which do contain their own data, even though it is not preserved between sessions (see CREATE TABLE and DECLARE LOCAL TEMPORARY TABLE).

As with a base table, the rows of a view are by definition unordered. Therefore, ORDER BY may not be specified in the query. Note that the query may access more than one base table and that therefore a view may combine data from several tables.

As is usual with database objects, views are part of a schema and can be created only by the schema owner. If the CREATE VIEW statement is part of a CREATE SCHEMA sequence and the view name is preceded by a schema name, the names must match. The name of the view must be distinct from all other table names—both base tables, including temporary tables, and views—in the same schema. Views can be based on other views, but at some point must refer to some set of base tables.

Let's look at some terminology. The tables or views directly referenced in a query—whether that query stands alone or is part of a view definition—are called the "simply underlying tables" of the query (or the view). These combined with all the tables they reference, and all the subsequently referenced tables—all the way down to and including the base tables that contain the data—are called the "generally underlying tables". The base tables—the ones that do not reference any other tables but actually contain the data—are called the "leaf underlying tables". View definitions cannot be circular. That is, no view can be among its own generally underlying tables.

The view also may not contain a target specification (a host variable, possibly accompanied by an indicator variable) or a dynamic parameter specification. (These are relevant only to Static and Dynamic SQL, respectively. If you want to pass parameters in this fashion, you probably want to use a cursor; see DECLARE CURSOR).

The list of columns is used to provide the columns with names that will be used only in this view. You may use it if you do not want to retain the names that the columns have in the underlying base table(s). You must name the columns whenever the following apply:

- Any two of the columns would otherwise have identical names.

- Any of the columns contain computed values or any values other than column values directly extracted from the under-lying tables, unless an AS clause is used in the query to name them.

- There are any joined columns with distinct names in their respective tables, unless an AS clause is used in the query to name them.

If you do name the columns, you naturally cannot use the same column name twice in the same view. If you name the columns, you must name all of them, so the number of columns in the name list has to be the same as that in the SELECT clause of the contained query. You may use SELECT * in the query to select all columns; if you do this, it will be converted internally to a list of all columns. This conversion is for your protection, because it means that if someone were to add a column to an underlying table using the ALTER TABLE statement, it would not change the definition of your view. Note that the columns in the view may not have a coercibility attribute of No Collating Sequence. This is only relevant for character string datatypes. Coercibility attributes are discussed under Collations in Part III.

Views and Privileges

Privileges exist on views just as on other tables. In order to create a view, you must have the SELECT privilege on every simply under-lying table referenced within it, including any underlying views. If you have this privilege with the GRANT OPTION for every such table, then you will also have it with GRANT OPTION on the view. Otherwise, you will own the view but still be unable to grant oth-ers to right to query it—it will basically be a view for your personal use. You can grant INSERT, UPDATE, and DELETE privileges on the view as well if you have these privileges on the underlying tables with GRANT OPTION, provided that the view is updatable (as explained below). The REFERENCES privilege works in a simi-lar manner: if you have it on all referenced columns, you have it on the view; and if you have it with GRANT OPTION, then you retain the grant option for the privilege on the view.

Inserting, Updating, and Deleting Values in Views

When you perform any of these operations on a view, the changes are transferred to the base table that contains the data. Such operations can be permitted only if the changes that must be made to the underlying table (always singular, as we shall see shortly) are unambiguous. The principle is that an insertion of or change to one row in the view must translate to an insertion of or change to one row in the leaf underlying table. If this is the case, the view is said to be updatable. The specific conditions outlined in the standard for a view to be updatable are these:

- It must be drawn on one and only one simply underlying table; in other words, no joins.

- It must contain one and only one query; in other words, no usage of UNION, EXCEPT, or INTERSECT.

- If the simply underlying table is itself a view, that view also must be updatable.

- The SELECT clause of the contained query may specify only column references, not value expressions or aggregate functions, and no column may be referenced more than once.

- The contained query may not specify GROUP BY or HAVING.

- The contained query may not specify DISTINCT.

- In SQL92, subqueries are permissible, but only if they do not refer to any of the generally underlying tables on which the view is based.

These are fairly stringent restrictions, and some products may relax some of them.

CHECK OPTION

The CHECK OPTION clause can be specified only for updatable views. It verifies that INSERT and UPDATE statements against the view do not populate the generally underlying tables with rows that will be excluded from the view. In other words, if I wanted a view of employees that would show only those working in London,

I could put WHERE city = 'London' in the query. If I then inserted a row into the view that had Barcelona in the city column, it would be inserted into the leaf underlying table but would not show up in my view. Usually, such an insertion is a mistake, so you normally should use CHECK OPTION with updatable views. With CHECK OPTION, INSERTs and UPDATEs are allowed only if they produce rows that satisfy the predicate of this view.

The CASCADED | LOCAL option determines whether the predicates of any underlying views are checked as well. You could have several layers of views between this view and the base table data. If an UPDATE or INSERT produces a row that violates the predicates of any of them, that row will not "trickle up" into the view. Should all of the predicates therefore be checked for every INSERT or UPDATE? The CASCADED option says yes, and it is the default. The LOCAL option will check only the predicate contained in this view. This does not override the predicates in the underlying views; if any of them excludes a row, it still will be added to the leaf underlying table without appearing in the present view. This can create subtle problems, as rows may disappear for reasons that are not obvious from examining the topmost view alone. For this reason, it is probably better in most cases to specify CASCADED or leave it as the default.

Note that CHECK OPTION is a sort of constraint. Unlike most types of constraints, however, it cannot be deferred. It will be effectively checked after every INSERT or UPDATE command.

Views and Security

Views are very useful to control what users do with the data. By granting access to views rather than the base tables, you can prevent users from seeing various rows and columns. In certain situations, you can use CHECK OPTION to effectively define constraints that are specific to various users. Place the constraints in the predicate of the view, specify CHECK OPTION, and give the users privileges on the view rather than the base table. Keep in mind that these users also will not see any existing rows that violate the constraint through the view, which may or may not be a problem.

Example

The following statement creates a read-only view called Price_ Variations based on the Fluctuations table (see the CREATE TABLE example). Since the view calculates the extent of price variation between the minimum and the maximum, and this is a calculated column, the output columns must be named. WITH CHECK OPTION cannot be specified, as the view is not updatable.

```
CREATE VIEW Price_Variations (item_id, item_name,
price_variation)
(AS SELECT item_id, name, max_price - min_price
 FROM Fluctuations
 WHERE start_price > end_price);
```

Conformance Levels

| Intermediate | Not required to allow specification of CAS-CADED or LOCAL for CHECK OPTION. If no specification is supported, it will default to CASCADED. |
| Entry | Not required to support UNION, EXCEPT, or INTERSECT, even for read-only views. Not required to support subqueries in updatable views. |

See Also   Part II: CREATE TABLE, DROP VIEW, GRANT, SELECT. Part III: Predicates. Appendix D.

DEALLOCATE DESCRIPTOR
(Dynamic SQL Only) Destroys a Descriptor Area

Syntax
```
DEALLOCATE DESCRIPTOR descriptor name;
```

Usage

The DEALLOCATE DESCRIPTOR statement deallocates, which is to say effectively removes, the named descriptor area, which must have been previously created with an ALLOCATE DESCRIPTOR statement. Descriptor areas are used in Dynamic SQL to provide information about and values for the parameters of dynamically generated SQL statements. For more information, see Descriptor Areas in Part III.

Conformance Levels

Intermediate   Implementations at this level are required only to support literals as descriptor names.

Entry   No Dynamic SQL or descriptor support is required.

See Also   Part II: ALLOCATE DESCRIPTOR, DESCRIBE, GET DESCRIPTOR, SET DESCRIPTOR. Part III: Descriptor Areas.

DEALLOCATE PREPARE
(Dynamic SQL Only) Destroys a Prepared Statement

Syntax

```
DEALLOCATE PREPARE prepared statement;
```

Usage

Prepared statements are statements generated from text strings at runtime. They are created using the PREPARE statement and destroyed using the DEALLOCATE PREPARE statement. If the prepared statement is currently referenced in a cursor, that cursor must be closed when the DEALLOCATE PREPARE statement is issued. The cursor and all prepared statements referencing it will be destroyed as well.

Conformance Levels

Intermediate   Implementations at this level are not required to support this statement.

See Also   Part II: ALLOCATE CURSOR, CLOSE, DECLARE CURSOR, OPEN, PREPARE.

DECLARE CURSOR
(Static or Dynamic SQL) Defines a Cursor

Syntax

```
DECLARE cursor name [ INSENSITIVE ] [ SCROLL ] CURSOR
FOR { SELECT statement
[ updatability clause ] }
  |{ prepared statement };

updatability clause::=
FOR { READ ONLY | UPDATE [ OF column list] } ]
```

Usage

The DECLARE CURSOR statement defines a *cursor*, an object used in applications to contain the output of a query and sometimes to perform updates on the tables referenced in the query. It is similar to a view in that its definition is a query and its content is the output of that query when it is opened (see OPEN). It differs from a view in that it does not act as a table, but rather as a way of breaking down the set-at-a-time operation of SQL into item-at-a-time operations for handling by an application. It is a sort of variable that stores the output of the query so that it can be processed by the application one row at a time.

The cursor name chosen must be unique within the module or compilation unit. The cursor can either be hard-coded (Static SQL) or created at runtime from a statement previously readied with a PREPARE statement (Dynamic SQL). In the former case, a SELECT statement and optional updatability clause will be specified. With the latter, a prepared statement containing the SELECT statement— and including the updatability clause if one is desired—will be used.

Ordering the Rows   Unlike those of a base table or view, the rows of an opened cursor have a definite order. If you wish, you may use an ORDER BY clause in the SELECT statement to impose an order. Otherwise, the order is implementation-dependent and possibly arbitrary. Even if your implementation provides a default ordering (which is common), for example by primary key, you should not consider it reliable unless your system documentation says it is. Generally, if the order of the rows is significant, you should use an

ORDER BY clause. ORDER BY allows you to sort the rows by any one or more columns of the cursor. You may specify ascending or descending independently for each column used to sort, with ascending as the default. For more detail on ORDER BY, see SELECT.

Sensitivity of Cursors   If you specify INSENSITIVE, the cursor's contents will be fixed once it is opened. Any changes made by other statements to the underlying data while the cursor is open will be ignored by the cursor. Only read-only cursors (explained below) can be defined as INSENSITIVE.

Scroll Cursors   If you specify SCROLL, you will not have to fetch the rows of the cursor in order once it is opened. SCROLL defines the cursor so that you can go back and forth through the rows when you fetch them. SCROLL can be specified only for read-only cursors.

Updating Cursors   A cursor is either updatable or read-only. Some cursors are not updatable by their nature and are therefore read-only even if this is not explicitly specified. If a cursor is updatable in principle, you can make it read-only with an updatability clause, although the reverse is not true. The updatability clause can also restrict the updatability of the cursor to specified columns. This clause can specify FOR UPDATE only if the cursor is updatable in principle. If the cursor is not updatable in principle, READ ONLY may be specified for clarity but will not change the behavior of the cursor. To be updatable in principle, a cursor must satisfy the following conditions:

- It may not specify INSENSITIVE, SCROLL, or ORDER BY.

- It must be drawn on one and only one simply underlying table (see CREATE VIEW). In other words, no joins.

- It must contain one and only one query. In other words, no use of UNION, EXCEPT, or INTERSECT.

- If the simply underlying table is a view, that view must itself be updatable.

- The SELECT clause of the contained query may specify only column references, not derived values or aggregate functions, and no column may be referenced more than once.

- The contained query may not specify GROUP BY or HAVING.

- The contained query may not specify DISTINCT.

A cursor that satisfies the above conditions is updatable in principle and by default permits UPDATE statements on all columns. Therefore, if FOR UPDATE is specified for such a cursor with no column list, it is simply for clarity and has no effect.

If you know that you will do no updating through an updatable cursor, declaring it read-only is a good idea. Data that might be changed must be locked, and this can slow down operations by other users. For the same reason, you may want to specify FOR UPDATE OF with a column list to lock only specific columns in the table.

Dynamic Cursors   Dynamic cursors are cursors created in Dynamic SQL at runtime. In Dynamic SQL you generally do not know, when you are writing the application, the specific content of the cursors the users will need. You may not even know how many cursors will need to be created. Therefore you can define cursors and have the SELECT statement and perhaps even the name filled in at runtime. You implement the latter option with the ALLOCATE CURSOR statement, which allows you to define any number of cursors with the same statement by simply executing the statement repeatedly with different values for the name parameter and query. See ALLOCATE CURSOR for more information on this topic.

With the Dynamic SQL version of DECLARE CURSOR, you define a cursor name in the code but leave the query to be filled in at runtime. In this case, you use a prepared statement in place of the SELECT statement and the updatability clause. The content of this prepared statement will in fact be a SELECT statement, possibly appended by an updatability clause, but the text of this statement will be generated dynamically at runtime by the application.

See PREPARE for information on how to define the query that the cursor will use.

Example

The following statement defines a scrollable, insensitive cursor called London_Clients, which contains the entries for all clients located in London. Because it is scrollable and insensitive, the cursor will automatically be read-only.

```
DECLARE London_Clients INSENSITIVE SCROLL CURSOR
FOR SELECT ID_NUM, NAME
  FROM Clients
  WHERE city = 'London';
```

Conformance Levels

Intermediate   Implementations at this level are not required to support insensitive cursors.

Entry   Implementations at this level are not required to support scroll cursors or updatability clauses (FOR UPDATE without a column list is implicit if the cursor is updatable; otherwise, read-only is implicit). They need not support Dynamic SQL or dynamic cursors at all.

See Also   Part I: Read-Only, Scrollable, Insensitive, and Dynamic Cursors. Part II: ALLOCATE CURSOR, CLOSE, CREATE VIEW, DEALLOCATE PREPARE, FETCH, OPEN, PREPARE, SELECT.

DECLARE LOCAL TEMPORARY TABLE
Defines a Local Temporary Table

Syntax

```
DECLARE LOCAL TEMPORARY TABLE qualified table name
( {column definition
| [table constraint ] }.,..
[ ON COMMIT { DELETE | PRESERVE } ROWS ] );
```

Usage

Temporary tables, unlike views, contain data of their own, but that data is not preserved between SQL sessions. In the case of declared local temporary tables, which are created with the DECLARE LOCAL TEMPORARY TABLE statement, the table definitions are not preserved either; the tables are defined at runtime (the other two types of temporary tables, which do have persistent definitions, are defined with the CREATE TABLE statement). The DECLARE LOCAL TEMPORARY TABLE statement is contained in some application SQL code, such as a module, or some Embedded SQL code.

When that code is executed, the declared table is created. When the module or compilation unit is exited, the definition and content of the declared local temporary table (which we will refer to as "declared tables" for the remainder of this discussion) is destroyed. In other words, a DELETE and a DROP TABLE statement are effectively executed. Not being a persistent part of the database, the definition of the declared table is not recorded in the INFORMATION_SCHEMA.

NOTE In the module language approach, all temporary table declarations must precede all procedures, which will contain the various other SQL statements used in the module.

A declared table does not reside in a schema as other tables do. The "schema" of which it is a part is derived in some implementation-dependent manner from the SQL-session identifier that invoked the module and the name of the module itself. Since you generally cannot know when writing Static SQL code what the SQL-session identifier will be, the standard provides a built-in variable that represents the containing schema. That variable is the word *MODULE*, which is to be prefixed to the declared table's name wherever referenced just as a schema name would be, for example, MODULE .MY_TABLE. This system allows a unique instance of the table to be defined for each session that invokes the containing module. Each such instance will be invisible to other sessions or modules. If Embedded or Dynamic SQL is used rather than the module language, support for declared tables is an implementation extension that should behave in a similar manner to the module approach.

The rules for columns, datatypes, constraints, defaults, and so on in declared tables are the same as for the other kinds of temporary tables described under CREATE TABLE. Likewise, the ON COMMIT clause operates in the same way as it does in CREATE TABLE: if DELETE ROWS (the default) is specified, the table is automatically emptied of values at the close of each transaction, although its definition will survive the transaction so that a second DECLARE TABLE within the same module will not be necessary. If PRESERVE ROWS is specified, the table will be emptied of values at the end of the session or when it is destroyed, whichever comes first. The table will be destroyed (dropped) when the module or compilation unit that contains the DECLARE statement is exited.

All of the conventional table privileges—INSERT, UPDATE, DELETE, SELECT, and REFERENCES—exist on declared tables but are not grantable. Therefore, each user will have these privileges on the versions of the table that she creates.

Example

The following statement creates a temporary table called Daily_Stats, which presumably will contain data to be used for further calculations by the application. The data inserted in the table will persist across transactions.

```
DECLARE LOCAL TEMPORARY TABLE Daily_Stats
(statnum   INTEGER NOT NULL PRIMARY KEY,
average    DECIMAL(4,2),
maximum    DECIMAL(4,2),
minimum    DECIMAL(4,2)
ON COMMIT PRESERVE ROWS   );
```

Conformance Levels

Intermediate   Implementations at this level are not required to support this statement.

See Also   Part II: CREATE SCHEMA, CREATE TABLE, DROP TABLE, GRANT. Part III: Authorization IDs.

DELETE
Removes Rows from Tables

Syntax

```
DELETE FROM table name
[  {  WHERE predicate }
|  {  WHERE CURRENT OF cursor name } ];
```

Usage

The DELETE statement can be coded directly or, in Dynamic SQL, be a prepared statement, which is a statement whose text is generated at runtime (see PREPARE). The DELETE statement removes rows from temporary or permanent base tables, views, or cursors. In the last two cases, the deletions are transferred to the base table from which the view or cursor extracts its data.

The WHERE CURRENT OF form is used for deletions from cursors. The row currently in the cursor is removed. This is called a *positioned deletion*. The WHERE *predicate* form is used for deletions from base tables or views. All rows that satisfy the predicate are removed at once. This is called a *searched deletion*. If the WHERE clause is absent, it is also a searched deletion, but all rows of the table or view are removed (be careful!). The following restrictions apply to both types:

- The Authorization ID performing the deletion must have the DELETE privilege on the table.

- If the deletion is performed on a view or cursor, that view or cursor must be updatable (see CREATE VIEW and DECLARE CURSOR).

- If the current transaction mode is read-only (see SET TRANSACTION), and the table being deleted from is not temporary, then the deletion is disallowed. Note that this logically should include views that are based on temporary tables, although the standard seems ambiguous on this point.

Using Searched Deletions The predicates used in DELETE statements, like those in SELECT and UPDATE, use one or more expressions—for example, `location = 'London'`—and test whether they are TRUE, FALSE, or (in the presence of NULLs) UNKNOWN for each row based on the values within that row. Each row for which the predicate is TRUE will be deleted.

NOTE If a row that satisfies the predicate for a searched deletion has been marked for deletion or update, by this or another transaction, through a cursor that is still open (see OPEN), it will produce the warning "Cursor operation conflict," but the deletion will proceed.

Using Positioned Deletions Positioned deletions use cursors and therefore only apply to Static or Dynamic, not to Interactive, SQL. You can use a positioned deletion if there is a cursor within the current module or compilation unit that references the table, and this cursor has been opened within the current transaction, has had at least one row FETCHed, and has not yet been CLOSEd (see OPEN and FETCH). The last row FETCHed will be deleted.

Using Prepared DELETE Statements   In Dynamic SQL, you generally do not know in advance the statements that will need to be issued. You may not even know the name of the table from which the values are being deleted when you write the code. For these situations, SQL provides the PREPARE statement, which you use to generate the text of dynamic statements at runtime. When you use PREPARE to generate a positioned deletion, the FROM table name clause of the DELETE statement may be omitted, and whatever table underlies the cursor will be assumed. This frees you from having to know the table name in advance, and the cursors can simply be generated dynamically as needed with the ALLOCATE CURSOR statement (see ALLOCATE CURSOR).

Example

The following statement removes from the Clients table everyone whose name begins with *W*:

```
DELETE FROM Clients
    WHERE NAME LIKE 'W%';
```

Conformance Levels

Intermediate   Implementations at this level are not
                  required to support prepared statements.

Entry   Implementations at this level are not
                  required to support Dynamic SQL.

See Also   Part II: ALLOCATE CURSOR, CREATE VIEW, DECLARE CURSOR, OPEN , PREPARE, SET TRANSACTION. Part III: Predicates.

DESCRIBE

(Dynamic SQL Only) Provides Information about a Prepared Statement

Syntax

```
DESCRIBE [ INPUT | OUTPUT ]
  SQL statement
   USING SQL DESCRIPTOR descriptor name;
```

Usage

The DESCRIBE statement stores information about the input or output parameters of the prepared SQL statement in the named SQL descriptor area, which previously must have been allocated with an ALLOCATE DESCRIPTOR statement. The prepared statement itself must have been created with a PREPARE statement. To access the information that DESCRIBE stores, use the GET DESCRIPTOR statement. If neither INPUT nor OUTPUT is specified, OUTPUT will be used by default.

The basic idea is that a given DESCRIBE statement examines either all input or all output parameters in the Dynamic SQL statement. It uses the context of how these parameters are used in the statement to figure out datatypes, nullability characteristics, and so on of the parameters. It then stores this information about the parameters in the descriptor area. Each item in the descriptor area describes one parameter. The actual value of the parameter is set with a SET DESCRIPTOR statement or automatically. For more information, see SET DESCRIPTOR and Part III: Descriptor Areas.

Describing Output Columns   You specify OUTPUT in order to provide information about the output columns of the statement. If the statement is not SELECT or FETCH, then the descriptor item COUNT is set to zero and the others are not set (this indicates a problem, as other statements will not use output parameters). Otherwise, COUNT is set to the number of output columns. If this number is greater than the number of descriptor items, a warning condition is raised and no other descriptor fields are set. Otherwise, the descriptor item areas are set in the same sequence as they appear in the SELECT list. Each descriptor item area will have values set as follows:

- TYPE is set to a code indicating the datatype. The codes are listed under Descriptor Areas in Part III.

- NULLABLE is set to 1 if the resulting column may contain NULLs or to 0 if it may not.

- NAME is set to the name of the column.

- UNNAMED is set to 1 if the name of the output column is implementation-dependent; otherwise, it is set to 0. (If the name is implementation-dependent, it's because the output column is not a simple replicant of an input column but is part of a value expression, aggregate function, union, or similar operation and has not been named in an AS clause. See SELECT for more information.)

How the other relevant fields are set depends on the datatype of the column. However, the settings of these fields for a particular datatype are the same whether DESCRIBE INPUT or DESCRIBE OUTPUT is specified, so they are explained later in this entry.

Describing Input Parameters   You specify DESCRIBE INPUT to provide information about the dynamic parameter specifications in the prepared statement. COUNT is set to the number of parameter specifications in the statement. If this number is greater than the number of allocated descriptor areas, a warning message is produced and the other descriptor areas are not set. Also, if this number is zero, the other descriptor areas are not set. Otherwise, they are set as follows:

• TYPE is set to the code listed under Descriptor Areas in Part III that matches the datatype of the column.

• NULLABLE is set to 1. This indicates that the input parameter may be NULL.

• NAME and UNNAMED are set to implementation-dependent values.

Settings That Are the Same for Either Input or Output   Whether you specify INPUT or OUTPUT, the DATA and INDICATOR are not relevant; these and other unused fields are set by DESCRIBE to implementation-dependent values. To set the DATA or INDICATOR fields, use the SET DESCRIPTOR statement. The values that depend on the datatype are described below for various datatypes. For more information on the meaning of these parameters, for example, precision and scale, see Datatypes in Part III.

If the datatype is any CHARACTER STRING type, then:

• LENGTH is set to the length (if fixed) or maximum length (if varying) of the string in characters.

• OCTET_LENGTH is set to the maximum possible length in octets (bytes).

• CHARACTER_SET_CATALOG, CHARACTER_SET_SCHEMA, and CHARACTER_SET_NAME are set to the catalog, schema, and name of the string's character set.

• COLLATION_CATALOG, COLLATION_SCHEMA, and COLLATION_NAME are set to the catalog, schema, and name of the string's collation.

Note that if the language being interfaced to is C or C++, the LENGTH and OCTET_LENGTH values will not include the implementation-defined string-termination character.

If the type is a BIT (binary) STRING, LENGTH is set to the length (if fixed) or maximum length (if varying) in bits, and OCTET_LENGTH is set to the maximum possible length in octets (bytes).

If any EXACT NUMERIC type is indicated, PRECISION and SCALE are set to the appropriate precision and scale.

If any APPROXIMATE NUMERIC type is indicated, PRECISION is set to the appropriate figure.

If a DATETIME type is indicated, then:

- LENGTH is set to the length in positions.

- DATETIME_INTERVAL_CODE is set to the code indicated in Part III: Descriptor Areas.

- PRECISION is set to the TIME precision or the TIMESTAMP precision, if either applies, that is, if the datatype is TIME or TIMESTAMP, respectively.

If an INTERVAL type is indicated, then:

- DATETIME_INTERVAL_CODE is set to the code indicated in Part III: Descriptor Areas.

- DATETIME_INTERVAL_PRECISION is set to the INTERVAL's leading field precision.

- PRECISION is set to the fractional seconds precision, if applicable.

Conformance Levels

| Intermediate | Implementations at this level are not required to support variables for descriptor names. |
| Entry | Implementations at this level are not required to support Dynamic SQL at all. |

See Also Part II: ALLOCATE DESCRIPTOR, DEALLOCATE DESCRIPTOR, GET DESCRIPTOR, SET DESCRIPTOR. Part III: Datatypes, Descriptor Areas.

DISCONNECT

Destroys Connections to the DBMS

Syntax

```
DISCONNECT connection | ALL | CURRENT;
```

Usage

The DISCONNECT statement terminates one or more connections between the current SQL-agent and the DBMS. If ALL is specified, it means all connections for the current user. If a connection is named, that connection is terminated; alternatively, you can specify either ALL connections or the CURRENT connection, by using those keywords. To start a connection, which will initially be the current one, use the SET CONNECTION statement while some connection is still current. If there is no current connection, of course, you use CONNECT to set a new current connection. In most implementations, CURRENT is also the default.

Conformance Levels

Intermediate   Implementations at this level are not required to support DISCONNECT.

See Also   Part II: CONNECT, SET CONNECTION.

DROP ASSERTION

Removes an Assertion from the Schema

Syntax

```
DROP ASSERTION constraint name;
```

Usage

The DROP ASSERTION statement is used to remove an assertion from the schema. Assertions are constraints that stand alone as objects, rather than being part of a table or domain definition; they are created with the CREATE ASSERTION statement. You can use assertions to ensure that a table is not empty, which you could not do from a constraint within the table itself. Assertions are also more logical for constraints that enforce business rules that are not a function of a particular table. The Authorization ID dropping the assertion must own the schema in which it resides.

Conformance Levels

Intermediate   Implementations at this level are not required to support DROP ASSERTION. But of course most of all DBMSs support some kind of DISCONNECT procedure.

See Also   Part II: CREATE ASSERTION. Part III: Authorization IDs, Constraints.

DROP CHARACTER SET
Destroys the Definition of a Character Set

Syntax

```
DROP CHARACTER SET character set name;
```

Usage

The DROP CHARACTER SET statement destroys a character set, which must have been previously defined with a CREATE CHARACTER SET statement. It must be issued by the owner of the schema that contains the character set, and no constraints, views, collations, or translations may be referencing the character set at the time it is dropped. If there are any, this statement produces an error, and the character set is not dropped. When the character set is destroyed, all Authorization IDs lose their privileges on it.

Conformance Levels

Entry   Implementations at this level are not required to support the DROP CHARACTER SET statement.

See Also   Part II: CREATE CHARACTER SET, CREATE SCHEMA. Part III: Authorization IDs, Collations.

DROP COLLATION
Destroys a Collation

Syntax

```
DROP COLLATION collation name;
```

Usage

The DROP COLLATION statement destroys a collation sequence, which must have been previously defined with a CREATE COLLATION statement. It must be issued by the Authorization ID that owns the schema in which the collation resides. Except in a COLLATE FROM clause, no view may reference it in a query; neither may any constraint—whether contained in a table definition, domain, or assertion—reference it in a predicate. If any views or constraints do so reference it, the DROP COLLATION statement is rejected with an error.

If collx is the name of the collation being deleted, other references to collx are dealt with as follows:

• The definitions of all other collations that reference collx are modified by deleting all THEN COLLATION collx or DESC (collx) clauses.

• All character-set definitions that reference collx are modified by deleting all COLLATION FROM collx or DESC (collx) clauses.

• The definitions of all column or domain definitions that reference collx are modified by deleting COLLATE collx clauses.

• All views and constraints that use a COLLATE FROM collx clause have that clause deleted.

Conformance Levels

Intermediate   Implementations at this level are not required to support the DROP COLLATION statement.

See Also   Part II: CREATE CHARACTER SET, CREATE COLLATION, CREATE SCHEMA. Part III: Collations, Constraints.

DROP DOMAIN

Destroys a Domain

Syntax

```
DROP DOMAIN domain name CASCADE | RESTRICT ;
```

Usage

The DROP DOMAIN statement destroys a domain, which must have been previously created with a CREATE DOMAIN statement. It must be issued by the owner of the schema in which the domain resides. If RESTRICT is specified, the domain must not be currently referenced by any tables, views, or constraints. If it is, the statement will get an error. If CASCADE is specified, the effects on all columns based on the domain are as follows:

- The datatype of the domain becomes the datatype of the column.

- If the column has no default value and the domain does, the default of the domain becomes the default of the column. If both the column and the domains have defaults, that of the column overrides that of the domain.

- Each constraint that is part of the domain is passed on to the column, provided that the Authorization ID dropping the domain has the necessary privileges to effect the change to the column. In other words, for each constraint C that is contained in the domain to be dropped, the following statement is effectively attempted under the privileges of the current SQL-session Authorization ID:

  ```
  ALTER TABLE table name ADD C;
  ```

- If the Authorization ID lacks the requisite privileges to execute this statement, the change is not made, but the domain is still dropped.

All users lose their privileges on the domain, and its definition is destroyed.

Conformance Levels

    Entry   Implementations at this level are not required to support the DROP DOMAIN statement.

See Also Part II: ALTER TABLE, CREATE DOMAIN, GRANT. Part III: Constraints.

DROP SCHEMA

Destroys a Schema

Syntax

```
DROP SCHEMA schema name CASCADE | RESTRICT ;
```

Usage

The DROP SCHEMA statement drops the named schema. The current Authorization ID must own the schema being dropped. If RESTRICT is specified, the schema must currently be empty of objects—permanent, global temporary, or created local temporary tables, as well as views, domains, assertions, character sets, collations, and translations—or the DROP SCHEMA statement will fail. If CASCADE is specified, any such objects are dropped along with the schema. This syntax form has the same effect as explicitly dropping each object with the appropriate DROP statement and specifying CASCADE where applicable (which would be for DROP TABLE, DROP VIEW, and DROP DOMAIN).

Conformance Levels

Entry   Implementations at this level are not required to support DROP SCHEMA.

See Also   Part II: CREATE SCHEMA, DROP ASSERTION, DROP CHARACTER SET, DROP COLLATION, DROP DOMAIN, DROP TABLE, DROP TRANSLATION, DROP VIEW.

DROP TABLE

Destroys a Base Table

Syntax

```
DROP TABLE table name CASCADE | RESTRICT ;
```

Usage

The DROP TABLE statement is used to drop the various kinds of tables that can be created with a CREATE TABLE statement: permanent base tables, global temporary tables, and created local temporary tables. Views are dropped with the DROP VIEW statement, and declared local temporary tables are automatically dropped at the end of the session wherein they are declared. The

Authorization ID that issues that statement must be the owner of the table or the DROP TABLE statement will produce an error.

If RESTRICT is specified, no views or constraints may currently be referencing the table to be dropped. If CASCADE is specified, such referencing objects will be dropped along with the table. For constraints, this means that the constraint itself will be dropped. If the constraint is contained in a table or domain definition, the containing object will not be dropped.

The definition of the table is destroyed and all users lose their privileges on it.

Conformance Levels

Entry   Implementations at this level are not required to support DROP TABLE.

See Also Part II: CREATE TABLE. Part III: Constraints.

DROP TRANSLATION
Destroys a Translation

Syntax
```
DROP TRANSLATION translation name;
```

Usage
The DROP TRANSLATION statement destroys a translation previously created using a CREATE TRANSLATION statement. The Authorization ID issuing the statement must own the schema in which the translation resides. The translation must not be currently referenced by any views or constraints or the DROP statement will produce an error. If any character sets or collations use a translation collation based on this translation, that collation is removed from their definitions. The translation definition is destroyed, and all users lose their privileges on it.

Conformance Levels

Intermediate   Implementations at this level are not required to support the DROP TRANSLATION statement.

See Also Part II: CREATE TRANSLATION. Part III: Collations.

DROP VIEW
Destroys a View

Syntax

```
DROP VIEW view name  CASCADE | RESTRICT ;
```

Usage

The DROP VIEW statement drops a view, which must previously have been created with a CREATE VIEW statement. The Authorization ID issuing the DROP VIEW statement must own the schema within which the view resides. If RESTRICT is specified, the view may not be referenced by any other views or by any assertions or the DROP statement will produce an error. If CASCADE is specified, such referencing objects are dropped along with the view. The view definition is destroyed, and all users lose their privileges on the view.

Conformance Levels

Entry   Implementations at this level are not required to support the DROP VIEW statement.

See Also   Part II: CREATE VIEW, CREATE ASSERTION.

EXECUTE
(Dynamic SQL Only) Executes a Prepared Statement

Syntax

```
EXECUTE [ GLOBAL | LOCAL ] prepared statement
[ INTO  { output parameter.,... }
   | { SQL DESCRIPTOR [GLOBAL | LOCAL ] descriptor name } ]
[ USING { input parameter.,... }
   | { SQL DESCRIPTOR  [ GLOBAL |LOCAL ] descriptor name
} ] ;
```

Usage

The EXECUTE statement executes a statement previously generated with the PREPARE statement. It provides values for any dynamic input and output parameters associated with the prepared statement. The USING clause is for input parameters and the INTO clause for output. A given EXECUTE statement will use either or both of these clauses depending on whether the prepared statement contains input parameters, output parameters, or both. Conceivably, the EXECUTE statement could use neither USING nor INTO, if no dynamic parameters are present in the prepared statement. This would be somewhat unusual, however, since such statements are generally better suited for EXECUTE IMMEDIATE. Prepared statements do not contain INOUT parameters (parameters functioning as both an INPUT and an OUTPUT). For more on prepared statements, see Part I: PREPARE. For either input or output parameters, you can use a descriptor area or a list of host-language variables (or parameters for the module approach; in this entry, we use the term *variables* for both approaches to simplify the discussion) to provide the values for the dynamic parameters embedded in the prepared statement.

The GLOBAL and LOCAL options refer to the scope of the prepared statement or descriptor area. If the scope is LOCAL, the statement or area is accessible only by statements within the module or compilation unit in which it was created (see Appendix B); otherwise, it is accessible to any statement in the session. If the scope of the statement or descriptor is GLOBAL, it must be specified. LOCAL is the default. Since the scope is technically part of the name, two prepared statements or descriptor areas may have the same names but a different scope and still be distinctly named.

IN the USING and INTO clauses, variables are preceded by colons (:) and may be appended by indicators. Any SQL descriptor areas used must previously have been allocated with an ALLO-CATE DESCRIPTOR statement and not yet deallocated with DEALLOCATE DESCRIPTOR.

The USING clause indicates from where the values for the dynamic input parameters contained in the prepared statement are to be taken. It will indicate either a list of variables that will have been assigned values by the host-language procedure calling the SQL EXECUTE statement or a descriptor area from which the values are to be drawn. If the former, the variables from the host language will be matched to the dynamic parameters (represented in the prepared statement by simple question marks) contained in the prepared statement on an ordinal basis. If the

latter, the descriptor items will be matched to the dynamic parameters on an ordinal basis.

The INTO clause indicates where the output from the prepared
statement will be stored. If output parameters are used, they will
be assigned values by the EXECUTE statement. The host-language
variables or descriptor items will be matched to the output columns
on an ordinal basis. The decision to use variables or descriptor
areas for input or output is actually two independent decisions;
the two approaches may be mixed.

Note that either, both, or neither of these clauses (USING and
INTO) may be used, but neither may be used more than once in a
given EXECUTE. The following rules apply:

- If the prepared statement contains dynamic input parameters,
  the USING clause must be present.

- If the prepared statement is a SELECT or FETCH statement,
  the INTO clause must be present. These are the statements
  that use output parameters.

- If the prepared statement is a SELECT, it must be of the single-
  row variety. SELECT statements that retrieve multiple rows
  should be put in dynamic cursors (see DECLARE CURSOR
  and ALLOCATE CURSOR).

- If the prepared statement references a created or declared
  local temporary table, this EXECUTE statement must be
  located in the same module or compilation unit as the
  corresponding PREPARE statement.

For the USING clause, if any, the following rules also hold:

- If a variable list is used, and its number of variables does not
  match the number of input variables in the prepared statement, an error is generated and the EXECUTE statement fails.

- If a descriptor area is used, the items within it must have been
  already set, including, for each item, either the DATA or the
  INDICATOR field, using a SET DESCRIPTOR statement.

- If a SQL descriptor area is used, the current value of COUNT
  in that area must equal the number of input parameters used in
  the prepared statement and must be between zero and the

MAX number of items specified when the descriptor was allocated, inclusively.

- If a descriptor area is used, the descriptor items naturally must match the parameters in the prepared statement. (See Part III: Descriptor Areas.)

- If an indicator parameter or the INDICATOR field of a descriptor item is negative, a NULL is placed in the matching input parameter in the prepared statement, and the value of the parameter or of the DATA field of the descriptor item is irrelevant. Otherwise, the value of the parameter or the DATA field of the descriptor area will be placed in the matching parameter.

- If the datatype of a descriptor item or parameter is not the same as the matching dynamic parameter of the prepared statement, an automatic CAST expression will be attempted to convert the parameter or descriptor item to the datatype of the dynamic parameter. The rules for CAST conversions are explained in Part III: CAST Expressions. If the CAST fails, an error is generated, and the EXECUTE statement fails.

- If a descriptor area is used, the values of the NAME and UNNAMED fields of the descriptor items are ignored.

For the INTO clause, the following rules apply:

- The number of listed output parameters, or the count of descriptor area items, as the case may be, must equal the number of output columns in the prepared statement.

- If a descriptor area is used, your implementation may require that you already have set its fields to match the dynamic parameter specifications in this prepared statement. If so, you would do this with the DESCRIBE or the SET DESCRIPTOR statement. These settings will become invalid once the DATA field is set by the EXECUTE statement. Hence, you must reset the descriptor each time you execute the prepared statement. Some implementations may relax this restriction.

- If the datatypes of the parameters or the value of the TYPE fields of the descriptor items do not match the datatypes of the output columns of the prepared statement, an automatic

CAST expression will be attempted, conforming to the principles outlined in Part III: CAST Expressions, to convert the value to the appropriate datatype. If the CAST expression fails, an error is generated, and the EXECUTE statement fails.

- If a descriptor area is used, the values in the fields of each of its items must accurately describe the output column value to be inserted into the item's DATA field (provided that the column is not NULL), possibly after the casting specified above.

- If output parameter variables are used, they must be able to hold the value produced by the casting specified above, or an error is produced.

- If the value of an output column is NULL, then either the descriptor item's INDICATOR field or the indicator appended to the variable, as appropriate, is set to -1. If variables are used without appended indicators and NULLs arise, an error is produced. In the presence of a negative indicator, the value of the descriptor item's DATA field, or of the variable, as appropriate, is implementation-dependent.

- If the value of the output column is not NULL, the indicator DATA field or the variable is set to that value, possibly after the casting specified above.

- If a descriptor area is used, and the value of an item after casting is a VARCHAR or BIT VARYING type, RETURNED_LENGTH is set to the length of the value in characters or bits, respectively, and RETURNED_OCTET_LENGTH to the length in octets (bytes).

Example

The following statement executes a prepared statement called stmt6, taking a series of values from a set of three input parameters and storing the results in a SQL descriptor area called Desc_11. The descriptor area has a global scope, but the prepared statement does not.

```
EXECUTE stmt6
USING :name, :city, :occup
INTO GLOBAL Desc_11;
```

Conformance Levels

Intermediate	Implementations at this level are required only to support literals (no variables) for descriptor names.
Entry	Implementations at this level are not required to support Dynamic SQL.

See Also   Part II: EXECUTE IMMEDIATE, PREPARE, SELECT.
Part III: CAST Expressions, Descriptor Areas.

EXECUTE IMMEDIATE

(Dynamic SQL Only) Prepares a Statement from a Text String and Executes It

Syntax

```
EXECUTE IMMEDIATE SQL statement variable;
```

Usage

The EXECUTE IMMEDIATE statement prepares a statement for execution from a variable containing a text string that expresses the statement to be executed. It then executes the statement, effectively combining the functionality of the PREPARE and EXECUTE statements, albeit with certain limitations—for example, the statement cannot be prepared once and executed repeatedly as can be done using the separate PREPARE and EXECUTE statements. Also, neither input nor output parameters may be used. This restriction implies that the statement to be executed cannot be SELECT or FETCH.

EXECUTE IMMEDIATE fails if any of the following conditions is TRUE:

- The datatype of the SQL statement variable does not correspond to a CHARACTER STRING type. To see which datatypes in your host language correspond to which SQL types, see Appendix E.

- The content of the SQL statement variable does not equal the text of a valid and legal (for the current Authorization ID) SQL statement.

- The SQL statement variable contains a comment. For information on comments, see Appendix D.

- The SQL statement contains one or more dynamic input parameters.

- The SQL statement is SELECT or FETCH.

- The SQL statement references a cursor that does not exist.

- The SQL statement references a cursor name that can match more than one cursor. This implies that one of the cursors is an extended dynamic (allocated) cursor whose name was generated at runtime.

If none of these conditions hold, the statement is prepared and immediately executed.

Example

The following statement takes a string variable called Delete_7, whose content is the text of a valid SQL statement (presumably DELETE), and executes it.

```
EXECUTE IMMEDIATE :Delete_7;
```

Conformance Levels

Entry   Implementations at this level are not required to support Dynamic SQL.

See Also   Part II: ALLOCATE CURSOR, DECLARE CURSOR, EXECUTE, PREPARE, SELECT.

FETCH

Retrieves a Row from an Open Cursor

Syntax

```
FETCH [ [ orientation ] FROM ]
cursor name INTO target spec .,... ;

orientation ::=
NEXT | PRIOR | FIRST | LAST |
{ ABSOLUTE | RELATIVE  offset }
```

Usage

The FETCH statement retrieves the values from one row of a cursor into the list of target specs in order, so that the first output column of the cursor goes in the first target spec, the second column in the second target, and so on. The target spec is an output parameter in the module language and a host-language variable in Embedded or Dynamic SQL. The cursor will have been created with a DECLARE CURSOR or an ALLOCATE CURSOR statement and opened with an OPEN CURSOR statement, before any rows are fetched.

Recall that the rows of cursors, unlike those of base tables or views, are by definition ordered, although this order may be arbitrary. At any time, an opened cursor has a position among the rows it contains; it may be before a row, on a row, or after the last row. When first opened, it is positioned before the first row. The FETCH statement repositions the cursor and then copies the values from the row on which it is currently positioned to the target specifications. By repositioning the cursor, the FETCH statement also determines which row of the cursor is the current row and therefore can be used in conjunction with the positioned versions of the DELETE and UPDATE statements to change the contents of the table retrieved by the cursor (assuming it is updatable; see DECLARE CURSOR).

The orientation specifies where the cursor is to be repositioned. NEXT is the default if the orientation is omitted and is, in any case, the only possibility unless SCROLL was specified for the cursor when it was defined (see DECLARE CURSOR). SCROLL may be specified only for read-only cursors. The offset is of an EXACT NUMERIC type with a scale of zero—in effect, an integer. This may be a literal or a host-language variable of an appropriate type—that is to say, a type that maps to SQL INTEGER. The options for orientation are defined as follows:

- If the cursor is currently positioned before the first row, NEXT moves the cursor onto that row. If it is on a row, NEXT moves it onto the next one. If it is after the last row, NEXT produces the no-data condition (explained below).

- If the cursor is currently positioned after the last row, PRIOR moves it onto that row. If it is currently positioned on a row other than the first one, PRIOR moves it onto the previous one. If it is currently positioned on or before the first row, PRIOR produces the no-data condition.

- FIRST moves the cursor onto the first row.

- LAST moves the cursor onto the last row.

- ABSOLUTE *offset* moves the cursor onto that row (i.e., if *offset* = 7, it moves to the seventh row). If *offset* is greater than the number of rows, the no-data condition is produced.

- RELATIVE *offset* moves forward *offset* rows if *offset* is positive or backward *offset* rows if *offset* is negative. If this option moves the cursor before the first or after the last row, the no-data condition is produced.

The no-data condition indicates that there is no row to be FETCHed in the indicated position. In this case, a warning message is produced, and the target specs are not set. Since rows are normally FETCHed until this happens, the no-data condition does not necessarily denote an error. FETCHing from an empty cursor also produces the no-data condition. When the no-data condition arises, the cursor position is defined as follows:

- If the last FETCH specified (or defaulted to) NEXT, specified LAST, or specified ABSOLUTE or RELATIVE using numeric arguments that were too large, the cursor is positioned after the last row.

- Otherwise, the cursor is positioned before the first row.

If an error arises during derivation of any derived columns in the cursor, the position of the cursor remains unchanged. Unless an orientation is specified, FROM is optional. It may be omitted; if included, it has no effect.

Example

The following statement moves the cursor Paris_Sales back three rows and places its output in a series of target specifications. It assumes Paris_Sales is a scrollable cursor.

```
FETCH RELATIVE -3
FROM Paris_Sales
INTO :name, :id_num, :num_of_clients;
```

Conformance Levels

Entry   Implementations at this level are not required to support orientations (in which case NEXT is effectively used) or to allow the word FROM. Also, they may require that only EXACT NUMERIC column values can be fetched into EXACT NUMERIC targets, rather than performing an automatic CAST.

See Also Part II: ALLOCATE CURSOR, CLOSE CURSOR, DECLARE CURSOR, OPEN.

GET DESCRIPTOR

(Dynamic SQL Only) Retrieves Information from a SQL Descriptor Area

Syntax

```
GET DESCRIPTOR descriptor name
{ simple target spec = COUNT }
/ { VALUE item number
  {simple target spec = desc field}.,.. };
```

Usage

The GET DESCRIPTOR statement retrieves information from SQL descriptor areas, which store information about input and output parameters for dynamically created SQL statements and can also store values for them. Each descriptor area describes all the input or all the output parameters of one statement. The content and structure of descriptor areas are described in detail in Part III: Descriptor Areas. By "simple target specifications" is meant host variables (or parameters for the module language) without appended indicator variables. The descriptor areas must first be allocated with the ALLOCATE DESCRIPTOR statement; then the information is stored in them with either the DESCRIBE or the SET DESCRIPTOR statement. The *descriptor name* can be either a literal or a host-language variable.

A descriptor area consists of a list of descriptor items and a COUNT field denoting the size of the list. Each descriptor item corresponds to one parameter or target specification in the statement and contains a number of fields:

- TYPE indicates the datatype. (Depending on the datatype, there may also be a variety of related fields providing descriptive

information such as the length. The irrelevant fields for a
given datatype, such as PRECISION for a character string, are
ignored.)

- DATA gives the actual content of the parameter or target if it
  is not NULL.

- INDICATOR will set to a negative value to indicate whether
  the parameter or target is NULL, in which case the value of
  DATA is irrelevant.

This statement will retrieve either the COUNT, which is the
number of descriptor items in the descriptor area, or specific information about a specific descriptor item. The items are listed in the
descriptor area in the order in which they are used in the statement
being described, so they can be referred to by this ordinal number
(*item number*). The fields of the item that you want to see are referred
to by name (*desc field*) as listed under Descriptor Areas in Part III.

Since it is the INDICATOR field of a descriptor item that establishes whether a value is NULL, neither the DATA field nor any of
the descriptive fields of the item can contain SQL NULLs. For any
given datatype, some of the fields in the item will be inapplicable.
These will be set to implementation-dependent defaults but not to
SQL NULLs. If you retrieve DATA and its value is NULL, you must
retrieve the INDICATOR in the same statement, or you will get an
error. Therefore, you should retrieve the INDICATOR whenever the
DATA value might be NULL, check the INDICATOR to see if it is
NULL, and have the program logic act appropriately. If the INDI-
CATOR is negative, and the descriptor item therefore NULL, the
value of DATA is implementation-dependent and does not matter.

You will also get an error if you specify an item number greater
than the maximum number of items in the descriptor area, i.e.,
the number of occurrences defined when the descriptor area was
allocated. If your item number is within this range but still greater
than the number of descriptor items actually used—the value of
COUNT—you will not get an error but merely a no-data condition. For an explanation of NO DATA, see Appendix F.

Example

The following statement retrieves the TYPE, NULLABLE, and
NAME fields from the seventh descriptor item (corresponding to

the seventh dynamic parameter in the described statement) into a series of target specifications.

```
GET DESCRIPTOR :Desc_7
VALUE 7
  :data_type = TYPE,
  :can_contain_nulls = NULLABLE
  :column_name = NAME;
```

Conformance Levels

Intermediate   Implementations at this level are not required to support the use of anything but literals for descriptor names.

Entry   Implementations at this level are not required to support Dynamic SQL.

See Also   Part II: ALLOCATE DESCRIPTOR, DEALLOCATE DESCRIPTOR, DESCRIBE, SET DESCRIPTOR. Part III: Datatypes, Descriptor Areas.

GET DIAGNOSTICS
Retrieves Diagnostic Information about the Previous SQL Statement

Syntax

```
GET DIAGNOSTICS { statement information item.,..}
| condition information;

statement information item ::=
simple target spec = NUMBER | MORE
| COMMAND_FUNCTION | DYNAMIC_FUNCTION
| ROW_COUNT

condition information ::=
EXCEPTION condition number
condition information item.,..

condition information item ::=
simple target spec = cond info item name

cond info item name ::=
CONDITION_NUMBER
```

```
| RETURNED_SQLSTATE
| CLASS_ORIGIN
| SUBCLASS_ORIGIN
| SERVER_NAME
| CONNECTION_NAME
| CONSTRAINT_CATALOG
| CONSTRAINT_SCHEMA
| CONSTRAINT_NAME
| CATALOG_NAME
| SCHEMA_NAME
| TABLE_NAME
| COLUMN_NAME
| CURSOR_NAME
| MESSAGE_TEXT
| MESSAGE_LENGTH
| MESSAGE_OCTET_LENGTH
```

condition number ::= simple value specification

Usage

The GET DIAGNOSTICS statement retrieves information from the DBMS regarding the exception and completion conditions of the immediately preceding SQL statement within the same session. Exception conditions are errors that prevent a statement from being executed; completion conditions are warnings that indicate possible errors but still allow the statement to execute. This information is stored in a diagnostics area and further clarifies the codes provided through SQLCODE or (preferably) SQLSTATE. It is in the form of various fields that are retrieved into simple target specifications—target specifications without indicator variables.

The statement information items provide information about the statement—which statement it was, how many rows were affected (for example, if it was an UPDATE statement), and so on. The condition information provides the SQLSTATE or SQLCODE value along with supplemental information—for example, if an error was a cursor conflict, you can find out the name of the cursor with which the conflict arose. Also, the diagnostics area can specify several error codes produced by the same statement, whereas SQLSTATE and SQLCODE can only specify one. The diagnostics area is discussed in detail in Appendix F.

Example

The following statement retrieves the error conditions for the previous statement, which we will assume was a prepared statement. It will find out the number of error or warning conditions this statement raised (NUMBER), whether this number exceeded what could be stored in the diagnostics area (MORE), and what the prepared statement itself was (DYNAMIC_FUNCTION). These values are stored in three target specifications.

```
GET DIAGNOSTICS
    :how_many_errors = NUMBER,
    :diagnostics_overflow = MORE,
    :prepared_statement = DYNAMIC_FUNCTION;
```

Conformance Levels

Entry   Implementations at this level are not required to support GET DIAGNOSTICS.

SQL89   Implementations at this level are not required to support SQLSTATE.

Non   Diagnostic areas are widely used but in a nonstandardized way.

See Also   Appendix F.

GRANT
Gives Privileges to Users

Syntax

```
GRANT privilege.,.. ON object name
TO { grantee.,.. } | PUBLIC
[ WITH GRANT OPTION ];

privilege ::=
  { ALL PRIVILEGES }
| { SELECT
| DELETE
| { INSERT [ (column name.,..) ] }
| { UPDATE [ (column name.,..) ] }
| { REFERENCES [ (column name.,..) ] }
| USAGE   }
```

```
object name ::=
[ TABLE ] table name
| DOMAIN domain name
| COLLATION collation name
| CHARACTER SET character set name
| TRANSLATION translation name
```

Usage

The GRANT statement gives the grantees—that is, Authorization IDs that represent users or, possibly, modules—the right to perform the specified actions on the named objects. The USAGE privilege applies to all other types of objects besides tables, whereas the other kinds of privileges apply only to tables. Tables here may be permanent base tables, temporary tables, or views. The Authorization ID issuing the GRANT, which we will refer to as the *grantor* for the remainder of this discussion, must have the privilege itself with the GRANT OPTION and may grant it with this option, which allows the grantee to grant the privilege further.

ALL PRIVILEGES confers all the applicable privileges that the grantor is entitled to grant. For global or created local temporary tables, only ALL PRIVILEGES may be specified. Privileges may not be granted on declared local temporary tables. PUBLIC denotes all Authorization IDs, present and future.

SELECT, INSERT, UPDATE, and DELETE allow the grantee to execute the statements of the same names on the object. USAGE confers the ability to use the object to define another object—for example, to use a translation to define a collation. REFERENCES confers the ability to use the table as a parent to a foreign key or to refer to it in a constraint. INSERT, UPDATE, and REFERENCES may be restricted to specified columns of the tables; if the list of columns is omitted, however, they apply by default to all columns, including columns added to the table later. If there are any columns that the grantor has not the right to confer (does not have the GRANT OPTION on), those columns are ignored by the GRANT, but the privilege is GRANTed on the others.

NOTE There is interest in a column-specific SELECT privilege for a future upgrade of the standard, and provision has been made for this in the current design of the standard INFORMATION_ SCHEMA, but the fields of the INFORMATION_SCHEMA provided for this purpose currently have no meaning.

Cascading of Privileges   Privileges can cascade up, meaning that privileges granted on some object can imply grants of privileges on other objects. These situations are covered by the following principles:

- If the grantee owns an updatable view and is being GRANTed privileges on its leaf underlying table (the base table wherein the data finally resides, regardless of any intervening views), these privileges will be GRANTed for the view as well. If specified, the GRANT OPTION also cascades up. There is only one leaf underlying table for an updatable view; see CREATE VIEW.

- If the grantee owns an updatable view that immediately references the table on which privileges are being GRANTed (in other words, if the reference appears in the FROM clause without an intervening view), these privileges also cascade up, including the GRANT OPTION if applicable.

- If the grantee owns a view, updatable or not, that grantee will already have the SELECT privilege on all tables referenced in its definition as well as on the view itself. If the grantee gains the GRANT OPTION on SELECT on all the referenced tables, he also acquires the GRANT OPTION on the SELECT privilege on the view.

- Likewise, the GRANT OPTION cascades up in domains. If a grantee owns a domain and acquires the GRANT OPTION on REFERENCES for all tables referenced in any domain constraints and on USAGE for all domains, character sets, collations, and translations referenced in the domain, that grantee gets the USAGE privilege on the domain with the GRANT OPTION.

- Likewise, if a grantee owns a collation or translation and gets the GRANT OPTION on the character set on which it is based, the GRANT OPTION cascades up to the collation or translation.

- The REFERENCES privilege cascades up in a more complex fashion. If the grantee owns a view and, after this GRANT statement has been executed, will have the REFERENCES privilege on every column referenced in the view, and if the grantor has the REFERENCES privilege on at least one column of each table referenced in that view, then the grantee gets the REFERENCES privilege on the view, with the GRANT OPTION if such was specified for this statement.

In all of the above situations, the grantor of the privilege is _SYSTEM, which denotes an automatic GRANT.

For each privilege that is GRANTed, a privilege descriptor is created. For column-specific privileges, a separate descriptor is generated for each column. The privilege descriptor indicates:

• The grantee that has received the privilege.

• The privilege itself (the action that can be performed).

• The object on which the privilege is GRANTed, which may be one of those listed above or a column.

• The grantor that conferred the privilege. For automatic GRANTs, this is the built-in value _SYSTEM.

• Whether the privilege is grantable (GRANTed with the GRANT OPTION).

Multiple identical privilege descriptors are combined, so that a privilege GRANTed twice by the same grantor need only be revoked (cancelled) once. Likewise, if two privilege descriptors differ only in that one confers the GRANT OPTION and the other does not, they are merged into a single privilege with the GRANT OPTION. If the grantor lacks the ability to GRANT the privileges attempted, a completion condition is raised—a warning that privileges were not GRANTed will appear. Revocation of privileges is also compli-cated. See REVOKE for details.

Example

The following statement gives the user (or, theoretically, the mod-ule) E-mail column-specific INSERT and UPDATE privileges with the GRANT OPTION on the Salespeople table:

```
GRANT INSERT(snum, name, city), UPDATE(name)
ON Salespeople
TO Emil
WITH GRANT OPTION;
```

Conformance Levels

Intermediate   Implementations at this level are not required to support privileges on character sets, domains, collations, or translations.

Entry   Implementations at this level are not required to support the optional word TABLE.

See Also Part II: CREATE CHARACTER SET, CREATE COLLATION, CREATE DOMAIN, CREATE TABLE, CREATE TRANSLATION, CREATE VIEW. Part III: Authorization IDs, Collations.

INSERT
INSERT rows into a table

Syntax

```
INSERT INTO table name
[ (column_name.,..) ]
{ VALUES(value.,..) }
| query
| {DEFAULT VALUES};
```

Usage

The INSERT statement enters one or more rows into *table name*. The rows are either the output of the query or a table value constructor. A table value constructor consists of the keyword VALUES followed by one or more row value constructors, separated by commas. A row value constructor is a parenthesized, comma-separated lists of values. Hence, the VALUES clause can be followed by one or more parenthesized lists of values, and each such parenthesized list constitutes a row to be INSERTed. For more on row and table value constructors, see Part III: Row and Table Value Constructors. In Entry SQL92 and older versions, the VALUES clause can take but a single list of values and INSERT but a single row unless a query were used.

Naturally, these rows must have the same datatypes as the columns being inserted into. The column name list identifies which columns of the table the values are being INSERTed into; all columns not in the list will have their default values INSERTed automatically. If any such columns cannot receive defaults (for example, if they have the NOT NULL constraint but have no other default value specified), the INSERT will fail. If the list is omitted, all columns of the table are the target of the INSERT. The number of columns and the order in which you list them must match the number and order of the output columns of the corresponding query or the number and order of the columns of all row value constructors in the VALUES clause version.

The Authorization ID under which this statement is issued must have the INSERT privilege on all named columns of the target table or on all such columns if the list is omitted. The table may be a view. If so, the view must be updatable (see CREATE VIEW), in which case the new rows are INSERTed into the base table ultimately containing the data from which the view is derived (the leaf underlying table). Keep in mind that the view may specify WITH CHECK OPTION, which restricts the values that can be inserted through it. In fact, there can be any number of intervening views before the base table is reached, and if these specify WITH CASCADED CHECK OPTION, they also can cause INSERTs to be rejected. (Views may be used in this manner as a security mechanism, enabling some users to make changes within tightly controlled parameters without constraining the base table itself.) Also, if the current TRANSACTION MODE is read-only, the table must be temporary or the INSERT is rejected.

Example

The following statement puts a row into the table Salespeople, using a single-row table value constructor. Even though table value constructors generally were not part of the pre-92 SQL standards, the particular language construction has been specified since SQL86.

```
INSERT INTO Salespeople (ID_num, lname, fname, city, country)
VALUES ( 1023, 'Blanco', 'Mercedes', 'Barcelona', 'Spain');
```

Conformance Levels

Intermediate   Implementations at this level may exclude references to the target table in the query expression, except where they are column qualifiers.

Entry   Implementations at this level may limit the table value constructor to that of a single row—in effect, to a row value constructor but with the VALUES keyword present. Also, EXACT NUMERIC types may be restricted to matching only other EXACT NUMERIC types (see Part III: Datatypes). Entry-level implementations are also allowed to exclude truncation, so that, for character string datatypes, the length of the target must be at least as great as the length of the value being INSERTed or the INSERT fails.

See Also   Part II: CREATE VIEW, SELECT, SET TRANSACTION. Part III: Authorization IDs, Datatypes, Predicates, Row and Table Value Constructors.

OPEN
(Static or Dynamic SQL) Readies a Cursor for Use

Syntax

```
OPEN cursor name [USING values source];
values source ::=
   parameter list
| {SQL DESCRIPTOR descriptor name}
```

Usage

The OPEN statement opens a cursor that will have been previously defined with a DECLARE CURSOR or (an alternative in Dynamic SQL) an ALLOCATE CURSOR statement. Any parameters or variables (including built-in variables such as CURRENT_USER) are filled in with their current values. The query contained in the cursor is executed and the data retrieved. The data is now ready to be processed one row at a time through the use of the FETCH statement.

If the cursor is INSENSITIVE, changes made to the data by other statements within the same transaction will not affect the content of the cursor while it is open. If it is not INSENSITIVE, whether such changes are visible is implementation-defined. You declare a cursor INSENSITIVE when defining it with the DECLARE CURSOR or the ALLOCATE CURSOR statement. The cursor will remain open until a CLOSE statement is issued or until the end of the transaction, regardless of whether all of its rows are FETCHed.

The USING clause only comes into play in Dynamic SQL and only if the query in the cursor uses dynamic input parameters, which are indicated with question marks (?). The OPEN CURSOR statement does not produce the output of the query; FETCH does that. Therefore, it cannot take output parameters, and all dynamic parameters in the statement must be input parameters. The USING clause specifies, in order, the values to put in the dynamic parameters. You have two options. One is to list a series of conventional variables (or parameters for the module language) passed from the application. You must prefix these with colons, and you may append indicators if you want to make it possible to insert NULLs into the dynamic parameters (see Parameters and Variables under Part III: Value Expressions, and Appendix C).

The other option is to take the values from a descriptor area. In this case, the words SQL DESCRIPTOR precede the name of the descriptor area. If a descriptor area is used, its COUNT field must equal the number of dynamic input parameters in the query. Otherwise, the number of variables listed in the USING clause (excluding indicators) must equal that of the dynamic input parameters in the query. In either case, the USING parameters or descriptor items must match or be converted to, in order, the datatypes of dynamic parameters in the query, based on the criteria for comparability of datatypes described in Part III: Datatypes.

Conformance Levels

Entry   Implementations at this level are not required to
         support Dynamic SQL and therefore not required
         to support dynamic cursors.

See Also   Part II: ALLOCATE CURSOR, CLOSE, COMMIT WORK.,
DECLARE CURSOR, FETCH, PREPARE, ROLLBACK. Part III:
Datatypes, Parameters and Variables.

PREPARE
(Dynamic SQL Only) Generates a SQL Statement from a Character String

Syntax

```
PREPARE [ GLOBAL | LOCAL ] SQL statement name
FROM character string variable;
```

Usage

In Dynamic SQL, you frequently cannot know beforehand the
SQL statements that will be required at runtime. Therefore, the
standard enables you to generate statements at runtime by first
storing the text of the desired statement in a character string variable and then converting this variable into a SQL statement. Providing a technique for generating proper SQL syntax based on the
actions of the user or application is the application's responsibility. Once the character string is generated, however, there are two
statements that can effect the conversion. EXECUTE IMMEDIATE
converts the character string and executes the statement at once.
The PREPARE statement creates a SQL statement from the text
that can then be repeatedly executed using EXECUTE or, if the
statement is a query, incorporated into a cursor using an ALLO-
CATE CURSOR or DECLARE CURSOR statement. Prepared statements can use dynamic parameters.

PREPARE neither provides values for input parameters nor
retrieves them for output parameters. EXECUTE, OPEN CURSOR,
and FETCH do so. This is one of the points of repeated execution
of prepared statements: you can repeat the statement with different values for the input parameters each time and get different
values for the output as well.

NOTE If a statement has already been prepared with the same name as the one we are attempting to prepare here, it will automatically be replaced, possibly without warning (no warning is required by the standard).

You have the option of specifying a scope of GLOBAL or LOCAL. The scope refers to the visibility of the prepared statement. If GLOBAL is specified, the prepared statement may be accessed by any EXECUTE, DECLARE CURSOR, or ALLOCATE CURSOR statement in the session. Otherwise, it may be accessed only from within the module or compilation unit. If the scope is not specified, LOCAL is the default. Two prepared statements with the same name but with different scopes are considered two distinctly named statements.

The character string stored in the variable must, once leading and trailing blanks are removed, match the text of some valid SQL statement without comments. It may use dynamic parameters, but all of the following criteria must be satisfied:

- No dynamic parameter may be contained in a SELECT clause.

- A dynamic parameter may not be used on both sides of a dyadic operator. That is to say, expressions such as ? = ? or ? > ? are prohibited.

- No dynamic parameter may be used in the following expressions:

    - ? COLLATE *collation* (See Collations in Part III.)

    - EXTRACT (*extract* field FROM ?) (See Datetime Value Functions in Part III.)

- No dynamic parameter specification may be the argument to an aggregate function (see Aggregate Functions in Part III).

- No dynamic parameter may be used in a row value constructor that is tested with the IS NULL predicate (see Predicates, Row and Table Value Constructors in Part III).

- No dynamic parameter may be the second element in a row value constructor used with the OVERLAPS operator (see Row and Table Value Constructors, Datetime Value Functions in Part III).

- No dynamic parameter may be the first operand of COA-LESCE or of the first WHEN condition in a CASE expression, or both operands of a NULLIF expression (see CASE Expressions in Part III).

- No dynamic parameter may be in the same column position for each row of a table value constructor, unless the statement is an INSERT and the constructor is used to generate values for it (see INSERT in this part, and Row and Table Value Constructors in Part III).

- If a dynamic parameter is a row value constructor used with an IN predicate, it may not be both the entire constructor and the first element in the list to be matched (see Predicates, Row and Table Value Constructors in Part III).

NOTE Since ALLOCATE CURSOR generates cursor names at runtime, these are allowed to duplicate the names of the more permanent cursors created with DECLARE CURSOR. The text of the prepared statement may refer to cursors of either type but will produce an error if the reference is ambiguous because of name duplication.

Once the conditions described above have been met, the statement is ready to be executed. Whether a prepared statement continues to be valid past the end of a transaction or needs to be prepared once again is implementation-dependent.

Example

The following statement converts the text string variable SQLstmt5 to the prepared statement Statement5. This statement will be accessible throughout the session. The content of the string variable is also shown. The statement uses a dynamic parameter for the city value that must be matched; this will be assigned a value when the statement is executed using an EXECUTE statement. The leading and trailing blanks will be removed automatically. As you can see, the statement terminator (;) is not part of the prepared statement.

```
SQLstmt5 ::= ' DELETE FROM Salepeople WHERE city = ? '
PREPARE GLOBAL Statement5 FROM :SQLstmt5;
```

Conformance Levels

Intermediate	Implementations at this level are not required to support any of the following as prepared statements: CREATE ASSERTION, DROP ASSERTION, CREATE COLLATION, DROP COLLATION, CREATE TRANSLATION, DROP TRANSLATION, SET SCHEMA, SET CATALOG, SET NAMES, SET CONSTRAINTS MODE, SELECT (used outside of cursors; in other words, a single-row SELECT).
Entry	Implementations at this level are not required to support Dynamic SQL at all.

See Also Part II: ALLOCATE CURSOR, DECLAIR CUSOR, EXECUTE, and EXECUTE IMMEDIATE. Part III: Predicates and Row and Table Value Constructors.

REVOKE

Removes the Privilege to Perform an Action

Syntax

```
REVOKE [ GRANT OPTION FOR ]
{ ALL PRIVILEGES } | { privilege .,..}
ON object
FROM PUBLIC | { grantee .,..}
 CASCADE | RESTRICT ;
```

Usage

The REVOKE statement removes privileges or the GRANT OPTION on them from Authorization IDs that will have previously received them with the GRANT statement. Authorization IDs generally refer to users but may also mean modules or compilation units (see Authorization IDs in Part III). The privileges follow the definitions and rules outlined under GRANT. The GRANT OPTION is the ability to grant the privileges received in turn to others. If GRANT OPTION FOR is specified, the grantee loses the ability to grant the named privileges on the named object but retains the privileges

themselves for his own use; if GRANT OPTION FOR is not specified, the grantee loses the named privileges. A grantee that loses a
privilege automatically loses GRANT OPTION as well, so a separate statement to REVOKE the GRANT OPTION is not necessary. If
no column list is given for a column-specific privilege, the REVOKE
statement applies to all columns on which the privilege (or GRANT
OPTION on the privilege) currently is held and which the issuer of
this statement has the authority to REVOKE.

NOTE Although REVOKE has been part of commercial SQL
implementations throughout the history of the language, it is
not required for Entry SQL92 and earlier SQL standards. In
practice, this means everyone supports it but may not follow
precisely what the standard specifies, especially in the area of
dependencies, where the standard is highly abstruse.

In any case, the revoker of the privilege will be the same Authorization ID that GRANTed it. To clearly explain CASCADE and
REVOKE, we must explain dependencies. Following are the basic
principles that govern dependencies. The standard is slightly more
complicated than this, but our explanation conforms to what you
are likely to actually find in practice.

- GRANT OPTION on a privilege includes subsets of that privilege. That is to say, if you have GRANT OPTION on SELECT
  for five columns of a table, you can GRANT SELECT on any of
  those five columns independently; you do not have to GRANT
  it on all of them.

- A privilege is either dependent or independent.

- An independent privilege is one directly GRANTed by the
  owner of the object in question or automatically GRANTed
  by the DBMS. Automatic GRANTs have a grantor of _SYSTEM
  and include such things as the GRANT of all privileges on an
  object to its creator. For more on automatic GRANTs, see GRANT.

- If a user (user A) is not the creator of an object but has GRANT
  OPTION on a privilege (privilege X), she can GRANT the privilege to user B. The privilege user B now has what is considered a separate privilege (privilege Y) that is directly dependent
  on privilege X.

- If user A GRANTed privilege X WITH GRANT OPTION, and user B GRANTs privilege Y to a third user (C, who now has privilege Z), privilege Z is directly dependent on privilege Y and indirectly dependent on privilege X.

- Several people can GRANT the same privilege to any given user. If these GRANTs differ only in their dependencies, that is, on who is GRANTing them, the privileges are merged, and we say that these privileges have multiple dependencies. The multiple dependencies are treated independently unless they are redundant (for example, the same GRANT executed twice by the same grantor to the same grantee would not result in two dependencies. If the grantors were different, it would).

- Privileges with GRANT OPTION are also merged with identical privileges without, but the GRANT OPTION has a separate dependency. Suppose user A GRANTs user B a privilege WITH GRANT OPTION, and user C GRANTs the same privilege without GRANT OPTION. If user A REVOKEs the privilege, user B still has it but without GRANT OPTION.

- Some objects require privileges on other objects. For example, to CREATE a VIEW, you must have the SELECT privilege on all columns of all tables directly referenced in the view. Likewise, to CREATE a DOMAIN using a particular COLLATION, you must have the USAGE privilege on that COLLATION. The objects that can have such dependencies are as follows:

  - Base tables can contain constraints that reference other tables. Such constraints rely on the REFERENCES privilege on those tables. Table constraints can also utilize domains, character sets, collations, and translations, all of which require the USAGE privilege.

  - Views require the SELECT privilege on all columns referenced in them. The query contained in a view can also make direct use of some other kinds of objects, such as domains (for CAST Expressions) or collations. These objects require the USAGE privilege.

  - Domains can use constraints, with the same consequences as for base tables.

  - Assertions use constraints, with the same consequences as for base tables.

- Note that some objects, like character sets, require privileges but do not depend on them.

- The above objects are said to be directly dependent on the privileges used to create them and indirectly dependent on any privileges on which those privileges depend.

- Consider a database full of privileges GRANTed like this. Picture each privilege as an oval having an arrow pointing to each other privilege that directly depends on it. Each independent privilege has a star on top of the oval. Now add rectangles indicating all objects that depend on privileges (other objects are not relevant). There are also arrows pointing to them from the privileges on which they directly depend. This type of picture is called a dependency graph; it may or may not actually be implemented by the DBMS as a data structure, but it is a useful tool for you to use to understand dependencies. (For complex schemata, having an application or tool that actually draws these things can be handy.)

- When a privilege or GRANT OPTION on one is REVOKEd, all privileges directly or indirectly dependent can be REVOKEd as well. All arrows indicating such dependencies are removed from the dependency graph. Arrows to objects that depend on these privileges are also removed.

- At this point, examine the graph and see if there are any privileges, other than independent privileges, or any objects with no arrows pointing to them. If so, these are "abandoned". Also, see if there are any groups of privileges and objects that point to one another but do not include any independent privileges. These also are abandoned. The principle is that *from any dependent privilege or object, you should be able to trace a path back through the arrows to an independent privilege. If you cannot, the privilege or object is abandoned.*

OK, now that you know all this, how do RESTRICT and CASCADE work? If the revocation of a privilege creates abandoned privileges or objects, the following happen:

- If the REVOKE statement specifies RESTRICT, then REVOKE fails and nothing is changed. REVOKE RESTRICT is the safe approach.

- If the REVOKE statement specifies CASCADE, then any or all of the following occur, depending on what dependencies exist. All abandoned privileges are automatically REVOKEd.

  - All abandoned views are dropped.

  - All abandoned constraints residing directly in tables are removed from those tables. This is achieved with an automatically executed ALTER TABLE statement, which may be how the CASCADE effect will show up in the logs. The tables are otherwise unaffected.

  - The same for abandoned constraints residing in domains. In effect, an ALTER DOMAIN statement is issued.

  - If an abandoned constraint resides in an assertion, the assertion is dropped.

NOTE It does not matter whether the user performing the REVOKE has the right to perform the above operations. They are automatic. You should keep the security implications of this in mind when GRANTing privileges.

Example

The following statement removes the SELECT privilege on Salespeople from Authorization ID Burns. Any dependent privileges are revoked, and dependent objects are dropped or altered as indicated.

```
REVOKE SELECT ON Salespeople FROM Burns CASCADE;
```

Conformance Levels

Entry   Implementations at this level are not required to support REVOKE.

Non   Most if not all nonconformant products do support REVOKE but it may not behave exactly as described here. The syntax is fairly, but not absolutely, standard.

See Also Part II: GRANT.

ROLLBACK
Ends a Transaction, Canceling All Changes

Syntax

```
ROLLBACK [ WORK ];
```

Usage

The ROLLBACK statement terminates the current transaction. A transaction is a group of one or more SQL statements that are effectively executed at the same instant and succeed or fail as a group. With ROLLBACK, they all fail, and their effects are canceled (the successful transaction-termination statement is COMMIT). ROLLBACK can never fail, but it can be overridden, if the SQL transaction is part of some implementation-dependent encompassing transaction. If this happens, you will get an invalid transaction state error. Otherwise, the ROLLBACK will proceed. All open cursors will be closed.

Conformance Levels

Entry   Implementations at this level may require the word
         WORK rather than having it be optional.

See Also   Part II: COMMIT WORK, SET TRANSACTION.

SELECT
Retrieves Rows from One or More Tables

Syntax

```
SELECT [DISTINCT]
{ { aggregate function |  value expression
  [AS column name]}.,..}
| {qualifier.*}
| *
INTO target spec.,..
FROM { {table name [AS] [correlation name]
[ (column name.,..) ] } }
| {subquery
```

```
    | joined table
    | table value constructor
    | {TABLE table name} }
          [AS] correlation name [(column name.,..)]}
     } .,..
    [ WHERE predicate ]
    [ GROUP BY {table name | correlation name}.column name
       [ COLLATE collation name ] ]
    [ HAVING predicate ]
    [ {UNION | INTERSECT | EXCEPT} [ALL]
    [CORRESPONDING [BY (column name.,..)] ]
    select statement | {TABLE table name}
    | table value constructor ]
    [ ORDER BY {{output column [ ASC | DESC ]}.,..}
       | {{positive integer [ ASC | DESC ]}.,..};
```

Usage

The SELECT statement is used to formulate queries—requests for information from the database. The issuer of the statement must have the SELECT privilege on all tables accessed. Queries may be stand-alone statements or used in the definitions of views and cursors. You can also use them as subqueries to produce values that will be used within other statements, including the SELECT statement itself. Sometimes, a subquery will be evaluated separately for each row processed by the outer query. Values from that outer row will be used in the subquery. Queries of this type are called correlated subqueries. For more information, see Subqueries in Part III.

The output of a query is itself a table, and the SELECT clause defines the columns of that table (the output columns). The output columns can either be taken directly from the table(s) on which the query operates, be derived from the values in those tables, or be direct value expressions not using the content of the tables.

The INTO clause is used only in Embedded SQL, Dynamic SQL, or the module language and only for queries that return but a single row. It simplifies operations for these queries by making a cursor.

The FROM clause determines the one or more tables from which the data will be taken or derived. These sources may include temporary or permanent base tables, views, or the results of subqueries and other operations that return tables.

The WHERE clause defines the criteria that rows must meet in order to be used for deriving the output. These criteria are defined using predicates, which are described later in this entry and discussed in more detail in Part III: Predicates.

The GROUP BY clause groups the output over identical values in the named columns. If the GROUP BY clause is used, every value expression in the output columns that includes a table column must be included in it, unless the columns are used as arguments to aggregate functions. GROUP BY is used to apply aggregate functions to groups of rows defined by having identical values in specified columns. If no GROUP BY clause is used, either all or none of those output columns in the SELECT clause based on tables must use aggregate functions. If all of them use aggregate functions, all rows satisfying the WHERE clause (if any) or all rows produced by the FROM clause (if there is no WHERE clause) are treated as a single group for deriving the aggregates.

The HAVING clause defines criteria that the groups of rows defined in the GROUP BY clause must satisfy to be output by the query. HAVING is meaningful only with GROUP BY, although some products may not reject the use of HAVING without GROUP BY.

UNION, INTERSECT, and EXCEPT are used to combine the output of multiple queries. They are explained in detail below.

ORDER BY forces the output of the one or more queries to emerge in a particular sequence.

The following list shows the order in which the clauses of the SELECT statement are effectively evaluated:

1. FROM

2. WHERE

3. GROUP BY

4. HAVING

5. SELECT

6. UNION or EXCEPT

7. INTERSECT

8. ORDER BY

9. INTO

The individual clauses are described in greater detail in the following sections, in the order in which they are specified in the syntax.

The SELECT Clause

The SELECT clause appears first but is not the first logical step. The other clauses produce a set of rows, the source rows, from which the output is to be derived. The SELECT clause determines which columns from these rows are output. It may directly output these columns, or it may use them in aggregate functions or value expressions. Value expressions can be NUMERIC, STRING, DATE-TIME, or INTERVAL; they may include CAST expressions, CASE statements, aggregate functions, and subqueries (for more information, see Part III: Aggregate Functions, CASE Expressions, CAST Expressions, and Value Expressions). If DISTINCT is specified, the rows are compared and, if any duplicate rows are found, only one copy appears in the output. This comparison occurs after all expressions have been evaluated, as the last step before output. The SELECT clause may contain any of the following:

- Aggregate functions, which are functions that extract single values from groups of column values—for example, SUM or COUNT.

- An asterisk (*), which means all of the columns of all tables listed in the FROM clause are output, in the order in which they appear in the FROM clause.

- A value expression, which in a SELECT clause usually is or includes a column name from one of the tables identified in the FROM clause. Either the column's value is directly output or it becomes part of some expression, such as AMOUNT * 3. The column name that you can specify with the AS clause is the name of the output column. If the output columns are directly taken from one and only one column referenced in the FROM clause, it will inherit the name of that column by default. You can override this name by using the AS clause, if desired. The names of columns not directly taken from input columns are implementation-dependent. You are not required to name any output columns. It makes no difference whether you include the word noiseword AS—if omitted, it is implied.

- The {qualifier.*} sequence, which produces all input columns as output columns, except that the common columns of any joined tables are removed. The qualifier is a name or correlation variable denoting a table referenced in the query. In order for the qualifier to have a point, this should be a joined table, probably created in the FROM clause using the join operators we will introduce later in this entry.

An output column from the query can contain NULLs if any of the following are true:

- It includes the name of a column that can contain NULLs.

- It is suffixed with an indicator parameter or an indicator variable. For example, *SELECT :prog-var:prog-var-indicator FROM tablename*.

- It contains a subquery.

- It contains a CASE, COALESCE, or NULLIF argument.

- It contains an aggregate function other than COUNT.

- The query contains an outer join (explained later in this entry).

Otherwise, the output column cannot contain NULLs. It is important to know whether NULLs may be present because, if you are using either Static or Dynamic SQL, you probably will want to use an indicator parameter or variable if NULLs may be encountered. If you don't, they could cause you an error (see Value Expressions in Part III).

NOTE In the last case listed above, the output column value would be NULL whenever no rows are selected from which the aggregate can be derived. With COUNT, the value in this situation is 0 rather than NULL.

The INTO Clause

You can use this clause whenever you know that a particular query will produce only one row and when you have a host-language into whose variables you can store the output. Situations where you know you will output only one row include when you are searching for a specific primary key value and when you are using aggregate functions with no GROUP BY clause. The *target specs* consists of host-language variables, possibly appended by indicator variables, that can hold the values in the output columns in the SELECT clause. The *target specs* should match the SELECT columns in the order given.

The FROM Clause

The FROM clause names the source tables for the query. These tables may be any of the following:

- Tables or views named and accessed directly.

- Tables derived on the spot with a subquery.

- Built-in joins (explained later in this entry).

- Table value constructors. This is a way to directly specify a set of values as constituting a table for the duration of this statement. See Part III: Row and Table Value Constructors.

- Explicit tables. These consist simply of the word TABLE followed by the name of a table or view. It is the equivalent of `SELECT * FROM tablename`.

You can follow tables specified with any of the above techniques with correlation names. A correlation name (also called a range variable or an alias) provides an alternative name for the table it follows. These names last only for the duration of the statement. They are an option of convenience for base tables and views but are required for tables produced by subqueries or table value constructors. They can be used to qualify ambiguous column references in the rest of the statement, as can the table names that they replace.

A join, explained later in this entry, is a technique for combining multiple tables into one. You may choose to join a table to itself, which is treated as a join of two identical tables; in this case, you will have to use correlation names to distinguish the two copies. The correlation name will prefix the column name—separated by a period, as usual (see Appendix D). The column name lists here are for renaming columns, just as they are in the SELECT clause. The names used here, however, are not for the output; they are for references to the columns made in the remainder of the statement, particularly in the WHERE clause. They are optional but may be required to clarify column references in some cases.

Joins

If more than one table is named in the FROM clause, they are all implicitly joined. This means that every possible combination of rows (one from each table) will, in effect, be derived, and that this concatenation will be the table on which the rest of the query operates. The concatenated table is called a Cartesian product or a cross join.

Usually, you want to eliminate most of the rows and focus on the data you want, typically in terms of some relationship. To do this, you can use the WHERE clause. As an alternative, you can use built-in join operators to perform the entire join in the FROM clause, treating the result as a derived table for processing by the rest of the query. For that matter, the two techniques can be combined, although this usually produces more confusion than it is worth. The old standard did not support built-in join operators, so if you have already learned to perform your joins by hand, you may find it natural to stick with that method. Otherwise, you are likely to find the built-in joins simpler for any of a group of standard operations.

First, let's look at the built-in join operators that you would use in the FROM clause. The syntax to create a joined table this way is as follows:

```
cross join ::=
table A CROSS JOIN table B

natural join ::=
table A NATURAL
  [join type] JOIN table B

union join ::=
table A UNION JOIN table B

specified join ::=
table A
  [join type] JOIN table B
   {ON predicate}
 | {USING (column name.,..)}

join type ::=
INNER
| { { LEFT | RIGHT | FULL } [OUTER] }
```

All of that just to replace a table name in the FROM clause! Nonetheless, it can be simpler than doing the same joins by hand, as you will see. The syntax above refers to a join of two tables (it is possible to join any number of tables, but these operations can be broken down into multiple joins of two tables). The result of this join is a table, which can be treated as a source table for the rest of the query. One and only one of the following is to be specified: CROSS, NATURAL, UNION, ON, or USING. The join type arguments (INNER, LEFT, and so on) serve to further qualify joins that use NATURAL, ON, or USING.

You can optionally place the entire join in parentheses. Why would you want to do this? Correlation names can follow either the entire join, to rename the table and possibly columns that result from it, or simply follow the individual tables being joined. Sometimes you must use correlation names for the individual tables to avoid ambiguity. If the join is parenthesized, a correlation name following it, outside the parentheses, applies to the result table of the join. Correlation names following the individual tables specified as part of the join apply to the tables and can be referenced in the join itself. In the absence or parentheses, a correlation name following a join is assumed to apply to the last table in the join, not the result table. The use of correlation names will become clearer in the examples that follow.

The two tables joined actually can be the same table, in which case the join is performed as though two identical tables are being joined. This is called a self-join and can be useful in some situations.

A join over a column is a join in which only those rows from the Cartesian product of *table A* and *table B* where the values in that column are the same are retained; these two columns are merged into one (the join column or common column). Naturally, the datatypes of the joined columns have to be comparable (as defined in Part III: Datatypes).

The joins fall into the following categories:

- A CROSS join, as defined above, is a straight Cartesian product. A CROSS join is shown in Table II.3.

- A natural join has a slightly different meaning in the SQL standard than it does in database theory generally. In theory, a natural join is a join of a foreign to its parent key. In the standard, a natural join is a join of two tables over all columns that have the same name, one in each table. You can make the standard joins the same as theoretical ones by making sure that all your foreign keys have the same names as their parents and that all other columns have unique names. Natural joins in either the standard or theoretical sense fall into the following categories, which in the standard are called join types. In all of these, the word OUTER, if used, is optional and has no effect:

- INNER, which means that only rows where matches are found are included in the output. This type is shown in Table II.4.

- LEFT [OUTER], which means that all rows from *table A* are included, with matching rows from *table B* where found and NULLs where not found. This type is shown in Table II.5.

- RIGHT [OUTER], which is the reverse of a LEFT OUTER join. All rows for *table B* are included with NULLs in rows unmatched in *table A*. This type is shown in Table II.6.

- FULL [OUTER]. This is a combination of LEFT and RIGHT OUTER. All rows from both tables are included, merged where matches are found, and filled out with NULLs where not. This type is shown in Table II.7.

- A UNION join consists of all columns of both tables, with no matching or Cartesian product derivation. You concatenate all of the columns from *table B* onto *table A*.. All the rows from *table A* are output, with NULLs in the columns from *table B*. Then all the rows from *table B* are output, with NULLs in the columns from *table A*. This is a fairly exotic type of join that sees little use. (Note that a UNION join is not the same as the UNION operator used to merge the output of multiple SELECT statements, described later in this entry.) This type is shown in Table II.8.

- A specified join uses ON or USING. Either of these can use the join types explained under natural joins:

  - USING is just like a natural join, except that you name the columns to be used in the join. The columns still have to have the same names in both tables. If your foreign and parent keys have the same names, but you may have other like-named columns as well (watch for common column names like "city" or "last name"), this is a way to restrict your join to the actual matching columns to directly name the columns to be joined. The standard calls this a named columns join. This type is shown in Table II.9.

- ON lets you specify a predicate, and the row combinations that satisfy that predicate are considered matched. This is pretty much the same way you hand-code a join in the main query anyway, but if you want to do all the work in the FROM clause, or if you want to have an easy way to embed joins, ON is your baby. The standard calls this a join condition, though all joins are over (written or implied) predicates (conditions). This type is shown in Table II.10.

The following tables show examples of the various join types. First, we introduce two tables that will be used to derive these joins: Salespeople and Customers, shown in Table II.2. The snum column in Customers is a foreign key referencing the column of the same name in Salespeople. The city column is not a key. The primary keys of the two tables are snum and cnum.

TABLE II.2: The two tables used as sources for the joins

Salespeople

Snum	Same	City	Comm
1001	Peel	London	.12
1002	Serres	San Jose	.13
1004	Motika	London	.11
1007	Rifkin	Barcelona	.15
1003	Axelrod	New York	.10

Customers

Cnum	Cname	City	Rating	Snum
2001	Hoffman	London	100	1001
2002	Giovanni	Rome	200	1003
2003	Liu	San Jose	200	1002
2004	Grass	Berlin	300	1002
2006	Clemens	London	NULL	1001
2008	Cisneros	San Jose	300	1007
2007	Pereira	Rome	100	1004

A CROSS Join

A complete CROSS join of these two tables would take 35 rows (seven rows in one table times five in the other). We're just going to show you enough to get the idea. In this and many other of these join examples, we are not including all columns of the joined tables. That would require the table to be too wide to make easily readable. The letters *s* and *c* are simple correlation names for the joined tables (not the result table).

```
Salespeople s CROSS JOIN Customers c
```

TABLE II.3: A Portion of a CROSS Join

S.snum	Sname	S.city	Cnum	Cname
1001	Peel	London	2001	Hoffman
1001	Peel	London	2002	Giovanni
1001	Peel	London	2003	Liu
1001	Peel	London	2004	Grass
1001	Peel	London	2006	Clemens
1001	Peel	London	2008	Cisneros
1001	Peel	London	2007	Pereira
1002	Serres	San Jose	2001	Hoffman
1002	Serres	San Jose	2002	Giovanni

A NATURAL INNER Join

The NATURAL INNER join retrieves all rows where both the city and snum columns of both tables have the same value. It is based on the fact that they have the same name. Although for an INNER JOIN, it does not strictly matter which table the commonly named columns come from (since the values are the same in both), it does matter for an OUTER JOIN, and the syntax requires you to specify. This mandates the use of correlation names.

Table II.4 shows a NATURAL join, in the standard, not theoretical, sense, of the Salespeople and Customers tables.

```
Salespeople s NATURAL INNER JOIN Customers c
```

TABLE II.4: A NATURAL INNER Join

Sname	S.snum	C.city	Cnum	Cname
Peel	1001	London	2001	Hoffman
Serres	1002	San Jose	2003	Liu
Peel	1001	London	2006	Clemens

A LEFT OUTER Join

Here is the previous example as a LEFT OUTER join:

```
Salespeople s NATURAL LEFT OUTER JOIN Customers c
```

TABLE II.5: A LEFT OUTER Join

Sname	S.snum	C.city	Cnum	Cname
Peel	1001	London	2001	Hoffman
Serres	1002	San Jose	2003	Liu
Peel	1001	London	2006	Clemens
Motika	1004	NULL	NULL	NULL
Rifkin	1007	NULL	NULL	NULL
Axelrod	1003	NULL	NULL	NULL

A RIGHT OUTER Join

Here is the previous example as a RIGHT OUTER JOIN:

```
Salespeople s NATURAL RIGHT OUTER JOIN Customers c
```

TABLE II.6: A RIGHT OUTER Join

Sname	S.snum	C.city	Cnum	Cname
Peel	1001	London	2001	Hoffman
Serres	1002	San Jose	2003	Liu
Peel	1001	London	2006	Clemens
NULL	NULL	Rome	2002	Giovanni
NULL	NULL	Berlin	2004	Grass
NULL	NULL	San Jose	2008	Cisneros
NULL	NULL	Rome	2007	Pereira

A FULL OUTER Join

Here is the previous example as a FULL (RIGHT and LEFT)
OUTER join:

```
Salespeople s NATURAL FULL OUTER JOIN Customers c
```

TABLE II.7: A FULL OUTER Join

Sname	S.snum	C.city	Cnum	Cname
Peel	1001	London	2001	Hoffman
Serres	1002	San Jose	2003	Liu
Peel	1001	London	2006	Clemens
Motika	1004	NULL	NULL	NULL
Rifkin	1007	NULL	NULL	NULL
Axelrod	1003	NULL	NULL	NULL
NULL	NULL	Rome	2002	Giovanni
NULL	NULL	Berlin	2004	Grass
NULL	NULL	San Jose	2008	Cisneros
NULL	NULL	Rome	2007	Pereira

A UNION Join

Here is a UNION join. Note that it is basically a way to concatenate the two tables, while keeping the result in a tabular structure:

```
Salespeople UNION JOIN Customers
```

TABLE II.8: A UNION Join

Snum	Sname	City	Cnum	Cname
1001	Peel	London	NULL	NULL
1002	Serres	San Jose	NULL	NULL
1004	Motika	London	NULL	NULL
1007	Rifkin	Barcelona	NULL	NULL
1003	Axelrod	New York	NULL	NULL

Continued on next page

TABLE II.8: A UNION Join (continued)

Snum	Sname	City	Cnum	Cname
NULL	NULL	NULL	2001	Hoffman
NULL	NULL	NULL	2002	Giovanni
NULL	NULL	NULL	2003	Liu
NULL	NULL	NULL	2004	Grass
NULL	NULL	NULL	2006	Clemens
NULL	NULL	NULL	2008	Cisneros
NULL	NULL	NULL	2007	Pereira

A Specified Join with USING

The following is a natural join in the theoretical sense between the two tables.

```
Salespeople s JOIN Customers c USING snum
```

TABLE II.9: A Specified Join with USING

Cnum	Cname	C.city	S.snum	Sname
2001	Hoffman	London	1001	Peel
2002	Giovanni	Rome	1003	Axelrod
2003	Liu	San Jose	1002	Serres
2004	Grass	Berlin	1002	Serres
2006	Clemens	London	1001	Peel
2008	Cisneros	San Jose	1007	Rifkin
2007	Pereira	Rome	1004	Motika

A Specified Join with ON

Here's a specified join using ON. Not a commonly useful predicate, but we got bored with simple equalities:

```
ON snum + 1000 = cnum
```

TABLE II.10: A Specified Join with ON

Snum	Sname	City	Cnum	Cname
1001	Peel	London	2001	Hoffman
1002	Serres	San Jose	2002	Giovanni
1004	Motika	London	2004	Grass
1007	Rifkin	Barcelona	2007	Pereira
1003	Axelrod	New York	2003	Liu

Note that all of these kinds of joins determine which rows are included in the output. Even joins over specified columns, such as natural and specified USING joins, actually retrieve all the columns of the underlying tables. The determination of which *columns* of these rows to include in the output is an independent matter determined by the SELECT clause.

Subqueries can be used in the FROM clause, but these may not use aggregate functions. WHERE clause subquery predicates are discussed in the next section and under Predicates in Part III.

The WHERE Clause

The WHERE clause contains a *predicate*, which is a set of one or more expressions that can be TRUE, FALSE, or UNKNOWN. NULLs compared to any value, including other NULLs, produce UNKNOWNs. Other values are compared according to collating sequence (for character string types), numerical order (for numeric types), chronological order (for datetime types), or magnitude (for interval types). These comparisons are expressed using the following operators: =, <, <=, >, >=, and <> (does not equal). Operators such as * (multiplication) or || (concatenation) may be applied depending on the datatype (see Datatypes in Part III).

In addition to the standard comparison operators, SQL provides the following special predicate operators. (These are explained in more detail in Part III: Predicates.) Assume that A, B, and C are all value expressions, which can be or include column names or be direct expressions (possibly using column names or aggregate functions) in the appropriate datatype. They could also be variables (Embedded SQL), parameters (module language), or dynamic parameters (Dynamic SQL). For more information, see Part III: Value Expressions. For example, assuming they are numbers, A could be 1000 (a direct expression, in this case, a literal), B could be snum (a column name), and C could cnum/2 (a value expression incorporating a column name). Following are the predicates.

BETWEEN

```
B BETWEEN A AND C
```

This statement is equal to (A <= B) AND (B <= C). A and C must be specified in ascending order. B BETWEEN C AND A would be interpreted as (C <= B) AND (B <= A), which would be FALSE if (A <= B) AND (B <= C) were TRUE, unless all three values were the same in which case, both component predicates would be TRUE. If any of the values is NULL, the predicate is UNKNOWN.

IN

```
A IN (C, D .,..)
```

This statement is TRUE if A equals any value in the list. If any of the values is NULL, the predicate is UNKNOWN.

LIKE

```
A LIKE 'string'
```

This statement assumes that A is a character string datatype and searches for the specified substring. Fixed and varying-length wildcards may be used (see Predicates in Part III). If A or the string is NULL, the predicate is UNKNOWN.

IS NULL

```
A IS NULL
```

This statement specifically tests for NULLs. Unlike most other predicates, it can only be TRUE or FALSE—not UNKNOWN. It is TRUE if A contains a NULL, FALSE otherwise.

SOME or ANY

```
A comp op SOME | ANY subquery
```

SOME and ANY have equivalent meanings. The *subquery* produces a set of values. If, for any value V so produced, *A comp op* V is TRUE, then the ANY predicate is TRUE. The comparison operators are the standard ones outlined above (=, <=, etc.)

ALL

```
A comp op ALL subquery
```

ALL is similar to ANY except, that all of the values produced by the *subquery* have to make A *comp op* V TRUE.

EXISTS

```
EXISTS subquery
```

This statement is TRUE if the *subquery* produces any rows, and FALSE otherwise. It is never UNKNOWN. To be meaningful, it must use a correlated *subquery* (explained later in this entry).

UNIQUE

```
UNIQUE subquery
```

If the *subquery* produces no identical rows, UNIQUE is TRUE; otherwise, it is FALSE. For the purposes of this predicate, identical rows are devoid of NULLs; otherwise, they are not identical.

MATCH

```
row value constructor MATCH arguments subquery
```

MATCH tests for the presence of the constructed row among those of the table produced by the *subquery*. The *arguments* allow you to specify FULL or PARTIAL matches and whether the matched row has to be unique. MATCH is examined in more detail in Part III under Predicates; also look at Row and Table Value Constructors.

OVERLAPS

```
row value constructor OVERLAPS row value constructor
```

OVERLAPS is a rather specialized predicate for determining when two date or time periods overlap. It must be used with DATETIME datatypes, possibly in conjunction with INTERVAL datatypes. Again, see Part III: Predicates.

Combining Predicates

These predicates are combined using the conventional Boolean operators AND, OR, and NOT. For TRUE and FALSE values, these predicates have the conventional results; if UNKNOWNs are involved, the results are those outlined in Part III: Predicates. Parentheses may be used to force an order of evaluation. When all is said and done, the rows selected by the WHERE clause, whether directly extracted from tables or based on Cartesian products, are the ones that go on to be processed by the subsequent clauses. For a given row to be SELECTed, it must make the predicate TRUE.

The GROUP BY Clause

The GROUP BY clause is used to define groups of output rows to which aggregate functions (COUNT, MIN, AVG, and so on) can be applied. If this clause is absent, and aggregate functions are used, the column names in the SELECT clause must all be contained in aggregate functions, and the aggregate functions will be applied to all rows that satisfy the query. Otherwise, each column referenced in the SELECT list outside an aggregate function will be a grouping column and be referenced in this clause. All rows output from the query that have all grouping column values equal will constitute a group (for the purposes of GROUP BY, all NULLs are considered equal). The aggregate function will be applied to each such group. Let's look at a simple example:

```
SELECT snum, AVG(amt), MAX(amt)
FROM Orders
GROUP BY snum;
```

This query assumes a table called Orders has one entry per order and includes a column indicating the salesperson (snum) and amount (amt) for each order. There will naturally be other columns as well, including, at the least, a PRIMARY KEY, since neither of these are suitable keys. Suffice it to say for our purposes that this query finds the average and the highest order amount for each salesperson. All orders with the same snum value—the same salesperson—constitute a group, and the highest and the average amount for each group are calculated and output. If there were also a date column called odate, giving the date of each order, and we wanted these figures calculated independently for each date, we could also make odate a grouping column. Then the aggregates would be calculated for each unique combination of snum and odate. Grouping can be done over joins, in which case table or correlation name prefixes to the column names may be necessary to resolve ambiguities.

If a COLLATE FROM clause is used, it will provide the collation defined for the output column derived from the grouping column. The coercibility attribute of the output column is then explicit. Naturally, the COLLATE CLAUSE can only be applied if the grouping column is a character set datatype. See Part III: Collations and Datatypes.

The HAVING Clause

Just as the WHERE clause defines a predicate to filter rows, the HAVING clause is applied after the grouping performed by GROUP BY to define a similar predicate for filtering groups based on the aggregate values. It is needed to test for aggregate function values, as these are not derived from single rows of the Cartesian product defined by the FROM clause, but from groups of such rows, and therefore cannot be tested in a WHERE clause.

UNION, INTERSECT, EXCEPT, and CORRESPONDING

These statements take entire SELECT statements (queries), minus any ORDER BY clauses, as arguments in this form:

```
query A {UNION | INTERSECT | EXCEPT} [ALL] query B
```

The output columns of each of the queries must be comparable (as defined in Part III: Datatypes) in the order specified—the first output column of *query A* with the first of *query B*, the second of each, and so on—because these columns will now be merged. If CORRESPONDING, described below, is used, the output columns can be in any order.

UNION includes any row output by either query. If ALL is specified, duplicate output rows are all retained. Otherwise, only one copy of each duplicate is retained.

EXCEPT outputs the rows from *query A*, except for any also produced by *query B*. These are eliminated from the output, and duplicates within the output of *query A* are output only once. If EXCEPT ALL is specified, the number of times a duplicate row appears in the output of *query B* is subtracted from the number of times it appears in *query A*, and it is output that many times—provided, of course, that the number is greater than zero.

If INTERSECT is specified, any rows that appear in the output of both *query A* and *query B* are output once each. Other rows are not output. INTERSECT ALL will have the duplicate rows appear the number of times that they appear in *query A* or the number they appear in *query B*—whichever is smaller.

Note that you may string together any number of queries with the above operators. You may also use parentheses to force an order of evaluation.

CORRESPONDING restricts the operation to columns in the SELECT clauses of the two queries whose names are the same and whose datatypes are comparable. (Of course, you may be able to force this by using the AS clause to assign names or a CAST expression to convert datatypes. See Part III: CAST Expressions.) If a list of columns is supplied with CORRESPONDING, they all must be commonly named and typed columns as just described. The operation is restricted to these columns. If no list is supplied, all such like named and typed columns are used.

In either case, only the like named and typed columns will be output. They will emerge in the order listed or, if no list is used, in the order in which they appear in the first query. With CORRESPONDING, it is not necessary for each SELECT list to have the same number of columns with matching datatypes in the same order—otherwise, it is necessary.

The ORDER BY Clause

Finally, the ORDER BY clause is used to sort the output. The rows are sorted according to the values in the columns listed here; the first column listed gets the highest priority, and the second column determines the order within duplicate values of the first, the third within duplicate values of the second, and so on. You may specify ASC (for ascending, the default) or DESC (for descending) independently for each column. Character sets will be sorted according to their collations. You may also use integers rather than names to indicate columns. The integers refer to the placement of the column among those in the SELECT clause, so that the first column is indicated with a 1, the fifth with a 5, and so on. If any output columns are unnamed, of course, you will have to use a number.

Possibly Nondeterministic Queries

In some cases, it is possible for the same query to produce different output tables on different implementations because of subtle implementation-dependent behaviors. Such queries are called *possibly nondeterministic queries*. A query is possibly nondeterministic if any of the following is true:

- It specifies DISTINCT and the datatype of at least one column of the source row is character string.

- One column of the source rows is of a character string datatype and is used in either the MIN or the MAX aggregate function.

- A character set column is used as a grouping column in GROUP BY or in a UNION.

- A HAVING clause uses a character string column within a MIN or MAX function.

- It uses UNION without specifying ALL.

- It uses INTERSECT or EXCEPT.

Possibly nondeterministic queries cannot be used in constraints (see Constraints in Part III).

Example

The following statement determines the total and average sales for each salesperson on each day of a given week, excluding days where the total was less than $100.00.

```
SELECT snum, SUM(amt), AVG(amt), odate
FROM Orders
WHERE odate BETWEEN '10-01-2000' AND '10-08-2000'
GROUP BY snum, odate
HAVING SUM(amt) > 100.00;
```

Conformance Levels

Intermediate — Implementations at this level are not required to support the use of table value constructors or the use of the TABLE clause (explicit tables). They are not required to support multiple specifications of DISTINCT in the same SELECT list. This would apply to uses of DISTINCT within aggregate functions. They are not required to support a COLLATE clause for GROUP BY, UNION joins, or CROSS joins. Nor are they required to support the use of subqueries to derive tables for the FROM clause.

Entry   Implementations at this level are not required to support the built-in join operators. If the FROM clause directly references a view based on aggregate data, and that view uses a GROUP BY clause, you may be restricted from referencing any other tables in the FROM clause, and WHERE, GROUP BY, HAVING, and further aggregates in the SELECT list of the present query may all be prohibited. Predicates may be prohibited from referencing aggregate functions. Qualifiers may be disallowed. EXCEPT, INTERSECT, and CORRESPONDING may all be excluded, and it may not be possible to make UNIONs of joins.

See Also   Part II: ALLOCATE CURSOR, CREATE VIEW, DECLARE CURSOR, GRANT. Part III: Aggregate Functions, Collations, Datatypes, Predicates, Row and Table Value Constructors, Subqueries. Appendix D.

SET CATALOG
Determines the Default Catalog

Syntax

```
SET CATALOG catalog name;
```

Usage

SQL schemata are grouped into catalogs, and these into clusters, although implementations have the option of allowing cross-cluster catalogs. This statement defines the default catalog within which the current session operates. Any unqualified schema names used in SQL statements will be implicitly qualified by this catalog name. The default prior to the use of this statement is implementation-defined. Once the leading and trailing blanks, if any, are removed, the catalog name must conform to the proper conventions for such names, which is to say it must be a properly formed SQL identifier (see Appendix D) and conform as well to any implementation-defined restrictions on catalog names.

Conformance Levels

Intermediate   Implementations at this level are not
                 required to support this statement or to
                 support catalogs.

See Also   Part I: Users, Schemas, and Sessions Part II: CREATE
SCHEMA, SET SCHEMA.

SET CONNECTION
Determines Which Connection is Active

Syntax

```
SET CONNECTION connection name | DEFAULT ;
```

Usage

The SQL92 standard gives you the ability to have more than one
simultaneous connection between a user and a DBMS. The connections are created with the CONNECT statement and destroyed
with DISCONNECT. Once you have created several connections
using CONNECT, you can use the SET CONNECTION statement
to switch between them. The named connection becomes current,
and the current one becomes dormant with no other change in its
state. The connection name may be a variable (Embedded SQL),
parameter (module language), or literal.

Conformance Levels

Intermediate   Implementations at this level are not
                 required to support this statement.

See Also   Part II: CONNECT, DISCONNECT.

SET CONSTRAINTS MODE
Determines When Constraints Are Checked

Syntax

```
SET CONSTRAINTS MODE constraint name.,... | ALL
[DEFERRED | IMMEDIATE];
```

Usage

Constraints are expressions involving table data, functioning as tests that must be satisfied for the data to be allowed into the database. They can be part of table definitions, domain definitions, or assertion definitions. When created as part of one of these objects, they are specified as DEFERRABLE or NOT DEFERRABLE. If they are NOT DEFERRABLE, they are effectively checked after every statement. Otherwise, checking can be deferred until the end of the transaction. This statement determines when the DEFERRABLE constraints are checked. If ALL is specified, the statement applies to all DEFERRABLE constraints. If not, it applies to the constraints that are named in the list. If IMMEDIATE is specified, all specified constraints are effectively checked now and after every subsequent statement. If DEFERRED is specified, all specified constraints are effectively checked at the end of the transaction. If any DEFERRED constraints are violated when you attempt to set their mode to IMMEDIATE, the SET CONSTRAINTS MODE statement fails.

Example

The following statement will cause all constraints to be checked immediately. If any are violated, the transaction will be rolled back.

```
SET CONSTRAINTS MODE ALL IMMEDIATE;
```

Conformance Levels

Intermediate   Implementations at this level are not
                    required to support this statement.

See Also   Part II: ALTER DOMAIN, ALTER TABLE, COMMIT WORK, CREATE ASSERTION, CREATE DOMAIN, CREATE TABLE, ROLLBACK.

SET DESCRIPTOR
(Dynamic SQL Only) Directly Stores Values in a Descriptor Area

Syntax

```
SET DESCRIPTOR  [GLOBAL | LOCAL] descriptor name
{ COUNT = integer }
| { VALUE item number
{ descrip item = value }.,.. };
```

Usage

This statement stores values in the descriptor area, or simply descriptors, or changes the number of parameters described therein. Descriptors are used in Dynamic SQL to provide and retrieve values for parameters of dynamically generated statements; see Part III: Descriptor Areas. A given descriptor describes either all dynamic input or all dynamic output parameters of a given statement. For each such parameter, there is one item consisting of a number of fields.

The descriptor shall have been previously created with an ALLOCATE DESCRIPTOR statement. GLOBAL or LOCAL refers to the scope and, if specified, must agree with the scope of the descriptor as defined in the ALLOCATE DESCRIPTOR statement that created it. If the scope is GLOBAL, it must be specified in this statement. LOCAL is the default and therefore optional. The following descriptor items cannot be changed by this statement but must be set automatically by the system: RETURNED_LENGTH, RETURNED_OCTET_LENGTH, NULLABLE, COLLATION_CATALOG, COLLATION_SCHEMA, COLLATION_NAME, and NAME.

If you set values other than DATA, the value of DATA becomes undefined. Therefore, a given SET DESCRIPTOR statement either sets the DATA field, which contains a value for the parameter, or sets the other fields that describe the parameter. In some situations, when you set certain fields, others are set automatically, as follows:

- If you set TYPE to CHARACTER or CHARACTER VARYING, then CHARACTER_SET_CATALOG, CHARACTER_SET_SCHEMA, and CHARACTER_SET_NAME are all set to the value for the default character set, and LENGTH is set to 1.

- If you set TYPE to BIT or BIT VARYING, then LENGTH is set to 1.

- If you set TYPE to DATETIME, then PRECISION is set to 0.

- If you set TYPE to INTERVAL, then DATETIME_INTERVAL_PRECISION is set to 2.

- If you set TYPE to NUMERIC or DECIMAL, then SCALE is set to 0 and PRECISION to the implementation-defined default value.

- If you set TYPE to FLOAT, then PRECISION is set to the implementation-defined default value. (This reflects the state of the standard as of this writing. The default SCALE of 0 may be subject to change.)

- If you set DATETIME_INTERVAL_CODE and TYPE to DATE-TIME, and you specify DATE, TIME, or TIME WITH TIME ZONE, then PRECISION is set to 0.

- If you set DATETIME_INTERVAL_CODE and TYPE to DATE-TIME, and you specify TIMESTAMP or TIMESTAMP WITH TIME ZONE, then PRECISION is set to 6.

- If you set DATETIME_INTERVAL_CODE and TYPE to INTER-VAL, then, if you specify DAY TO SECOND, HOUR TO SEC-OND, MINUTE TO SECOND, or SECOND, PRECISION is set to 6, and if you do not specify one of the above, PRECISION is set to 0.

For all of the above cases, fields not mentioned may be automatically set to implementation-dependent values. In any case, the above are defaults that generally can be overridden by subsequently setting the descriptor field directly with this statement. When a group of descriptor fields are set in a single statement, they are set in the following order: TYPE, DATETIME_INTERVAL_CODE, DATETIME_INTERVAL_PRECISION, PRECISION, SCALE, CHARACTER_SET_CATALOG, CHARACTER_SET_SCHEMA, CHARACTER_SET_NAME, LENGTH, INDICATOR, and DATA. So, for example, the default PRECISION created when you set TYPE can be overridden with a PRECISION specification in the same statement. Note that this effect is independent of the order in which the fields are listed in the SET DESCRIPTOR statement.

Naturally, the datatypes of the values being set must match those of the descriptor item targets, and values being inserted into the DATA field must match the description of that field given by the other items, as least for TYPE, LENGTH, OCTET_LENGTH, PRECISION, and SCALE. Also note that the values of the descriptor area items following a failed SET DESCRIPTOR statement are implementation-dependent; this differs from most statements, which definitely leave the data in its previous state if they fail. Also, there may be implementation-dependent restrictions on changing fields previously set by a DESCRIBE statement. DESCRIBE is an alternative way to set descriptor areas; it automatically derives values by examining a prepared statement.

Example

The following statement sets the TYPE (to the code for CHARAC-TER) and LENGTH fields of the fourth item (which would describe the fourth dynamic parameter) of the descriptor area called State-ment5_Desc. The scope of GLOBAL must be specified, as it is part of the descriptor name.

```
SET DESCRIPTOR GLOBAL :Statement5_Desc VALUE 4
TYPE = 1, LENGTH = 25;
```

Conformance Levels

Intermediate   Implementations at this level may require a descriptor name to be a literal—a simple name. Otherwise, it could be a variable.

Entry   No Dynamic SQL support is required.

See Also   Part II: ALLOCATE DESCRIPTOR, DESCRIBE, GET DESCRIPTOR. Part III: Descriptor Areas.

SET NAMES
Sets the Default Character Set

Syntax

```
SET NAMES character set name;
```

Usage

The SET NAMES statement defines the default character set used for SQL statements. Trailing and leading blanks are removed, and then the character set name must identify a character set suitable for SQL text. The default remains in force for the duration of the session or until a new one is defined. The character set name may be a variable or parameter.

Conformance Levels

Intermediate   Implementations at this level are not required to support this statement.

See Also   Part II: CREATE CHARACTER SET, CREATE SCHEMA.

SET SCHEMA
(Dynamic and Interactive SQL) Sets the Current Schema

Syntax

```
SET SCHEMA schema name;
```

Usage

The SET SCHEMA statement defines the schema that will be used by default to qualify unqualified object names in interactive or prepared SQL statements. After leading and trailing blanks are removed, the schema name must identify an existing schema to which the current Authorization ID has access. The schema name may be prefixed with a catalog name; if so, both the schema and the catalog are set, and the named schema naturally must reside within the named catalog. Otherwise, some implementation-defined default catalog containing the schema will apply. It may be useful to override this default because schema names need only be unique within their catalogs. You could have a development and a production schema with the same name in different catalogs, for example. The default schema remains in force until a new one is defined or until the end of the session.

Conformance Levels

Intermediate   Implementations at this level are not required to support this statement.

See Also   Part II: CREATE SCHEMA, SET CATALOG.

SET SESSION AUTHORIZATION

Changes the Authorization under Which Statements Are Executed

Syntax

```
SET SESSION AUTHORIZATION Authorization ID;
```

Usage

Once leading and trailing blanks are removed, the Authorization ID named in the statement must be one that the current Authorization ID can access and switch to. The rules for determining which other Authorization IDs, if any, an Authorization ID may switch to are implementation-defined. If the switch is legal, the SQL-session Authorization ID—the value of the built-in variable SESSION_USER—is changed, as are the Authorization IDs controlling access to temporary tables.

Conformance Levels

SQL89   Implementations at this level are not required to support this statement.

See Also   Part III: Authorization IDs.

SET TIME ZONE
Defines the Local Time Zone Displacement

Syntax

```
SET TIME ZONE interval value | LOCAL;
```

Usage

Time zones in SQL are used for clock arithmetic and for time stamps. The default time zone for your session is implementation-defined. This statement changes that time zone. The INTERVAL value must be of the INTERVAL HOUR TO MINUTE type and must be between '-12:59' and '+13:00'. The time zone will be incremented or decremented by the indicated amount. Alternatively, LOCAL returns you to the initial default.

Conformance Levels

Entry   Implementations at this level are not required to support this statement.

See Also   Part III: Datetime Value Functions, Sessions.

SET TRANSACTION
Sets the Attributes of the Next Transaction

Syntax

```
SET TRANSACTION { ISOLATION LEVEL
  { READ UNCOMMITTED
  | READ COMMITTED
  | REPEATABLE READ
  | SERIALIZABLE }
| { READ ONLY | READ WRITE }
| { DIAGNOSTICS SIZE num of conditions } }.,.. ;
```

Usage

The SET TRANSACTION statement specifies whether a transaction shall be read-only or read/write, what the level of isolation from concurrent transactions will be, and how many conditions to allocate for the diagnostics area for the transaction. It must be specified while no transaction is active, and it will apply to the subsequent transaction. If you specify ISOLATION LEVEL, you will follow it with one of these: READ UNCOMMITTED, READ COMMITTED, REPEATABLE READ, or SERIALIZABLE. You may also specify READ ONLY or READ WRITE or allocate a diagnostics area by specifying DIAGNOSTICS SIZE. You may specify any or all of these, separated by commas.

The ISOLATION LEVELs determine whether and how this transaction will be affected by concurrent transactions—transactions from different SQL sessions that are accessing the same data. There are three phenomena that the isolation levels are designed to address:

- Dirty Read: One transaction modifies a row, and another reads it before the change is committed. If the transaction is rolled back (canceled), the change does not take place, and the second transaction has read a row that never really existed.

- Non-repeatable Read: One transaction reads a row. A second transaction deletes or modifies it and COMMITS before the first one does. Now the first transaction could perform the same read and get different results.

- Phantom: One transaction reads a group of rows that satisfy a predicate. Another INSERTs or UPDATEs rows, so that they too satisfy the predicate. Now the same query performed by the first transaction will get different results.

Table II.11 shows which isolation levels permit which of these phenomena.

TABLE II.11: Isolation Levels and Permitted Reads

ISOLATION LEVEL	Dirty Read	Non-Repeatable	Phantom
READ UNCOMMITTED	Yes	Yes	Yes
READ COMMITTED	No	Yes	Yes
REPEATABLE READ	No	No	Yes
SERIALIZABLE	No	No	No

READ ONLY and READ WRITE simply refer to the updatability of the transaction—whether the transaction is permitted to make changes to the structure or content of the database or merely to extract data. If you know that no writes will be necessary, declaring the transaction READ ONLY may improve the performance of this or of concurrent transactions.

When specifying ISOLATION LEVELs and updatability, you must conform to the following principles:

- If you omit the ISOLATION LEVEL, SERIALIZABLE is implied.

- If READ WRITE is specified, the ISOLATION LEVEL may not be READ UNCOMMITTED.

- If the ISOLATION LEVEL is READ UNCOMMITTED, the transaction is READ ONLY by default; otherwise it is READ WRITE by default.

- The number of conditions must be a positive integer.

The DIAGNOSTICS SIZE clause allocates a number of items within which diagnostics information may be stored. This information can be retrieved with the GET DIAGNOSTICS statement. The content of diagnostics areas and the specific error codes are listed in Appendix F.

Example

The following statement will specify that the subsequent transaction can write as well as read data, that it will have a REPEATABLE READ isolation level, and that room for 14 error messages will be allocated in the diagnostics area.

```
SET TRANSACTION ISOLATION LEVEL REPEATABLE READ,
READ WRITE, DIAGNOSTICS SIZE 14;
```

Conformance Levels

Entry   Implementations at this level are not required to support this statement.

See Also   Part II: COMMIT WORK, GET DIAGNOSTICS, ROLLBACK.

UPDATE

Changes the Values in a Table

Syntax

```
UPDATE table name
SET { column name =
{ value expression
|  NULL
|  DEFAULT }}.,..
[ {WHERE predicate }
| {WHERE CURRENT OF cursor name } ];
```

Usage

This statement changes one or more column values in an existing row of a table. The table may be a temporary or permanent base table or a view. Any number of columns may be set to values, and the whole *column name* = *value expression* clause is followed by a comma if there is another such to follow. As an alternative to an explicit value, the column may be set to NULL or to the DEFAULT defined for the column (see CREATE TABLE) or the domain (see CREATE DOMAIN). The *value expression* may refer to the current value in the columns. Any such references refer to the values of all of the columns before any of them were updated by this statement.

This allows you to do such things as double all column values (if numeric) by specifying

```
column name = column name * 2
```

Value expressions also can use subqueries, CASE expressions, and CAST expressions (see Value Expressions in Part III).

The UPDATE will be applied to all rows that fulfill the WHERE clause or, if the WHERE clause is omitted, to all rows. The WHERE clause is one of two types. The WHERE predicate form is like the WHERE predicate clause in the SELECT statement (see SELECT in Part II and Predicates in Part III). It uses an expression that can be TRUE, FALSE, or UNKNOWN for each row of the table to be updated, and the UPDATE is performed wherever it is TRUE. The WHERE CURRENT OF form can be used in Static or Dynamic SQL if an updatable cursor directly (in other words, not through views) referencing the target table is open and positioned on a row (see OPEN, FETCH). The UPDATE is applied to the row on which it is positioned. When using WHERE CURRENT OF in Dynamic SQL, you can omit the table name from the UPDATE clause, and the table in the cursor is implied.

In either case, for the UPDATE to be successful, the following conditions must be met:

- The issuer of the statement must have the UPDATE privilege on each column of the table that is being set (see GRANT).

- If the target table is a view, it must be updatable (see CREATE VIEW).

- If the current transaction state is read-only, the target table must be temporary.

- If the UPDATE is done through a cursor that specifies ORDER BY, it may not set the values of any columns specified in the ORDER BY clause.

- The value expression in the SET clause must not, directly or through views, reference the leaf-underlying table (the base table where the data ultimately resides) of the target table.

- The value expression may not use aggregate functions save in subqueries (see Aggregate Functions, Subqueries in Part III).

- Each column of the target table can be altered only once by a given UPDATE statement.

- If the UPDATE is on a cursor that specified FOR UPDATE, each column being set will have been specified or implied by that FOR UPDATE (see DECLARE CURSOR).

- If the UPDATE is made through a view, it may be constrained by a WITH CHECK OPTION clause (see CREATE VIEW).

Example

The following statement doubles the commission of salespeople in Hong Kong and sets their salary to some default value already defined for the column.

```
UPDATE Salespeople SET comm = comm * 2, salary = DEFAULT
WHERE city = 'Hong Kong';
```

Conformance Levels

Intermediate	Implementations at this level are not required to support UPDATEs on cursors that use ORDER BY. In an UPDATE using the WHERE predicate that is made on a view, neither the predicate nor the value expression in the FROM clause can reference the leaf-underlying table. Also at this level, letting the table name be implied for a Dynamic SQL UPDATE using WHERE CURRENT OF may be disallowed.
Entry	No support for Dynamic SQL is required. Neither is support for specifying DEFAULT in place of a value expression. Also, matches of the value expression to the column in which it is being put are defined fairly tightly, so that for character strings, the value expression may not be longer than the column (no truncation allowed), and exact numeric types cannot be updated to approximate numerics. (That is, there are no automatic conversions; see Datatypes in Part III.)

See Also Part II: CREATE TABLE, CREATE VIEW, DECLARE CURSOR, FETCH, GRANT, OPEN, SELECT. Part III: Aggregate Functions, Datatypes, Predicates, Subqueries, Value Expressions.

Common Elements

This part of the reference contains detailed information about the elements of SQL statements; it supplements what is listed in Part II under the statements themselves, as material included in this section is common to several statements.

Both sections are extensively cross-referenced. References that appear in UPPERCASE letters are to statement entries in Part II; those in Mixed Case are to the entries for other SQL elements in this part.

Aggregate Functions
Calculate a Single Value from a Set of Values

Syntax

```
aggregate function ::=
{ COUNT (*) } |
{{   AVG
|   SUM
|   MAX
|   MIN
|   COUNT }
([DISTINCT | ALL] value expression) }
```

Usage

Aggregate functions, sometimes called set functions, take a group of values in the SELECT or HAVING clause of a query (which can be a subquery) and produce a single value. The group will be either one defined with a GROUP BY clause or all of the values produced by the query. (Queries are requests for information from the database and are implemented in SQL with the SELECT statement, as discussed in Part II. This discussion will assume you understand the basics of queries.)

The COUNT function has two forms. The first listed above, which uses the asterisk (*), counts the number of rows output by the query. It does not count individual column values and pays no attention to whether rows are DISTINCT or whether NULLs are included. The other form of COUNT and all of the other functions automatically disregard NULLs, although they should raise a completion condition (send a warning message) when this happens.

> **NOTE** The elimination of NULLs is performed after the value expression is evaluated, so NULLs in the data may be counted if the value expression uses CASE or COALESCE expressions. For that matter, values could be eliminated based on a predicate specified in a NULLIF expression, although they are normally eliminated based on the predicates in the WHERE clause of the containing query.

If DISTINCT is specified for these aggregates, duplicate values will be counted only once in the aggregate figure; otherwise, duplicate values are treated the same as other values, regardless of whether ALL is specified (ALL is the default). Let's examine the role of the functions:

- The second form of COUNT counts all non-NULL column values.

- AVG takes the average (mean) of all the values. This function and SUM (below) may not be applied to CHARACTER STRING, BIT STRING, or DATETIME datatypes, although they may be applied to INTERVAL and, naturally, NUMERIC datatypes.

- SUM totals the values. It may be applied to the same datatypes as AVG.

- MAX returns the largest of the values, based on the rules for comparisons outlined under Predicates. MAX may be applied to any datatype and will follow the rules for comparison specified for comparison predicates under Datatypes.

- MIN is the reverse of MAX. It returns the least of the values.

You should also be aware of a number of rules. Among these rules are the following:

- If the query returns no rows—or no rows in a given group—so that the aggregate function has no data to be applied on, COUNT produces a zero, and the other functions produce NULLs.

- The value expression may not itself contain an aggregate function or a subquery.

NOTE The effect of taking an aggregate of an aggregate—for example, the highest average—can often be achieved by defining a view using the innermost aggregate (AVG) and then putting the outermost aggregate (MAX) in the query on (rather than the query within) the view.

- If the aggregate function is used in a subquery, the value expression may contain an outer reference, but if it does, no other column references are allowed in the same expression. (An outer reference is a reference in a subquery to values in a containing query; see Subqueries.) An aggregate using an outer reference also must be contained either directly in a SELECT clause or in a subquery in a HAVING clause (see SELECT in Part II). If the latter, it must be contained in a subquery defined in the HAVING clause (not the WHERE), and the table referenced must come from that query at the same level of nesting as that HAVING clause.

- The result of COUNT is an INTEGER. Other aggregates inherit the datatypes of their value expressions, although the precision is implementation-defined in the case of SUM and both the precision and scale are implementation-defined in the case of AVG, with the value expression's precision and scale being the minimum values allowed. For an explanation of precision and scale, see Datatypes.

- If SUM produces a value that is out of range for its datatype, you will get an error.

When contained in the SELECT list of a query that does not use GROUP BY, the aggregate functions are applied to the whole output of the query. If GROUP BY is used, each set of rows that has equal values for the column or group of columns specified in the GROUP BY clause constitutes a group, and the aggregate functions are applied independently to each such group. HAVING filters groups based on aggregate rather than individual values. GROUP BY and HAVING are explained in more detail under Part II: SELECT.

Conformance Levels

Intermediate — Implementations at this level may require the value expression to be a simple column reference if DISTINCT is specified.

Entry — Implementations at this level need not allow ALL to be specified for COUNT and may require that the value expression contain a column reference to the output columns of the SELECT clause (which it normally does, except when using an outer reference). If the value expression uses an outer reference, implementations may require that expression to be a simple column name. No value expression may generally contain an aggregate function (for example, in the view referenced; this may prevent you from using views to take aggregates of aggregates as suggested, although many products don't enforce this restriction).

See Also   Part II: SELECT. Part III: Collations, Datatypes, Predicates, Subqueries, Value Expressions.

Authorization IDs
Determine the Privileges under Which Statements Are Issued

Usage

An Authorization Identifier (Authorization ID) is a unique identifier that is associated with a SQL session, a set of owned objects, and a set of privileges on objects. Its format is that of an identifier as outlined in Appendix D. Up to three Authorization IDs may be active at any given moment in a session. You can refer to these in statements by the built-in user value functions SESSION_USER, SYSTEM_USER, and CURRENT_USER.

The SESSION_USER is the Authorization ID named in the USER clause of the CONNECT statement that initiated the session. If the CONNECT statement lacked a USER clause, or if the session was initiated in some implementation-defined manner, then the SESSION_USER is implementation-defined. The SESSION_USER can be changed with the SET SESSION AUTHORIZATION statement; the restrictions on this are implementation-defined.

The CURRENT_USER (also referred to simply as the USER) is the Authorization ID whose privileges determine what can actually be done. By default, it is the same as the SESSION_USER, but there are two exceptions: in CREATE SCHEMA sequences and in the module language. Either a schema definition or a module may specify an Authorization ID, which will become the CURRENT_USER while that CREATE SCHEMA statement or module is being executed.

The SYSTEM_USER is the user as defined by the operating system. It is derived in an implementation-dependent manner and is provided primarily so that there is a way to map DBMS users to operating system users, as there is no requirement that there be consistent name usage or a one-to-one correspondence between the two. Indeed, there frequently is not.

When a CREATE SCHEMA is issued under the privileges of an Authorization ID, that Authorization ID becomes the owner of the schema and the objects within it. Objects include base tables, views, domains, assertions, character sets, collations, and translations.

This owner will have the right to create new objects in the schema. As the owners of objects, Authorization IDs may GRANT privileges on them to other users, subject to one restriction (explained below). They may also have privileges on other objects, which will have been explicitly or implicitly GRANTed (through a GRANT to PUBLIC, for example) by the owners of those objects (see GRANT in Part II). Whenever a statement is issued on an object, the privileges of the CURRENT_USER are evaluated, and an error is produced if sufficient privileges to perform the operation do not exist.

> **NOTE** If you create an object that references other objects—such as a domain referencing a character set or a view referencing a base table—that you do not own, you will be prevented from granting any privileges on your own object that imply grants of privileges on the referenced objects unless you have the GRANT OPTION on the implied privileges (for more detail, see GRANT and the various CREATE statements in Part II).

Conformance Levels

SQL89   Each statement and each schema is associated with an Authorization ID, effectively corresponding to the current user, but how this association is determined is implementation-defined.

Non   A widely used convention is that Authorization IDs may have system-level privileges as well as privileges on objects.

See Also Part II: CREATE ASSERTION, CREATE CHARACTER SET, CREATE COLLATION, CREATE DOMAIN, CREATE SCHEMA, CREATE TABLE, CREATE TRANSLATION, CREATE VIEW, GRANT, REVOKE. Part III: Value Expressions. Appendix B.

CASE Expressions
Allow Values to Be Specified Conditionally

Syntax

```
{CASE value expression
{ WHEN value expression
  THEN   { value expression | NULL } }...)
```

```
| {CASE
{ WHEN predicate
  THEN   { value expression | NULL } }...}
[ ELSE { value expression | NULL } ]
    END }
/ { NULLIF (value expression, value expression) }
| { COALESCE (value expression.,..) }
```

Usage

A CASE expression is used in a SQL statement in place of a value
when there is more than one possible value you might want to
use depending on conditions. CASE is the most general form; it
allows you to define either a predicate or a value expression you
attempt to match and then to set the value as desired if the predicate is TRUE or the match occurs. NULLIF and COALESCE both
represent situations that could be covered by the CASE form, but
they are more elegantly expressed using these forms.

The CASE Form

The CASE form takes one or more WHEN and THEN clauses of
either of the two forms and one optional ELSE clause. The WHEN
clauses are all tried in sequence. As soon as one succeeds, the matching THEN clause provides the value of the CASE expression. If none
of the WHEN clauses succeed, the ELSE clause provides a value. If
the ELSE clause is omitted, ELSE NULL is implied. At least one of the
THEN clauses or the ELSE clause must specify a result other than
NULL (otherwise, since NULL is the default ELSE value, the CASE
expression would always produce NULLs and would therefore be
senseless). The CASE form is terminated with the keyword END.

All of the WHEN clauses in a given CASE expression must be of
the same form—either *value expression* WHEN *value expression* or
WHEN *predicate*. In the first form, the WHEN condition is satisfied
whenever the value expression in a WHEN clause equals the value
expression in the CASE clause. This means, of course, that the datatypes of all the value expressions following WHEN clauses must be
comparable to the first value expression. (Datatypes are comparable
if they are convertible.) In the second form, the WHEN condition
is satisfied whenever the predicate is TRUE. In both forms, the
value expression in the THEN clause indicates the value that will

be the result of the CASE expression if the matching WHEN condition is satisfied, and the value expression in the ELSE clause indicates the value that will result if none of the WHEN clauses are satisfied. If more than one WHEN condition is satisfied, the first one in the statement is used to determine which THEN clause produces the result.

The datatype of the result of the CASE expression depends on the datatypes of the values contained in the various THEN clauses and the ELSE clause, if any. We will call these the *candidate values*. The candidate values must all be comparable. The following are the criteria that the candidate values must meet and that determine the datatype of the result:

- If any of the candidate values are CHARACTER strings, they must all be CHARACTER strings using the same repertoire. The result will be a CHARACTER string. If any of them is a BIT string, they must all be BIT strings, and the result will be, too.

- If they are CHARACTER or BIT strings and any of them are varying-length, the result is a varying-length CHARACTER or BIT string, respectively; otherwise, the result is a fixed-length CHARACTER or BIT string equal in length to the longest of the specified strings (measured in characters or bits as appropriate).

- If they are all EXACT NUMERIC, the result will be EXACT NUMERIC with a scale equal to the largest of their scales and an implementation-defined precision.

- If any of them is APPROXIMATE NUMERIC, they must all be EXACT or APPROXIMATE NUMERIC, and the result will be APPROXIMATE NUMERIC with an implementation-defined precision.

- If any of them is a DATETIME type, they all will be the same DATETIME type, and this will be the type of the result.

- If any of them is an INTERVAL, they all will be INTERVALs. If any specifies YEAR or MONTH, they all will specify only YEAR or MONTH. If any specifies DAY, HOUR, MINUTE, or SECOND (precision), then none of them will specify YEAR and MONTH. Within these parameters, the precision of the result includes all time units from the largest to the smallest specified by any of the THEN clauses.

The NULLIF and COALESCE Forms

The NULLIF form compares the two values given to it. If they are equal according to the principles outlined under comparison predicates (see Predicates), NULL is the result. Otherwise, the result is the first value. If V1 and V2 are the two values, NULLIF (V1, V2) is equivalent to the following CASE expression:

```
CASE WHEN V1=V2 THEN NULL ELSE V1 END
```

COALESCE takes a series of comparable values and returns the first one that is not NULL or returns NULL if there is none such. Again using V1 and V2, COALESCE (V1, V2) is equivalent to:

```
CASE WHEN V1 IS NOT NULL THEN V1 ELSE V2 END
```

COALESCE expressions with more than two values as arguments are equivalent to CASE expressions with more THEN clauses, one for each argument. If V1, V2, and so on to *Vn* (where *n* is an arbitrary number) are the arguments, the equivalent CASE expression is:

```
CASE WHEN V1 IS NOT NULL THEN V1
ELSE COALESCE (V2, . . . ,Vn ) END
```

In other words, try each value in sequence. If its value is NULL, perform the COALESCE operation with the remaining values until you find a non-NULL value or until there are no values left, in which case COALESCE returns a NULL.

Conformance Levels

Entry   Implementations are not required to support CASE expressions at this level.

See Also   Part III: Datatypes, Predicates.

CAST Expressions
Used to Convert from One Datatype to Another

Syntax

```
CAST ( { value expression | NULL }
  AS { datatype | domain } )
```

Usage

Use this expression in place of a value expression when the result of that value expression needs to be converted to another datatype or domain. If the CAST is into a domain, the Authorization ID performing the action must have the USAGE privilege on that domain.

We can call the datatype of the value expression we are converting from the source datatype (SD) and the datatype we are converting to—or the datatype of the domain we are converting to, as the case may be—the target datatype (TD). Not all conversions are allowed. Table III.1 shows which conversions are valid. There are three possibilities: Y (yes) means that the conversion is valid without restriction, N (no) means that the conversion is not valid, and M (maybe) means that the conversion is valid if certain conditions to be outlined are met. The source datatypes are listed vertically along the left edge, while the targets are listed horizontally across the top.

TABLE III.1: Valid Datatype Conversions

	EN	AN	VC	FC	VB	FB	D	T	TS	YM	DT
EN	Y	Y	Y	Y	N	N	N	N	N	M	M
AN	Y	Y	Y	Y	N	N	N	N	N	N	N
C	Y	Y	M	M	Y	Y	Y	Y	Y	Y	Y
B	N	N	Y	Y	Y	Y	N	N	N	N	N
D	N	N	Y	Y	N	N	Y	N	Y	N	N
T	N	N	Y	Y	N	N	N	Y	Y	N	N
TS	N	N	Y	Y	N	N	Y	Y	Y	N	N
YM	M	N	Y	Y	N	N	N	N	N	Y	N
DT	M	N	Y	Y	N	N	N	N	N	N	Y

The following abbreviations are used: EN = EXACT NUMERIC, AN = APPROXIMATE NUMERIC, C = CHARACTER (Fixed- or Varying-length), FC = Fixed-length CHARACTER, VC = Varying-length CHARACTER, B = BIT STRING (Fixed- or Varying-length), FB = Fixed-length BIT STRING, VB = Varying-length BIT STRING, D = DATE, T = TIME, TS = TIMESTAMP, YM = YEAR-MONTH INTERVAL, DT = DAY-TIME INTERVAL.

The following are the applicable restrictions:

- If SD is INTERVAL and TD is EXACT NUMERIC, then SD is allowed only one DATETIME field.

- If SD is EXACT NUMERIC and TD is INTERVAL, then TD is allowed only one DATETIME field.

- If SD and TD are both CHARACTER STRINGS, they must have the same character repertoires.

- If TD is a CHARACTER STRING, the collating sequence of the result is the default collating sequence for its repertoire, and the result is coercible (See Collations).

If NULL or the result of the value expression is specified, the result of the CAST expression is NULL. This helps you to define empty columns of appropriate datatypes where needed—for example, in queries combined in a UNION expression (see SELECT in Part II) without having to actually define columns or insert data. If NULL is not specified, the target value (TV, the value that will result from the CAST expression) is derived from the source value (SV, the value of the value expression) following the specifications outlined below.

If the target datatype (TD) is EXACT NUMERIC then:

- If the source datatype (SD) is EXACT or APPROXIMATE NUMERIC, and SV can be represented in TV without losing any leading digits, the conversion to a number of equivalent value in the new type is effected; otherwise, an error—numeric value out of range—is produced. Trailing digits can be rounded or truncated, although which of these will be done is implementation-defined.

- If the source datatype (SD) is a CHARACTER STRING, then leading and trailing blanks are removed, and what is left must be the character representation of an optionally signed exact number.

- If the source datatype (SD) is INTERVAL, then the same rules as outlined above for EXACT and APPROXIMATE NUMERICs apply.

If the target datatype (TD) is APPROXIMATE NUMERIC, then the rules are the same as outlined above for EXACT NUMERICs, except that the source datatype may not be an INTERVAL.

If the target datatype (TD) is a CHARACTER STRING, then let its length, if it is fixed-length, or its maximum length, if it is varying-length, be called the target length (TL). The target length is measured in the number of characters. The following stipulations apply:

- If the source datatype is EXACT or APPROXIMATE NUMERIC, the character repertoire of the target must include all of the characters actually used to represent the number. (It need not include all that could be used to express a number of that type, although it normally would. So, for example, if the character repertoire did not include the minus sign, you would have no problem unless a negative number were actually encountered.)

- If the source datatype is EXACT or APPROXIMATE NUMERIC, and the number of characters needed to represent the source value (SV) is shorter than the target length, the SV is padded with blanks; if SV is longer, an error is produced. If the source is APPROXIMATE NUMERIC and its value is zero, the representation will be x '0E0' (zero exponent zero).

NOTE Some host languages interpret 0E0 as 1. This obviously will garble APPROXIMATE NUMERIC zeros produced by SQL and introduce subtle or dramatic errors. When building applications, you should handle these zeros as a special case, unless you know that your host language adopts the same convention as SQL.

- If the source datatype is fixed or variable-length STRING, and the number of characters in the source value exceeds the target length, truncation occurs and produces a warning, unless the truncation is only of trailing blanks.

- If the source datatype is BIT STRING, things get complicated. Let's call the length of the source value (SV) in bits the source length (SL) and the bit length of the character with the shortest bit length in the form-of-use of the target datatype (TD) the minimum character length (MCL). SL is divided by MCL, and the remainder is the number of zero-valued bits that are appended to the source value (SV). If that remainder (and thus the number of such bits added) is not zero, then a warning—implicit zero-bit padding—is raised. In any case, the BIT STRING is converted according the form-of-use of the target datatype. If the resulting string is of a different length than the target length (TL), then either truncation (if it is too long) or zero-bit padding (if too short) occurs, and an appropriate warning condition is raised.

- If the source datatype is DATETIME or INTERVAL, then it is converted to the shortest character string that can express its value with the appropriate precision. If this character string is longer than the target length, an error is produced; no truncation is allowed in this case. Otherwise, if it is shorter, it is padded with blanks. Again, the character repertoire of the target must be able to express the character string produced from the DATETIME or INTERVAL source.

If the target value (TV) is BIT STRING, then let SL be the length of the source value in bits and TL be the length in bits of either the target value, if the target is fixed-length, or of the maximum target value, if it is varying-length. The source value (SV) is converted to a BIT STRING. If this string is longer than TL, truncation occurs. If it is shorter and the target is fixed-length, it is padded on the right with zero-bits. In either of these cases, an appropriate warning condition is raised.

If the target datatype (TD) is DATE, then:

- If the source datatype is CHARACTER STRING, leading and trailing blanks are removed, and if the remaining string represents a valid DATE value, the conversion is effected. Otherwise, an error is produced.

- If the source datatype is DATE, the conversion is automatic.

- If the source datatype is TIMESTAMP, the target value is set to the YEAR, MONTH, and DAY fields of the source value, adjusted by the time-zone displacement if any.

If the target datatype is TIME, then:

- If the source datatype is CHARACTER STRING, leading and trailing blanks are removed, and if the remaining string represents a valid TIME value, the conversion is effected. If not, an error is produced.

- If the source datatype is TIME, and if the target specifies WITH TIME ZONE, the implied or explicit time-zone displacement of the source is inherited. Otherwise, the target inherits the time-zone displacement of the current SQL session.

- If the source is TIMESTAMP, the target value is set to the HOUR, MINUTE, and SECOND fields of the source value. If the target specifies WITH TIME ZONE, the implied or explicit time-zone displacement of the source is inherited. Otherwise, the target inherits the time-zone displacement of the current SQL session.

If the target datatype is TIMESTAMP, then:

- If the source datatype is CHARACTER STRING, leading and trailing blanks are removed, and if the remaining string represents a valid TIMESTAMP value, the conversion is effected. Otherwise, an error is produced.

- If the source datatype is DATE, the values of its YEAR, MONTH, and DAY fields become the values of the same fields in the target. The HOUR, MINUTE, and SECOND fields of the target are set to zero. If WITH TIME ZONE is specified for the target, the time-zone displacement for the current SQL session is inherited.

- If the source datatype is TIME, the values of its HOUR, MINUTE, and SECOND fields become the values of the same fields in the target. The YEAR, MONTH, and DAY fields of the target are set to those produced by an execution of CURRENT_DATE (see Datetime Value Functions). If WITH TIME ZONE is specified for the target, the explicit or implied time-zone displacement for the source is inherited.

If the target datatype is INTERVAL, then:

- If the source datatype is EXACT NUMERIC, and if the source value can be represented in the target without the loss of leading significant digits, the conversion is effected. Otherwise, an error is produced.

- If the source datatype is CHARACTER STRING, leading and trailing blanks are removed, and, if the result is a valid INTERVAL value, the conversion is effected. Otherwise, an error is produced.

- If the source datatype is INTERVAL, and the precisions of the source and target are the same, the conversion is automatic. If not, the source is converted to a single number expressed in its least significant (smallest) units. If this number cannot be converted to the precision of the target without loss of precision of its most significant field, an error is produced. Otherwise, the conversion is effected.

Finally, if the target datatype is contained in a domain, the target value produced must satisfy any constraints in that domain.

Conformance Levels

Entry   Support for CAST expressions is not required at this level.

See Also   Part II: CREATE DOMAIN. Part III: Datatypes, Datetime Value Functions.

Collations
Objects in the Schema That Define Collating Sequences

Usage

Character sets in SQL are normally sortable, which means they can be placed in some order, called a *collating sequence*, and compared in terms of it—for example, 'a' < 'b' means 'a' precedes ' b' in the collating sequence. A *collation* is a schema object that defines a collating sequence used on a character set. In most cases, it is desirable to design the collating sequence to approximate alphabetical order, although this necessarily will be imperfectly realized with many character sets. Each character has a unique place in the collating sequence, and a given letter in upper- and lowercase is two different characters. The default collations for the standard ASCII and EBCDIC character sets place all the characters of one case before all the characters of the other because they collate in terms of the encoding—the numeric values that constitute the internal representation of the characters. For this reason, it may be desirable to define custom collations for these character sets (if your implementation has not done this for you already), as well as for any others that you may use.

Where You Use Collations

You use the CREATE COLLATION statement to define a collation (see Part II: CREATE COLLATION). You must have the USAGE privilege on all character sets and translations referenced in that statement. You will now have the USAGE privilege on your collation and possibly will be able to share it with others using the GRANT statement (see Part II: GRANT).

Once created, a collation may be referenced in a number of statements in a COLLATE clause following the value expression to which it is to apply. The syntax of the COLLATE clause is:

```
COLLATE collation name
```

For example, this can be used in a CREATE CHARACTER SET statement to define the default collating sequence for that character set. It also can define a default for a domain that overrides that of the character set or for a column that overrides that of its domain, if any (see CREATE DOMAIN, ALTER DOMAIN, CREATE TABLE, and ALTER TABLE in Part II). Any of these, in turn can be overridden with COLLATE clauses appended to value expressions, which can include column references, aggregate functions, scalar subqueries, CASE expressions, and CAST specifications (see Value Expressions, Subqueries, CASE Expressions, and CAST Expressions), and string value functions, such as SUBSTRING, FOLD, CONVERT, TRANSLATE, and TRIM (see String Value Functions). These value expressions are used in the SELECT and GROUP BY clauses of queries (see SELECT in Part II) and in predicates (see Predicates).

Coercibility

Each collating sequence has a coercibility attribute with one of the following values:

- An *explicit* coercibility attribute means that a COLLATE clause has directly specified the collation in the statement at hand. For example, a COLLATE clause in the GROUP BY list in a query will determine the collating sequence used to sort the output rows, if such sorting is performed (see SELECT in Part II). This is an explicit collation and overrides any other.

- An *implicit* coercibility attribute means that the collation is implied. The results of CONVERT and TRANSLATE expressions, as well as column references, are implicit.

- A *coercible* value for the coercibility attribute means that the collation can be overridden by an explicit or an implicit collation on the same character set. In general, value specifications, the targets (results) of CAST expressions, and columns following a collating sequence are coercible by default.

- An attribute of *no collating sequence* means that the character set cannot be meaningfully sorted. No value expression with this coercibility attribute may be referenced in the query expression contained in a view (see CREATE VIEW in Part II) or used with comparison predicates (see Predicates). Actually, every character set defined in the database has a collating sequence—by default the order of the binary numbers that represent the characters in the encoding. Characters without a collating sequence can arise, however, as the result of certain operations (see Collations).

The following tables show how the collating sequence and coercibility are determined whenever operators are used on character strings or whenever characters strings are compared. A collating sequence labeled "default" indicates the default collating sequence, and X means any collating sequence. Of course, if the coercibility attribute is "no collating sequence", the collating sequence does not exist.

Table III.2 shows the rules for monadic operators. These are operators that reference only a single string, namely FOLD and TRIM. SUBSTRING is also treated for this purpose as a monadic operator, with the string being examined considered the operand. The leftmost two columns of the table indicate the coercibility and collating sequence for the character string before the operator is applied. For each such combination, the resulting coercibility and collating sequence are shown on the right.

Table III.3 shows the coercibility and collating sequences that result from using operators that take two strings as arguments and produce a string as a result; these are called *dyadic operators*. In this and Table III.4, X means any collating sequence of the first operand, Y means any collating sequence of the second operand, and Y<> X means Y does not equal X.

Table III.4 shows how comparison of character strings with differing collations will be collated.

TABLE III.2: Collating Sequences and Coercibility Rules for Monadic Operators

Operand		Result	
Coercibility	Collating Sequence	Coercibility	Collating Sequence
Coercible	Default	Coercible	Default
Implicit	X	Implicit	X
Explicit	X	Explicit	X
No Collating Sequence		No Collating Sequence	

TABLE III.3: Collating Sequences and Coercibility Rules for Dyadic Operators

Operand 1		Operand 2		Result	
Coercibility	Collating Sequence	Coercibility	Collating Sequence	Coercibility	Collating Sequence
Coercible	Default	Coercible	Default	Coercible	Default
Coercible	Default	Implicit	Y	Implicit	Y
Coercible	Default	No Collating Sequence		No Collating Sequence	

Continued on next page

TABLE III.3: Collating Sequences and Coercibility Rules for
Dyadic Operators (continued)

Operand 1		Operand 2		Result	
Coercibility	**Collating Sequence**	**Coercibility**	**Collating Sequence**	**Coercibility**	**Collating Sequence**
Coercible	Default	Explicit	Y	Explicit	Y
Implicit	X	Coercible	Default	Implicit	X
Implicit	X	Implicit	X	Implicit	X
Implicit	X	Implicit	Y <> X	No Collating Sequence	
Implicit	X	No Collating Sequence		No Collating Sequence	
Implicit	X	Explicit	Y	Explicit	Y
No Collating Sequence		Any, except Explicit	Any	No Collating Sequence	
No Collating Sequence		Explicit	X	Explicit	X
Explicit	X	Coercible	Default	Explicit	X
Explicit	X	Implicit	Y	Explicit	X
Explicit	X	No Collating Sequence		Explicit	X
Explicit	X	Explicit	X	Explicit	X
Explicit	X	Explicit	Y <> X	Not Permitted: Invalid Syntax	

TABLE III.4: Collating Sequences Used for Comparisons

Comparand 1		Comparand 2		Collating Sequence Used for Comparison
Coercibility	**Collating Sequence**	**Coercibility**	**Collating Sequence**	
Coercible	Default	Coercible	Default	Default
Coercible	Default	Implicit	Y	Y

Continued on next page

TABLE III.4: Collating Sequences Used for Comparisons (continued)

Comparand 1		Comparand 2		Collating Sequence Used for Comparison
Coercibility	Collating Sequence	Coercibility	Collating Sequence	
Coercible	Default	No Collating Sequence		Not Permitted: Invalid Syntax
Coercible	Default	Explicit	Y	Y
Implicit	X	Coercible	Default	X
Implicit	X	Implicit	X	X
Implicit	X	Implicit	Y<> X	Not Permitted: Invalid Syntax
Implicit	X	No Collating Sequence		Not Permitted: Invalid Syntax
Implicit	X	Explicit	Y	Y
No Collating Sequence		Any, except Explicit	Any	Not Permitted: Invalid Syntax
No Collating Sequence		Explicit	X	X
Explicit	X	Coercible	Default	X
Explicit	X	Implicit	Y	X
Explicit	X	No Collating Sequence		X
Explicit	X	Explicit	X	X
Explicit	X	Explicit	Y<>X	Not Permitted: Invalid Syntax

Operations that involve more than two operands, for example CASE expressions with more than two THEN clauses, are treated for the purpose of determining collation as a series of dyadic operations. The first two operands are compared, and the resulting collating sequence and coercibility attribute are used in comparison to the third operand, and so on until all the operands have been included in the comparison.

Conformance Levels

Intermediate   Support for explicit collations is not
                 required at this level.

See Also Part II: CREATE CHARACTER SET, CREATE COLLATION, DROP COLLATION, Part III: Datatypes, Predicates, String Value Functions.

Constraints
Put Restrictions on the Data That May Be Entered into Tables

Syntax

```
table constraint ::=
[ CONSTRAINT constraint name ]
{ PRIMARY KEY  (column name.,..)}
| { UNIQUE (column name.,..)}
| { FOREIGN KEY  (column name.,..)
REFERENCES table name [(column name.,..)]
[ referential specification ] }
| { CHECK predicate }
[ [NOT] DEFERRABLE ] ]
column constraint ::=
[ CONSTRAINT constraint name ]
{ NOT NULL }
| { PRIMARY KEY }
| { UNIQUE }
| { REFERENCES table name [(column name)]
[ referential specification ] }
/ { CHECK predicate }
  [ [ INITIALLY DEFERRED | INITIALLY IMMEDIATE ]
[ [NOT] DEFERRABLE ] ]

referential specification::=
[ MATCH { FULL | PARTIAL } ]
[ ON UPDATE { CASCADE
```

```
           | SET NULL
           | SET DEFAULT
           | NO ACTION } ]
    [ ON DELETE { CASCADE
           | SET NULL
           | SET DEFAULT
           | NO ACTION } ]
```

Usage

Constraints define conditions that data must meet in order to be entered into the database. They can be included in the definitions of columns, temporary or permanent base tables, domains, or assertions. Although constraints cannot be used in views, views also offer facilities for controlling column values (see CREATE VIEW in Part II). Table constraints apply to one or more columns of one or more tables; they are used in table definitions, domains, and assertions. Column constraints apply to single columns, except for the REFERENCES constraint, which applies to two columns—the referencing column and the referenced column—which are usually in separate tables. Column constraints follow the definition of the constrained column within its table definition (for REFERENCES, this is the table containing the referencing rather than the referenced column). There are equivalent table constraints for all column constraints. Domains and assertions use only CHECK constraints.

You may optionally name the constraint; this will allow you to drop or alter it later by referring to its name. If the constraint is not named, an implementation-dependent default name will be generated (this was not true in SQL89).

If the data is in such a state that a deferred constraint is violated, and a statement causes the constraint to be checked, one of two things happens. If the statement that causes the constraint to be checked is COMMIT WORK, the transaction is rolled back. Otherwise, the statement that causes the constraint to be checked will fail. This includes SET CONSTRAINTS MODE itself, so if you want to know whether a constraint has been violated, you can attempt to change the constraint's mode and see if you get an error.

In general, all references in table constraints to columns are to columns in the table where the table constraint resides. (The exceptions are in some CHECK predicates and the REFERENCES list within FOREIGN KEY constraints.) The meanings of the various table constraints are as follows:

- PRIMARY KEY means that the group of one or more named columns is the unique identifier for the table. The combination of values in a PRIMARY KEY is constrained to be distinct for each row; duplicates and NULLs will be rejected. Only one PRIMARY KEY constraint may exist for a given table. Formally speaking, PRIMARY KEY is equivalent to the following CHECK constraint (see Predicates):

```
CHECK(UNIQUE (SELECT key columns FROM table name)
AND
(key columns) IS NOT NULL)
```

- UNIQUE is like PRIMARY KEY, except that any number of UNIQUE constraints may coexist in the same table. For Entry-level SQL92, columns that take the PRIMARY KEY or the UNIQUE constraint must be declared NOT NULL. The NULL check need not be built into the constraint, as above. However, at Intermediate-level and in SQL99, NOT NULL is implied for PRIMARY KEY and optional for UNIQUE. Here is the CHECK constraint that is the equivalent to UNIQUE:

```
CHECK(UNIQUE (SELECT key columns FROM table name))
```

- FOREIGN KEY names a group of columns in this table that will be a foreign key referencing a group of columns in this or another table. The group of columns in the referenced table must have either the PRIMARY KEY or the UNIQUE constraint. In the former case, the column name list can be omitted from the REFERENCES clause—the table's PRIMARY KEY is the default. The referenced columns must be of the same datatypes as the referencing columns, in the specified order. A table may reference itself, which enables circular relationships. This constraint is discussed in more detail below.

- CHECK defines a predicate that will refer to one or more values from one or more tables, unless it is contained in a domain. If the predicate is FALSE when the constraint is checked, the constraint is violated. This constraint is also discussed in more detail below.

These are the definitions of the column constraints:

- NOT NULL means that the column may not contain the NULL value.

- PRIMARY KEY is the same as the table-constraint version, except that no column list may be used. As a column constraint, it automatically applies only to the column whose definition it follows.

- UNIQUE is the same as the table-constraint version, also with the proviso that a column list need not and cannot be used.

- REFERENCES is the column-constraint version of the FOREIGN KEY constraint. A referencing column list is not used; the column being constrained is the referencing column. A referenced column list, if used, will have only one column. If the referenced column has the PRIMARY KEY constraint, it need not be named.

- CHECK is also the same as the table-constraint version, except that all column references in the predicate must be to the constrained column unless they are contained in subqueries (see Subqueries).

The FOREIGN KEY and REFERENCES Constraints

As noted above, these are two variations on the same constraint, and we will use the term "FOREIGN KEY constraint" to refer to both of them unless otherwise noted.

A FOREIGN KEY constraint requires that all values present in the foreign key be matched by values in the parent key—in other words, that the foreign key have referential integrity. This means that someone using a set of columns as a parent key is placing controls on what can be done with those columns. For this reason, the REFERENCES privilege on those columns is required to define a foreign key on them. In addition, the following rules must be satisfied:

- Each column in the foreign key must reference a column of the same datatype in the parent key. The columns must be specified in the same order in the FOREIGN KEY and in the UNIQUE or PRIMARY KEY constraints, and no column may be specified more than once.

- If the foreign key table is a persistent base table, the parent key table must also be such a table.

- If the foreign key table is a global local temporary table, the parent key table must also be such a table.

- If the foreign key table is a created local temporary table, the parent key table must be either a global or created local temporary table.

- If the foreign key table is a declared local temporary table, the parent key table can be any sort of temporary table.

- If the parent key table specifies ON COMMIT DELETE ROWS, the foreign key table must do so as well.

In addition to the above, there are two issues that must be addressed in ensuring that the values in the foreign key are matched in the parent:

- What is meant by a match?

- What happens when a change to the parent key data is attempted that would affect the match?

The first of these two questions is addressed by the *match type*, determined by the MATCH FULL or PARTIAL clause. The second is addressed by *referential triggered actions*, determined by the ON UPDATE and ON DELETE clauses.

Match Types

A match, of course, basically means that the values in any row of the foreign key are present in some row of the parent. The complexity arises when NULLs are factored in. NULLs in principle represent data items whose values are unknown. Strictly speaking, then, we cannot say whether they match known data items or even each other. There is considerable debate in this area, which we won't go into here. Suffice it to say that NULLs don't match anything—not even other NULLs. Other than that, the standard lets you take one of three approaches:

- If the MATCH clause is omitted, then a partially NULL foreign key is acceptable regardless of whether there are parent key values that match. Otherwise, all of the values in the foreign key must be present in some row of the parent.

- If MATCH FULL is specified, then each row of the foreign key must be entirely NULL, or it must have no NULLs and be entirely matched by some row of the parent key.

- If MATCH PARTIAL is specified, then the foreign key may be partially NULL, and the non-NULL values of each row of the foreign key must match the corresponding values in the parent key. Since parent key values may be identical in those columns where they match the foreign key and differ in others, it is possible for more than one parent key row to match the same foreign key row. Such parent key rows are called *nonunique matching rows*; others are *unique matching rows*. Notice that unique matching rows are unique *in the parent key*; it is possible for more than one foreign key row to reference the same parent key row, and, for each foreign key that matches only one such row, this parent key row will be the unique matching row. A parent key row may be a unique matching row of some group of foreign key values and a nonunique matching row of others, since the matches could be based on different non-NULL columns in the foreign keys. Unique and nonunique matching rows work differently with referential triggered actions, as discussed below (don't worry, we have examples coming).

To illustrate the types of matches, we will use the Client_Phone table shown in Table III.5. In this table, the combination of ID_NUM and PHONE is the primary key. We will also use another table, shown in Table III.6, that tracks each phone call made to a client. This table has a foreign key (CLIENT_ID, PHONE) that references Client_Phone (ID_NUM, PHONE). The primary key of the Calls_to_Clients table is CALL_ID.

TABLE III.5: The Client_Phone Table

ID_NUM	Phone	Type	Avail
1809	415 555 8956	home	after 6 P.M.
1809	510 555 6220	work	9-5 MF
1996	212 555 0199	work	app. 10-7
1996	212 555 7878	cell	any
1777	503 555 2279	fax	any
1777	503 555 9188	home	after 7 P.M.

TABLE III.6: The Calls_to_Clients Table

Call_ID	Client_ID	Phone	Made_By
2201	1809	415 555 8956	Terrence
2202	1809	· NULL	Liu
2204	NULL	212 555 0199	MacLeish
2207	NULL	NULL	MacLeish
2209	1811	503 555 9188	Liu

Rows of Calls_to_Clients are identified by CALL_ID; those of Client_Phone are identified by the combination of PHONE and ID_NUM. However, we will refer to them simply by their order as shown to make the discussion less awkward. For each of the three types of MATCH specification (FULL, PARTIAL, and neither), the following list identifies the rows of Client_Phone that each row of Calls_to_Clients matches and, for PARTIAL, whether it matches them uniquely (in other words, whether the matching Client_Phone rows are unique matching rows).

- If FULL is specified, call 2201 matches the first row, and call 2207 is an acceptable foreign key value, but it does not match anything (foreign keys can be NULL). The other rows of Calls_to_Clients violate referential integrity and would be rejected.

- If PARTIAL is specified, call 2201 matches the first row, and call 2207 is still an acceptable, unmatched value. In addition, call 2202 matches the first and second rows, and call 2204 uniquely matches the third row. Call 2209 violates referential integrity and would be rejected.

- If neither FULL nor PARTIAL is specified, call 2201 matches the first row. None of the other calls match any row, but since the foreign keys are partially or entirely NULL, they would not be rejected.

As you can see, omitting the MATCH clause produces the most tolerant and possibly the most problematic behavior. It is usually safest and least confusing to specify MATCH FULL by default.

For column constraints, or for foreign keys where all columns have the NOT NULL constraint, MATCH clauses are ignored, and the effect is the same as if none were used.

Referential Triggered Actions

The referential triggered actions specify what happens when a change to a parent key could affect its match with a foreign key. The ON UPDATE and ON DELETE versions allow you to specify this effect separately for UPDATE and for DELETE statements. (INSERT statements, of course, don't directly affect referential integrity, since the rows generated could not have been previously referenced.) You may specify at most one ON DELETE and one ON UPDATE clause in a given constraint. The options are discussed in the following paragraphs.

CASCADE makes the same change to the foreign key as is made to the parent. If the operation is DELETE, the entire row of the foreign key table is deleted; if UPDATE, the changes made to the parent key table cause the same changes in the corresponding columns of the foreign key table. If MATCH PARTIAL is specified and the triggered action is ON DELETE CASCADE, only the unique matching rows are deleted. If MATCH PARTIAL is specified and the triggered action is ON UPDATE CASCADE, the change is made to all unique matching rows, provided that this change can be cascaded consistently to all matching rows.

If SET NULL is specified with an ON DELETE triggered action, then all foreign key columns in matching rows—or all in unique matching rows if MATCH PARTIAL is specified—are set to a value of NULL. With an ON UPDATE triggered action, then, if no match type was specified, those columns that reference altered values are set to NULL. Otherwise, if MATCH FULL is specified, the entire referencing foreign key is set to NULL. If MATCH PARTIAL is specified, then only the columns that reference altered values are set to NULL and only for unique matching rows.

SET DEFAULT works almost like SET NULL, except that the columns are set to the default value specified in their table definition or in their domain definition (see CREATE TABLE and CREATE DOMAIN in Part II). A second difference from SET NULL is that, when MATCH FULL is specified with an ON UPDATE SET DEFAULT triggered action, the change is made only to those columns whose referenced values have been altered, not to all columns of the foreign key. Note that, since NULLs don't match anything, they don't reference anything, and that therefore a change to a column in the parent key that is NULL in the foreign key will leave the foreign key NULL rather than install its default value.

NO ACTION is the default if you do not specify a triggered action. NO ACTION specifies that no automatic change will be made to the foreign key data in response to changes in the parent key. If such changes would leave the data without referential integrity—in other words, if the FOREIGN KEY constraint would be violated—the changes are not allowed.

We will use Tables III.5 and III.6 again to illustrate the operation of referential triggered actions. If the second and third rows of the Client_Phone table are deleted, then:

- If FULL or neither is specified, there are no matching rows, and therefore no changes to the Calls_to_Clients table are made. If a triggered action of NO ACTION is specified, the delete is still allowed because there are no matches.

- If PARTIAL were specified, then, since call 2202 is a nonunique matching row of row 2, it would not be changed by any referential action and, if NO ACTION were specified, would not prevent the deletion of row 2, as it would still have a valid reference to row 1. The deletion of row 3, on the other hand, would be rejected because 2204 is a unique matching row of row 3 (of course, if the deletions of rows 2 and 3 were part of the same statement or transaction, the one rejection would cause both to fail). If SET CASCADE were specified, the deletion of row 3 would cause call 2204 to be deleted also.

- If SET NULL were specified, the CLIENT_ID and PHONE for call 2204 would be set to NULL; for SET DEFAULT, the PHONE column would be set to the default of the column or domain.

Let's say we updated rows 1 and 3 in Table III.5 to the following:

ID_NUM	PHONE	TYPE	AVAIL
NULL	415 555 8956	home	after 6 PM
1996	212 555 8888	work	app. 10–7

- If MATCH FULL is specified, the change to row 3 would have no effect on the Calls_to_Clients table, nor would it be rejected: there are no matching rows. If ON UPDATE CASCADE is specified, the update would be rejected, because the attempt to cascade the change of row 1 to NULL to the foreign key in Calls_to_Clients would produce a partially NULL foreign key there, which is not permissible for MATCH FULL. Likewise, NO ACTION would fail, because it would leave call 2201 without a valid reference. If SET NULL or SET DEFAULT is specified, the CLIENT_ID and PHONE columns of Calls_to_Clients would both be set to NULL or to default values, respectively.

- If neither FULL nor PARTIAL is specified, the effects are the same as for MATCH FULL with two exceptions:

  - If CASCADE is specified, the update will be permitted, and the CLIENT_ID column for call 2201 in Calls_to_Clients will be set to NULL.

  - If SET NULL is specified, only the CLIENT_ID will be set to NULL, whereas with MATCH FULL the PHONE column would be set to NULL as well.

- If MATCH PARTIAL is specified, then the effects deriving from the update of row 1 are the same as if neither were specified. For the update of row 3, if NO ACTION is specified, the update would be rejected, as it would leave call 2204 without a valid reference (it would still contain the old phone number, which is not now present in the parent key). If CASCADE, SET NULL, or SET DEFAULT is specified, the PHONE column for 2201 would be set to the new phone number, to NULL, or to a default value, respectively.

This changes the first ID_NUM and the third PHONE values; the referential triggered actions follows in the next section.

The CHECK Constraint

Formally speaking, a CHECK constraint is violated if the following predicate is TRUE:

```
EXISTS ( SELECT * FROM tables WHERE NOT (predicate))
```

where *tables* are the tables referenced in or containing the constraint, and *predicate* is the predicate contained in the constraint (see Predicates). Notice that if the predicate is UNKNOWN, EXISTS will be FALSE and the constraint will be satisfied (see "Three-Valued Logic" in the Predicates entry).

If the CHECK constraint is contained in a domain, the keyword VALUE will be used instead of a column reference. Whenever a column based on that domain is updated, the constraint will be checked by substituting the name of that column for the keyword VALUE and checking the value in the row that is under examination by the constraint.

A CHECK constraint must also meet the following criteria:

- If it is contained in a permanent base table or a domain, then the predicate may not reference temporary tables.

- If it is contained in a global temporary table, then the predicate can reference only global temporary tables.

- If it is contained in a created local temporary table, then the predicate can reference only global or created local temporary tables.

- If it is contained in a declared local temporary table, then it may not reference a permanent base table.

- If it is contained in a temporary table definition that specifies ON COMMIT PRESERVE ROWS, then it may not reference a temporary table that specifies ON COMMIT DELETE ROWS.

- It may not reference a datetime value function or a user value function.

- It may not use a query that is possibly nondeterministic (see SELECT in Part II).

- The creator of the CHECK constraint must have the REFERENCES privilege on any columns named in the constraint.

- If a table is referenced in the constraint, but no columns from it are specifically indicated (for example, if SELECT * is used), the creator of the CHECK constraint must have the REFERENCES privilege on at least one column of that table.

- If the text of the predicate is too long for the allocated space in the INFORMATION_SCHEMA, it is truncated and a warning condition is raised.

When Constraints Are Checked

A constraint is defined when created as either DEFERRABLE or NOT DEFERRABLE. If neither is specified, NOT DEFERRABLE is the default. A constraint that is NOT DEFERRABLE is checked after every statement (INSERT, UPDATE, or DELETE) that may produce values in violation of it. A DEFERRABLE constraint can be checked immediately or at the end of each transaction; that is, its mode may be either IMMEDIATE or DEFERRED (the mode of constraints that are NOT DEFERRABLE is always effectively IMMEDIATE).

Constraints whose mode is IMMEDIATE are checked whenever a statement is issued that may produce values that violate the constraint or one (SET CONSTRAINTS MODE) that directly mandates the immediate checking of the constraint. A constraint's mode at the beginning of a session is determined by whether INITIALLY IMMEDIATE or INITIALLY DEFERRED was specified when it was created. The SET CONSTRAINTS MODE statement can then be used to change the mode of a DEFERRABLE constraint at any time. The two clauses—DEFERRABLE or NOT DEFERRABLE and INITIALLY IMMEDIATE or INITIALLY DEFERRED—may be specified in either order.

Conformance Levels

Intermediate   Implementations at this level are not required to support temporary tables. FOREIGN KEY constraints need not allow the MATCH type to be specified or to support ON UPDATE referential triggered actions. It may be required that the order of the columns as named in the FOREIGN KEY constraint match the order they were named in the PRIMARY KEY or UNIQUE constraint. Intermediate-level implementations do not have to allow subqueries in the predicate of a CHECK constraint, and they may allow that predicate to access tables without the constraint creator having the REFERENCES privilege on them. They might not support ALTER DOMAIN.

Entry   Implementations at this level are not required to support user naming of constraints. If PRIMARY KEY or UNIQUE is specified, NOT NULL must be specified for each column in the constraint (the old approach from SQL89). Entry-level implementations are not required to support referential triggered actions. They are not required to support adding and dropping table constraints or to support domains.

SQL89   Constraints are not named.

See Also Part II: ALTER DOMAIN, ALTER TABLE, CREATE ASSERTION, CREATE DOMAIN, CREATE TABLE, CREATE VIEW, DELETE, ROLLBACK, SELECT, SET CONSTRAINTS MODE, UPDATE. Part III: Predicates, Subqueries.

Datatypes
Definitions and Characteristics of SQL Datatypes

Syntax

```
datatype ::=
{ {CHARACTER[(length)]}
| {CHAR[(length)]}
| {CHARACTER VARYING(length)}
| {CHAR VARYING(length)}
| {VARCHAR(length)}
[CHARACTER SET(repertoire name | form-of-use name )] }
| {NATIONAL CHARACTER[(length)]}
| {NATIONAL CHAR[(length)]}
| {NCHAR[(length)]}
| {NATIONAL CHARACTER VARYING(length)}
| {NATIONAL CHAR VARYING(length)}
| {NCHAR VARYING(length)}
| {BIT[(length)]}
| {BIT VARYING(length)}
| {NUMERIC[ (precision[, scale]) ]}
| {DECIMAL[ (precision[, scale]) ]}
| {DEC[ (precision[, scale]) ]}
| INTEGER
```

```
| INT
| SMALLINT
| {FLOAT[(precision)]}
| REAL
| {DOUBLE PRECISION}
| DATE
| {TIME[(precision) ]
[ WITH TIME ZONE ]}
| {TIMESTAMP[(precision)]
[ WITH TIME ZONE ]}
| {INTERVAL interval qualifier
```

Usage

Every column of every table in a SQL database must have a data-type. The datatype will be part of either the column definition itself (see Part II CREATE TABLE) or the definition of the domain on which the column is based (see Part II CREATE DOMAIN). The SQL standard takes a two-tiered approach to datatypes. Officially, there are seven basic datatypes, but most of these have several variations that go by different names, and it is the names of the variations that you use when you specify a datatype for a column or a domain. For clarity, we will define each variation as a separate datatype and consider the larger groupings categories. The DBMS itself, however, does not necessarily distinguish datatypes within categories. The category plus values for the relevant arguments (*precision*, *length*, and so on) can be sufficient to define the datatype. Therefore, INTEGER in the standard is usually referred to as "EXACT NUMERIC with scale 0," a decimal number with no digits following a decimal point, and the datatypes of SQL items (such as descriptor area fields) are officially defined as such. The categories are as follows:

> **CHARACTER STRING**   All datatypes that represent text, whatever the character set used.

> **NATIONAL CHARACTER**   Effectively the same as the CHARACTER STRING types, except that the character set is some implementation-defined set that corresponds to the language that will be in most general use. For our purposes, we will put these types in the same category with CHARACTER STRING for the remainder of this discussion.

BIT STRING   Straight binary data.

EXACT NUMERIC   Numbers that represent exact figures.

APPROXIMATE NUMERIC   Numbers expressed in scientific notation (mantissa and exponent) that represent approximate figures.

DATETIME   Dates, times, or combinations of both.

INTERVAL   The quantity of time between various dates and times.

The specific types for each of the categories are described in later sections of this entry.

Comparability of Datatypes

If values are to be compared, or if columns are to be joined or combined to be using UNION, EXCEPT, or INTERSECT operators (see Part II: SELECT), the values or columns must be of comparable datatypes. All datatypes within categories other than CHARACTER, NATIONAL CHARACTER, DATETIME, or INTERVAL are comparable (the restrictions on DATETIME and INTERVAL comparability are discussed under "DATETIME Types" and "The INTERVAL Type", respectively, later in this section). CHARACTER and NATIONAL CHARACTER types are comparable, within or between the CHARACTER and NATIONAL categories, if they use the same character repertoire. EXACT NUMERIC and APPROXIMATE NUMERIC are also comparable. If datatypes are not comparable, they can in some cases be converted by using a CAST expression (see CAST Expressions for a table of the valid type conversions).

CHARACTER STRING Types

CHARACTER STRINGs can be fixed- or varying-length. CHARACTER STRINGs are set off in SQL statements with single quotes (apostrophes—not left and right single quotes in the standard, though some products relax this restriction) before and after. Blank spaces between quotes represent blank spaces, and single quotes themselves are represented within a string with a concatenation of two single quotes ('') for each single quote expressed. Double quotes are different characters than pairs of single quotes and do not require this special treatment within strings.

NATIONAL CHARACTER STRING types behave in the same way as CHARACTER STRING types, except that, when specified as literals in SQL statements, NATIONAL CHARACTER types are preceded by an N and a space. The CHARACTER STRING and NATIONAL CHARACTER STRING datatypes are each described below along with any arguments, other than character set specifications, that may be appended to them when they are specified:

- CHARACTER [(*length*)], which can be abbreviated CHAR, is a fixed-length text string. The length is a positive integer specifying the number of characters that the column holds. It is effectively a maximum; values of lesser length will be padded with blanks. Although the *length* argument is technically optional, the default (and the minimum) is 1, so it is usually necessary.

- NATIONAL CHARACTER [(*length*)] is the NATIONAL CHARACTER STRING equivalent of CHARACTER. It can be abbreviated NATIONAL CHAR or NCHAR.

- CHARACTER VARYING (*length*), also known as CHAR VARYING and VARCHAR, is a text string of varying length. Here the *length* argument literally specifies a maximum and is not optional; it can be anything from 1 to the implementation-defined maximum. The length of the data value can be anything from 0 to the value of *length*.

- NATIONAL CHARACTER VARYING, NATIONAL CHAR VARYING, and NCHAR VARYING are all names for the NATIONAL CHARACTER STRING equivalent of VARCHAR.

For all of the types listed above, there will be some implementation-defined maximum for the *length* argument.

If a character set specification is used, it will be of the following form:

```
CHARACTER SET(repertoire name | form-of-use name )
```

In other words, either the repertoire or the form-of-use may be specified and the other will be implied. Which repertoires and forms-of-use are supported and how they are associated is implementation-defined. They may follow national or international standards, or they may themselves be implementation-defined. If the character set specification is omitted, some default will apply.

Every implementation is required to support a character repertoire called SQL_TEXT. This will contain all the characters necessary to express the SQL language, plus all characters contained in other character sets supported by the implementation.

BIT STRING Types

BIT strings, of course, are binary numbers—sequences of zeros and ones. Long BIT strings containing complex data—for example, digitized images or sound—are often called BLOBS (Binary Large Objects). There are two bit datatypes (that's "two bit" not "two-bit"): BIT and BIT VARYING. Each is followed by a parenthesized positive integer indicating the length in bits. BIT strings are fixed-length. The length may be omitted, but the default is 1, so usually a length will need to be specified. Unlike fixed-length CHARACTER strings, fixed-length BIT strings impose a minimum as well as a maximum length. In other words, any attempt to insert a string shorter than the indicated length will produce an error. BIT VARYING strings are varying-length, and the length, which will be the maximum length, must be specified. There will be some implementation-defined length that cannot be exceeded in any case. (Some implementations may not enforce this restriction.)

BIT strings can be represented in SQL statements in binary or hexadecimal form. Hexadecimal is a base-16 number system where each digit represents four binary digits; it provides a more concise and readable way to express binary values. The characters used to represent hexadecimal (or hex) are the digits 0–9 and the letters A–F. (Either upper- or lowercase letters A–F may be used to the same effect.) If a BIT string literal is represented in a SQL statement in binary form, it will be preceded by the letter B; if it is hex, it will be preceded by the letter X and delimited with single quotes.

BIT strings in the standard can be compared and thus sorted. The details for how this is done are described under Predicates.

EXACT NUMERIC Types

EXACT NUMERIC numbers have a specified or implied precision and scale. The precision is the total number of significant digits used to express the number; the scale is the number of significant digits to the right of the decimal point. Naturally, the scale cannot exceed the precision. Also, the precision may be either binary, meaning that it is expressed as the bit-length of the number, from which the number of digits can be derived, or decimal, in which case it directly indicates the number of digits. The scale is decimal. If the precision is omitted, an implementation-defined default applies; if the scale is omitted, the default is 0, which means that the number is effectively an INTEGER and the decimal point is dropped. The EXACT NUMERIC types are these:

- NUMERIC [(*precision*[, *scale*])]. This may specify neither precision nor scale, specify both precision and scale, or just specify precision and leave scale as the default, which is 0. The precision, whether specified or default, is decimal rather than binary.

- DECIMAL [(*precision*[, *scale*])], also known as DEC. This is very similar to NUMERIC, but with the subtle difference that the implementation may choose a precision greater than that specified. NUMERIC specifies an actual precision; DECIMAL specifies a minimum precision. Of course, in either case the precision could be omitted in favor of the implementation's default.

- INTEGER, also known as INT. The scale is 0, and the precision is an implementation-defined default. Whether this default is decimal or binary is also implementation-defined.

- SMALLINT. This is the same as INTEGER except that the precision may be less than that of INT. Whether the precision actually is less is implementation-defined. INT and SMALLINT precisions will be either both decimal or both binary—whichever the implementation chooses.

APPROXIMATE NUMERIC Types

APPROXIMATE NUMERIC numbers are expressed in scientific notation and have a precision, but no scale as such. The mantissa and the exponent are both signed, and the sign and magnitude of the exponent essentially determine the scale. The precision is binary (see EXACT NUMERIC above) and is that of the mantissa. The number of digits that can be in the exponent (not, properly speaking, a precision) is implementation-defined. The capital letter E (without quotes; this is not a text string) is the exponentiation symbol. The APPROXIMATE NUMERIC types are as follows:

- FLOAT [(*precision*)]. The precision you specify here is a minimum. The implementation is free to exceed it. There is, however, an implementation-defined maximum precision, and the precision you specify here cannot exceed that number. For FLOAT and only FLOAT, the precision is always binary. This means the number you give will be the number of bits rather than a number of digits.

- REAL. For this type, the precision is decimal and implementation-defined.

- DOUBLE PRECISION. Here, too, the precision is decimal and implementation-defined but is greater than that of REAL.

In any case, there will be some implementation-defined maximum precision that applies to all the above types.

DATETIME Types

DATETIME types in SQL consist of multiple fields representing different parts of an expression indicating the date and/or time. These are delimited with separators—minus signs (-) separate the fields of a date, and colons (:) those of a time. Where dates and times are combined, the two are separated with a blank space.

DATETIME values are comparable if they have the same fields. Individual fields of DATETIME values can be accessed with the EXTRACT expression. (See Numeric Value Functions. Although it works on DATETIMEs, EXTRACT produces a numeric result and is so considered a numeric value function.) There are three DATETIME datatypes:

- DATE is a set of three integer fields: YEAR, MONTH, and DAY. Four positions are allocated for years and two each for months and days, in the format *yyyy-mm-dd*. With separators, the total number of positions is 10.

- TIME [(*precision*)] [WITH TIME ZONE] is also a set of three numeric fields: HOUR, MINUTE, and SECOND. With separators, the length is 8 positions. You can optionally use the precision argument to specify fractional seconds up to an implementation-defined maximum number of positions, which will be at least 6. SECOND is therefore a DECIMAL; the other fields are INTEGERs. When fractional seconds are used, the total number of positions in the TIME item increases by the positions of the fractional seconds plus 1 to account for the decimal point. You can also optionally specify a time zone displacement. This indicates an amount to offset the time to account for divergence from UCT (Universal Coordinated Time). The time zone displacement adds two new fields— TIMEZONE_HOUR and TIMEZONE_MINUTE—to the value of the TIME datatype. The possible values for TIMEZONE_ HOUR are integers ranging from -12 to +13. For TIMEZONE_ MINUTE, they are 0 to 59. In effect, the sign on the TIME-ZONE_HOUR field applies to both. If WITH TIME ZONE is omitted, the default for the session applies. The addition of a time zone increases the length of the column by 6 positions.

• TIMESTAMP [(precision)] [WITH TIME ZONE] is a combination of DATE and TIME. Fractional seconds and time zones are options just as with TIME. The length of the TIMEZONE datatype is 19 positions plus whatever is added by fractional seconds or the time zone option.

When values for any of these types are given as literals in a SQL statement, they are surrounded by single quotes and preceded by the name of the type followed by a blank space. For example, a TIMESTAMP value would look like this:

```
TIMESTAMP '2000-07-12 10:38:54'
```

The possible values for DATETIME fields are shown in Table III.7.

TABLE III.7: Valid Values for DATETIME Fields

Field Name	Valid Values
YEAR	0001 to 9999
MONTH	01 to 12
DAY	Within the range 1 to 31, but further constrained by the values of the MONTH and YEAR fields, according to the rules for well-formed dates in the Gregorian calendar

Continued on next page

TABLE III.7: Valid Values for DATETIME Fields (continued)

Field Name	Valid Values
HOUR	00 to 23
MINUTE	00 to 59
SECOND	00 to 61.9..., where 9... means repeating 9s for as many digits as are specified by the precision
TIMEZONE_HOUR	00 to 13
TIMEZONE_MINUTE	00 to 59

NOTE DATETIME datatypes allow dates in the Gregorian format to be stored in the date range 0001–01–01 CE (Common Era, the same as AD in ISO nomenclature) through 9999–12–31 CE. The range for SECOND allows for as many as two "leap seconds". Interval arithmetic that involves leap seconds or discontinuities in calendars will produce implementation-defined results (we hope).

The syntax for assigning a value to the TIME ZONE is to append

```
AT {TIME ZONE interval } | LOCAL
```

to the end of the DATE value. LOCAL indicates that the time zone should be the default for the session. If the entire AT clause is omitted, LOCAL is the default. If TIME ZONE is specified, it will be indicated with a value of type INTERVAL containing the fields HOUR and MINUTE. INTERVALs are described in the following section.

The INTERVAL Type

INTERVALs are datatypes that denote the quantity of time between two DATETIME values. For example, between 12:00 and 12:30 is an interval of 00:30, or a half-hour. DATETIME values can be incremented or decremented by INTERVALs or added or subtracted to produce INTERVALs. The fields of the INTERVAL are numbers as in the DATETIME fields, but the numbers can be signed to indicate a direction in time. When used as literals, INTERVALs are preceded by the word *INTERVAL* and delimited with single quotes. The separators used are the same as for the DATETIME types. The definition of an INTERVAL includes an interval qualifier that indicates which fields of the DATE and TIME fields are to be included in the INTERVAL. The syntax diagram of this element is:

```
interval qualifier ::=
range of fields | single field

range of fields ::=
{ { YEAR | DAY | HOUR | MINUTE }
[(precision)] }
TO { YEAR | MONTH | DAY | HOUR | MINUTE }
| { SECOND [(precision)] }

single field ::=
{ { YEAR | MONTH | DAY | HOUR | MINUTE }
[(precision)] }
| { SECOND [(leading precision[, frac precision])] }
```

In other words, the interval qualifier may specify either a range of fields or a single field. If it specifies a range, the field before TO is called the *start field,* and the field following TO is called the *end field.* The start and end fields may be the same, in which case the effect is the same as if a single field had been specified.

The start field may not be SECOND. If you want seconds as the only field, specify SECOND as a single field. The optional precision argument following the start field is a positive integer indicating the number of positions to place in the leading field. The default is 2. The optional precision argument following the SECOND field represents the fractional precision—the number of digits to the right of the decimal point that will be used to represent the value. The following criteria must be met:

- The start field must be of equal or greater significance than the end field, where the descending order of significance of the fields is YEAR, MONTH, DAY, HOUR, MINUTE, SECOND.

- All fields falling between the start and end fields in the descending order of significance are included. In other words, an interval cannot be DAY, MINUTE without the intervening HOUR.

- If the start field is YEAR, the end field must be MONTH.

- The start field cannot be MONTH.

In effect, these restrictions mean that INTERVALs are either any single DATETIME field, YEAR possibly subdivided into MONTH, or fields less significant than MONTH, possibly subdivided into fields that are less significant still. YEAR and DAY are always either start fields or single fields. INTERVALs with YEAR and/or MONTH fields are called *year-month INTERVALs*; others are called *day-time INTERVALs*. Year-month and day-time INTERVALs are not comparable to each other in the terms discussed at the beginning of this entry. However, other INTERVALs are comparable.

For single-field INTERVALs, you may specify any DATETIME field, again with the optional precision. If the single field is SECOND, the precision can have two parts—the leading precision and the fractional (frac) precision. The former is the number of digits preceding the decimal point, with a default of 2. The latter is the number following the decimal point, with a default of 6.

The length of the INTERVAL is calculated according to the following principles:

- If the interval qualifier is a single field, the INTERVAL is the length of that field. If that field is SECOND, the length is the leading precision plus the fractional precision plus 1 (for the decimal point); otherwise, the length equals the specified or implied precision.

- All fields between the start and end fields have a length of 2, but each adds 3 positions to the length of the INTERVAL because of the necessary separator.

- The length of an INTERVAL that uses a range of values is calculated as follows: add the start field precision, the length of the end field (which is calculated just as though the end field were a single field as described above) plus 1 (for the separator), and the length of the intervening fields plus separators, which is 3 for each intervening field.

Anything that can be expressed in the precision specified or implied is a valid value for the start field or the sole field of an INTERVAL. YEAR and DAY are always start or sole fields. The valid values for the fields when not used as start or sole fields are shown in Table III.8.

TABLE III.8: Valid Values for Intervening and End Fields in INTERVAL Items

Field	Valid Value Range
MONTH	-1 to 11
HOUR	-23 to 23
MINUTE	-59 to 59
SECOND	-59.9… to 59.9…, where 9… means repeating 9s for as many digits as are specified by the precision

Operations Involving DATETIMEs and INTERVALs

Arithmetic operators can be used on DATETIMEs and INTERVALs. The result will be a value expression that can be used in SQL statements where value expressions normally are—for example, among the output columns of queries or as values to be placed into a table with an INSERT statement. (See Value Expressions in PART II.) Table III.9 defines the operations that are possible.

TABLE III.9: Valid Operators Involving DATETIMEs and INTERVALs

Operand 1	Operator	Operand 2	Result Type
DATETIME	-	DATETIME	INTERVAL
DATETIME	+ or -	INTERVAL	DATETIME
INTERVAL	+	DATETIME	DATETIME
INTERVAL	+ or -	INTERVAL	INTERVAL
INTERVAL	* or /	NUMERIC	INTERVAL
NUMERIC	*	INTERVAL	INTERVAL

These operations, of course, also obey the natural rules associated with dates and times according to the Gregorian calendar. The meanings are as follows:

- DATETIME - DATETIME = INTERVAL. This compares two DATE-TIMEs and finds the INTERVAL of time between them. The two DATETIMEs must be comparable (as defined under DATE-TIME earlier in this entry). If the first DATETIME is chronologically later, the INTERVAL is positive.

- DATETIME (+ or -) INTERVAL = DATETIME. This increments (+) or decrements (-) the DATETIME by the INTERVAL. If the DATETIME has a TIME ZONE component, it is preserved in the resulting DATETIME value.

- INTERVAL + DATETIME = DATETIME. This is equivalent to DATETIME + INTERVAL described above.

- INTERVAL (+ OR -) INTERVAL = INTERVAL. Adds or subtracts the numbers in the various fields of the INTERVALs. Keep in mind that INTERVAL values are signed and that subtracting a negative increases the value of the answer.

- INTERVAL (* or /) NUMERIC = INTERVAL. NUMERIC here means any EXACT or APPROXIMATE NUMERIC type. The various fields of the INTERVAL are multiplied or divided by the NUMERIC figure and values are converted to appropriate units and carried into fields of greater or lesser significance as necessary.

- NUMERIC * INTERVAL = INTERVAL. This is the equivalent of INTERVAL * NUMERIC, described above.

For example, the following expression increments the value of a DATETIME value by a year-month INTERVAL value:

```
DATE '2000-11-28' + INTERVAL '0002-4'
```

This will evaluate to the following DATETIME value:

```
DATE '2003-03-28'
```

In addition to the above operations, time periods can be compared to see whether they overlap. This is done with the OVERLAPS predicate as described in the Predicates entry of this part.

Compatibilities with Other Languages

When it needs to pass values to or from an application, SQL will either use variables (in Embedded SQL), parameters (in the module language), or dynamic parameters (in Dynamic SQL). However, the datatypes supported by various languages differ both from each other and from the SQL datatypes. In particular, DATETIME and INTERVAL are supported by none of the languages specified in the standard. Also, SQL values can be NULL, which has no equivalent in most languages because NULLs produce UNKNOWN values in comparisons, whereas even values such as zero or an empty string will produce TRUE or FALSE values in comparisons in conventional languages. Indicator variables are appended to conventional variables to indicate the presence of NULLs and allow the application to respond appropriately. The details of how to pass SQL values through variables or parameters, as well as the exact equivalents for SQL datatypes in the various standard-supported languages, are outlined in Appendices A and B.

Conformance Levels

Intermediate   At this level, support for BIT STRINGs is not required, CHARACTER STRINGs need not allow character set specifications, and DATE-TIME and INTERVAL datatypes need not support a specified precision for fractional seconds.

Entry   At this level, support for varying-length character strings, as well as NATIONAL CHARACTER, DATETIME, and INTERVAL datatypes is not required, although VARCHAR, DATE, and TIME are very widely supported, sometimes augmented with TIMESTAMP and INTERVAL. Also, empty strings may be disallowed, although most implementations do allow them.

See Also   Part II: CREATE CHARACTER SET, SELECT. Part III: CAST Expressions, Collations, DATETIME Value Functions, Predicates. Appendix A, B.

Datetime Value Functions
Functions That Produce Date and Time Values

Usage

Datetime value functions are used in place of value expressions and produce system-determined values when referenced. There are three kinds, one for each of the DATETIME datatypes:

- CURRENT_DATE. The date according to the system clock. The datatype of this item is DATE.

- CURRENT_TIME [(*precision*)]: The time according to the system clock. The current session TIME ZONE is automatically included. The precision argument, if supplied, specifies the decimal fractions of a second to be included in the time. This follows the principles outlined in the Datatypes entry under "DATETIME Types". The datatype of this item is TIME WITH TIME ZONE.

- CURRENT_TIMESTAMP [(*precision*)]: A combination of CURRENT_DATE and CURRENT_TIME. The precision argument has the same meaning as specified under CURRENT_TIME. The datatype of this item is TIMESTAMP WITH TIME ZONE.

Conformance Levels

Intermediate	Implementations at this level are not required to allow a specification of the fractional seconds for CURRENT_TIME or CURRENT_TIMESTAMP.
Entry	Implementations at this level are not required to support datetime value functions.

See Also   Part III: Datatypes, Value Expressions.

Descriptor Areas

(Dynamic SQL Only) An Effective Way to Deal with Dynamic Parameters

Usage

Dynamically-generated SQL statements can often use dynamic parameters as input or output parameters. There are two ways to set the values for the input parameters or retrieve them from the output parameters. You can use host-language variables (or parameters in the module language), or you can use descriptor areas. This entry is concerned with descriptor areas.

A *descriptor area*, sometimes just called a *descriptor*, consists of a series of items, each of which stores information about a single dynamic parameter. Each item has a number of fields: one field can hold a value for the parameter, another indicates whether it is NULL, and the rest provide descriptive information, such as the datatype, length, and so on of the parameter. Which of these fields are relevant depends on the datatype of the parameter.

When you execute a dynamic statement, you can specify that a descriptor area is to be used for all input parameters, all output parameters, or both. In the case of "both" you use a separate descriptor area for input and for output. You specify a descriptor for the input parameters with the USING clause, and you specify one for the output parameters with an INTO clause. These clauses are the same for any of the statements that use them, and either of them can take a list of host-language variables or the name of a descriptor area. The statements that use these clauses are as follows:

- EXECUTE is used to execute statements previously assembled with the PREPARE statement. The prepared statements can include most SQL statements, including queries that are known to produce only one row of output (single-row queries). EXECUTE can use either USING or INTO. INTO would be used only for queries.

- OPEN CURSOR in Dynamic SQL can execute a cursor that was dynamically created with either a DECLARE CURSOR or an ALLOCATE CURSOR statement. Such a cursor may have dynamic input parameters, and these will be given values with a USING clause in the OPEN CURSOR statement.

- FETCH is the statement that actually retrieves the data from open cursors. Therefore, it will use an INTO clause to store the output columns of the query in the cursor. FETCH retrieves the cursor contents one row at a time.

Of course, a given statement can have either, neither, or both kinds of dynamic parameters. The upshot is that a given descriptor area handles either all input or all output parameters for a given statement. A single descriptor does not handle both kinds of parameters, nor would it normally be used for more than one statement, though it could if the parameters for the statements were the same. However, you can execute the same statement repeatedly with different values specified in or entering the descriptor, which is largely the point.

Descriptor areas are created with the ALLOCATE DESCRIPTOR statement. When you create (allocate) a descriptor, you specify the maximum number of items it can hold. The values in the fields can either be manually specified with the SET DESCRIPTOR statement or automatically set with the DESCRIBE statement. However, for input parameters, you must use SET DESCRIPTOR to set the values. DESCRIBE cannot do this. The normal situation would be to:

- Use DESCRIBE to initialize the descriptor.

- Use SET DESCRIPTOR to change any fields you think you need to change.

- For input parameters, use SET DESCRIPTOR again to set the DATA field. You cannot set the DATA field, which actually contains the value for the parameter, at the same time as the other descriptor fields.

You can retrieve the content of the descriptor with the GET DESCRIPTOR statement.

The fields of a descriptor area item are shown in Table III.10.

TABLE III.10: The Descriptor Area Fields

Name Of Field	Datatype
TYPE	INTEGER
LENGTH	INTEGER
OCTET_LENGTH	INTEGER
RETURNED_LENGTH	INTEGER
RETURNED_OCTET_LENGTH	INTEGER
PRECISION	INTEGER
SCALE	INTEGER
DATETIME_INTERVAL_CODE	INTEGER
DATETIME_INTERVAL_PRECISION	INTEGER
NULLABLE	INTEGER
INDICATOR	INTEGER

Continued on next page

TABLE III.10: The Descriptor Area Fields (continued)

Name Of Field	Datatype
DATA	Matches datatype and description specified by the values in the following fields: TYPE, LENGTH, PRECISION, SCALE, DATETIME_INTERVAL_CODE, DATETIME_INTERVAL_PRECISION, CHARACTER_SET_CATALOG, CHARACTER_SET_SCHEMA, and CHARACTER_SET_NAME
NAME	CHARACTER string with character set SQL_TEXT and length not less than 128 characters
UNNAMED	INTEGER
COLLATION_CATALOG	CHARACTER string with character set SQL_TEXT and length not less than 128 characters
COLLATION_SCHEMA	CHARACTER string with character set SQL_TEXT and length not less than 128 characters
COLLATION_NAME	CHARACTER string with character set SQL_TEXT and length not less than 128 characters
CHARACTER_SET_CATALOG	CHARACTER string with character set SQL_TEXT and length not less than 128 characters
CHARACTER_SET_SCHEMA	CHARACTER string with character set SQL_TEXT and length not less than 128 characters
CHARACTER_SET_NAME	CHARACTER string with character set SQL_TEXT and length not less than 128 characters

Most of the fields apply only to particular datatypes and therefore may or may not be relevant depending on the value of the datatype of the parameter, which is specified in the TYPE field. The values in those fields that are not relevant are implementation-dependent.

The fields that do not depend on the value of TYPE are described below:

- TYPE itself, naturally, will always be present and indicate the datatype of the parameter following the codes indicated in Table III.10.

- NULLABLE indicates whether the parameter may contain NULL values. A value of 1 indicates that it may, and a value of 0 indicates that it may not.

- INDICATOR is a descriptor field that indicates whether the parameter actually does contain a NULL. If NULLABLE is 1, you should always check this value (for output parameters) or set it when you want to specify NULLs (for input parameters). If an output parameter is NULL, and the INDICATOR field is not retrieved (with the GET DESCRIPTOR statement, naturally), an error is produced. A negative INDICATOR value means that the parameter is NULL, and the value of DATA is irrelevant; otherwise, the parameter is not NULL, and the value of DATA must be appropriate for its datatype and description as indicated in the other fields. This applies to both input and output parameters, so INDICATOR fields may be set negative to insert NULLs.

- DATA is the content of the parameter. Its value must match the description given by the TYPE and other relevant fields (precision and so on), unless the INDICATOR field shows that it is NULL, in which case its value is implementation-defined and effectively undefined (and irrelevant).

- NAME indicates the name of the parameter.

- UNNAMED specifies whether the name of the parameter is implementation-dependent or imposed. The name is imposed if SQL syntax dictates what the name is—for example, if it is taken directly from a column name or specified with an AS clause (see Part II: SELECT). If the name is implementation-dependent, UNNAMED is set to 1; otherwise, it is set to 0.

The numeric codes for the various datatypes as used in the TYPE field are shown in Table III.11.

TABLE III.11: Valid Values for the TYPE Descriptor Field

Datatype	Code
Implementation-defined	< 0
BIT	14
BIT VARYING	15
CHARACTER	1
CHARACTER VARYING	12
DATE, TIME, or TIMESTAMP	9
DECIMAL	3
DOUBLE PRECISION	8
FLOAT	6
INTEGER	4
INTERVAL	10
NUMERIC	2
REAL	7
SMALLINT	5

The CODE number indicates the datatype of the parameter specified on the left in the above table. The fields that are relevant for the various datatypes indicated by TYPE are defined below:

- If TYPE indicates NUMERIC, then PRECISION and SCALE are the precision and scale values for the NUMERIC datatype.

- If TYPE indicates DECIMAL, then PRECISION and SCALE are the precision and scale values for the DECIMAL datatype.

- If TYPE indicates FLOAT, then PRECISION is the precision value for the FLOAT datatype.

- If TYPE indicates BIT or BIT VARYING, then LENGTH is the length or maximum length value for the BIT datatype.

- If TYPE indicates CHARACTER or CHARACTER VARYING, then LENGTH is the length or maximum length value for the CHARACTER datatype, CHARACTER_SET_NAME indicates the

character set on which it is based, and CHARACTER_SET_
CATALOG and CHARACTER_SET_SCHEMA indicate the
catalog and schema where that character set resides. Likewise, COLLATION_NAME, COLLATION_CATALOG, and
COLLATION_SCHEMA contain the same information for
the collation of the character set.

- If TYPE indicates DATE, TIME, or TIMESTAMP, then DATE-
  TIME_INTERVAL_CODE is a code specified in Table III.10, and
  PRECISION is the fractional seconds precision, if any, of the
  TIME or TIMESTAMP.

- If TYPE indicates INTERVAL, then DATETIME_INTERVAL_
  CODE is a code specified in Table III.11, and DATETIME_
  INTERVAL_PRECISION and PRECISION are the leading field
  precision and fractional seconds precision, if any, respectively.

All implementation-defined datatypes are negative numbers,
and the set of fields that are relevant for such types is also
implementation-defined.

For DATETIME and INTERVAL datatypes, the DATETIME_
INTERVAL_CODE is used to indicate which fields are present in
the DATETIME or INTERVAL. The meaning of the value in the
field can vary depending on whether the datatype is DATETIME
or INTERVAL. The possible values for DATETIMEs are shown in
Table III.12, while those for INTERVALs are shown in Table III.13.

TABLE III.12: Valid Values for DATETIME_INTERVAL_CODE if
the Datatype Is DATE

Datetime Datatype	Code
DATE	1
TIME	2
TIME WITH TIME ZONE	4
TIMESTAMP	3
TIMESTAMP WITH TIME ZONE	5

TABLE III.13: Valid Values for DATETIME_INTERVAL_CODE if the Datatype Is INTERVAL

Interval Fields	Code
DAY	3
DAY TO HOUR	8
DAY TO MINUTE	9
DAY TO SECOND	10
HOUR	4
HOUR TO MINUTE	11
HOUR TO SECOND	12
MINUTE	5
MINUTE TO SECOND	13
MONTH	2
SECOND	6
YEAR	1
YEAR TO MONTH	7

Conformance Levels

Entry   Support for Dynamic SQL, which is where descriptor areas are used, is not required at this level. In fact, most products support it, but not necessarily conforming to the specifications of the standard.

See Also   Part II: ALLOCATE DESCRIPTOR, DEALLOCATE DESCRIPTOR, DESCRIBE, GET DESCRIPTOR, SET DESCRIPTOR, Part III: Predicates (for discussion of three-valued logic and NULLs), Datatypes. Appendix C.

Numeric Value Functions
Functions That Produce Numeric Values

Syntax

```
numeric value function ::=
{ POSITION (character string IN character string) }
```

```
| {EXTRACT ( datetime field
 FROM {datetime value expression | interval value
expression} ) }
| {CHAR_LENGTH | CHARACTER_LENGTH (string value
expression)}
| {OCTET_LENGTH (string value expression) }
| {BIT_LENGTH (string value expression) }
```

Usage

Numeric value functions operate on nonnumeric datatypes but produce numeric results. They can be used in SQL statements wherever numeric value expressions are used. When a numeric value expression produces a number, it is said to equal that number. The rules are outlined in the following paragraphs.

POSITION

For POSITION, both strings must have the same character repertoire but not necessarily the same character set. In other words, their collating sequences and forms-of-use may differ. The result is an INTEGER. If either string is NULL, POSITION is also NULL. If the first string is a subset of the second, POSITION is set to the character position in the second string where the first string begins. All matches after the first are ignored. If the first string is empty, POSITION = 1. If no match is found, POSITION = 0. For example, the following expression finds the starting position of the first occurrence of 'press' in 'Express':

```
POSITION ('press' IN 'Express')
```

The resulting value would, of course, be 3.

EXTRACT

For EXTRACT, if the DATETIME or INTERVAL on which the extract is performed is NULL, EXTRACT is NULL as well. Otherwise, EXTRACT equals the value of the field specified. The fields that can be extracted are YEAR, MONTH, DAY, HOUR, MINUTE, SECOND, TIMEZONE_HOUR, and TIMEZONE_MINUTE. The last two can be extracted only from DATETIME values of type TIME or TIMESTAMP that specify WITH TIME ZONE. If the extracted field is SECOND, the datatype of EXTRACT is EXACT NUMERIC with some implementation-defined precision and scale, such that the fractional seconds can be expressed without truncation. Otherwise, the datatype is INTEGER. For example, the following expression produces an integer corresponding to the month value of the INTERVAL literal:

```
EXTRACT MONTH FROM INTERVAL '2010-05'
```
The resulting value would, of course, be 05.

CHARACTER_LENGTH

CHARACTER_LENGTH may be abbreviated as CHAR_LENGTH. The string literal, string datatype, or other value expression on which it operates, is a CHARACTER or BIT STRING as specified under String Value Functions in this section. If the string value function output (hereafter *string*) is NULL, then CHAR_LENGTH is NULL. Otherwise, if the string is a CHARACTER datatype, CHAR_LENGTH returns the number of characters in it, which will be an INTEGER.

NOTE An empty character string is not NULL; it will produce a CHAR_LENGTH of zero. For BIT STRINGs, CHAR_LENGTH is equivalent to OCTET_LENGTH.

OCTET_LENGTH

OCTET_LENGTH also is NULL if the string is NULL. Otherwise, OCTET_LENGTH is the BIT_LENGTH of the string divided by 8 and rounded up to the nearest INTEGER. Octets are sequences of 8 bits each, and in some obscure circles are called *bytes* (although people have been known to take liberties with the definition of bytes, which is why the standard went for octets).

BIT_LENGTH

BIT_LENGTH, too, returns NULL if the string is NULL. Otherwise, it returns an INTEGER indicating the number of bits used to represent the value, which will be zero for a zero-length (as opposed to NULL) string.

Conformance Levels

Intermediate   Support for POSITION and BIT_LENGTH is
                   not required at this level.

Entry   Support for numeric value functions is not
                   required at this level.

See Also   Part III: Datatypes, String Value Functions, Value
Expressions.

Predicates
Predicates are expressions that can be TRUE, FALSE, or UNKNOWN.

Syntax

```
predicate ::=
[(] [NOT]
{ comparison predicate
| between predicate
| in predicate
| like predicate
| null predicate
| quantified comparison predicate
| exists predicate
| unique predicate
| match predicate
| overlaps predicate    }
[AND | OR predicate ] [)]
[IS [NOT] truth value]

truth value ::=
TRUE | FALSE | UNKNOWN
```

Usage

Predicates are expressions that apply comparison operators (the
comp op element shown in the syntax) and/or SQL predicate operators (IN, EXISTS, and so on) to values, to produce a truth value of
TRUE, FALSE, or UNKNOWN. Predicates may be either a single
such expression or a combination of any number of them using
the standard Boolean operators AND, OR, and NOT, as well as the
special SQL operator IS, and possibly using parentheses to impose

an order of evaluation. Predicates are used in the WHERE and HAVING clauses of SELECT statements and subqueries to determine which rows or aggregate groups are to be selected (see SELECT in Part II and Subqueries in this section), in constraints to determine whether a constraint is violated (see Constraints), and in the UPDATE and DELETE statements to determine on which rows the change should be made (see the UPDATE and DELETE entries in Part II). The individual types of predicates are explained in separate sections later in this entry.

Many of these predicates use row value constructors, which are parenthesized lists of one or more values. We note here that the parentheses may be omitted if a list contains but a single value. For more information, see Row and Table Value Constructors.

Three-Valued Logic (3VL)

With the exceptions of the EXISTS, IS NULL, UNIQUE, and MATCH predicates, predicates in SQL can be TRUE, FALSE, or UNKNOWN. UNKNOWNs arise when NULLs are compared to any value including other NULLs. Since we don't know what the value is, we can't say what the result of the comparison should be. UNKNOWN truth values can be operated on by the Boolean operators AND, OR, and NOT, as well as by the SQL operator IS, with the results shown in Tables III.14 through III.17.

TABLE III.14: Truth Values Using NOT in Three-Valued Logic

Expression	Truth Value
NOT TRUE	FALSE
NOT FALSE	TRUE
NOT UNKNOWN	UNKNOWN

TABLE III.15: Truth Values Using OR in Three-Valued Logic

OR	TRUE	FALSE	UNKNOWN
TRUE	TRUE	TRUE	TRUE
FALSE	TRUE	FALSE	UNKNOWN
UNKNOWN	TRUE	UNKNOWN	UNKNOWN

TABLE III.16: Truth Values Using AND in Three-Valued Logic

AND	TRUE	FALSE	UNKNOWN
TRUE	TRUE	FALSE	UNKNOWN
FALSE	FALSE	FALSE	FALSE
UNKNOWN	UNKNOWN	FALSE	UNKNOWN

TABLE III.17: Truth Values Using IS in Three-Valued Logic

IS	TRUE	FALSE	UNKNOWN
TRUE	TRUE	FALSE	FALSE
FALSE	FALSE	TRUE	FALSE
UNKNOWN	FALSE	FALSE	TRUE

In Table III.14, the expression on the left produces the truth value on the right. The other tables should be read like multiplication tables; the value indicated at the intersection of a column and a row is that produced by applying the operation (OR, AND, or IS) to the values indicated on the left and on top.

The rules of thumb (which cover most but not all combinations, hence the tables) are these:

- TRUE OR anything is TRUE.

- FALSE AND anything is FALSE.

- Any truth value ANDed or ORed with itself produces itself.

- IS is TRUE if the two truth values are the same and FALSE otherwise.

It is important to keep in mind that NULLs can not only be stored in the database, they can be generated by queries or CAST expressions (see CAST Expressions). In particular, outer joins (see Part II: SELECT) can insert NULLs into the output of a query, even if none are present in the tables being joined. Outer joins merge the rows of two tables wherever matching values are found in one or more columns. Where no matches are found for a row from one of the tables, that row may be included (depending on the type of outer join) but with NULLs inserted into the columns whose values would have been taken from the other table had there been a match. Although useful, three-valued logic is problematic and controversial (if you love a good fight, the legitimacy of 3VL is the biggest one in SQL.) The IS operator is provided primarily to give you a way to test for UNKNOWNs and ensure that the results are either TRUE or FALSE. As IS never produces an UNKNOWN.

Among the problems to be careful of in 3VL is its inability to generalize. Consider this predicate:

```
X > 1 OR X < 2
```

Obviously, any integer X will make this predicate TRUE. If X is NULL, however, the predicate will still come out UNKNOWN, as its two components would individually be UNKNOWN, and UNKNOWN AND UNKNOWN is UNKNOWN. This is one of the arguments against 3VL.

When all is said and done, the predicate will finally be either TRUE, FALSE, or UNKNOWN. Rows are selected by SELECT statements or subqueries if their values make the predicate in the WHERE clause TRUE. Likewise, rows are changed by INSERT or UPDATE statements if their values make the predicate in the WHERE clause TRUE. The predicate in the HAVING clause of a SELECT statement applies to values derived from groups of rows (see SELECT in Part II , and Aggregate Functions in this section); groups are selected for output if their values make the predicate TRUE. Constraints, however, are satisfied if the predicate is either TRUE or UNKNOWN; only a truth value of FALSE violates a constraint.

Comparison Predicates

```
comparison predicate ::=
row value constructor comp op row value constructor

comp op ::=
=
| <
| <=
| >
| >
| <>
```

NOTE The syntax for a row value constructor is shown under Row and Table Value Constructors.

Comparison predicates compare two sets of one or more values that are in the form of simple value expressions, subqueries, or row value constructors. A row value constructor is a sequence of one or more values. Each row value constructor must have the same number of values and in such an order that the values in corresponding positions are of comparable datatypes (see Datatypes for the precise definition of comparability). Each such pair of values is called a *pair of corresponding values*. For subqueries, the values produced by the subquery are treated as though they were the content of a row value constructor. Likewise, for simple value expressions, although, in this case, the row value constructor would have only one element. For the rest of this discussion, we shall speak mostly in terms of row value constructors, but the substance applies to sets of values specified by any of these techniques, unless otherwise stated or clear from context.

If either or both of a pair of corresponding values is NULL, the result of the comparison of those two values is UNKNOWN. Otherwise, the two values are compared in terms of the comparison operator, which will be one of the following: =, <, <=, >, >=, <>, and the resulting expression is evaluated as TRUE or FALSE. NUMERIC values are compared according to their algebraic values. CHARACTER STRINGs are compared according to their collating sequences, as determined by the rules specified under Collations in Table III.4. If the strings are of unequal length, then the shorter is padded prior to comparison according to the pad attribute of the applicable collating sequence. If the attribute is PAD SPACE (the default), the shorter string is padded with whatever character in the repertoire is defined as the blank space character. If the attribute is NO PAD, then the shorter string is padded with some implementation-dependent character from outside the character set that collates lower than any character within it. Then the strings are compared.

Two strings are equal if they collate the same. For example, the following two strings are not the same but would be considered equal, provided that they were collated with the PAD SPACE attribute:

```
'Weston'
'Weston
```

In some cases, it is possible for two strings of unequal length or representing different sequences of characters to collate the same. If such strings are referenced in an aggregate function, are subject to exclusion by a DISTINCT argument in a SELECT clause, are used in UNION, INTERSECT, or EXCEPT operations, or are used in a GROUP BY clause to partition aggregate groups (for all of these, see SELECT in Part II), which of these distinguishable but equal values is used is implementation-dependent.

BIT STRINGs are compared bit by bit until the first difference is found or until the end of at least one of the strings is reached. On the first bit difference, the BIT STRING value that equals 1 is the greater. If there is no bit difference and the strings are of unequal length, then the longer string is greater. If there is no bit difference and no difference in length, then the strings are equal.

DATETIMEs are compared according to their placement in chronological time. A later date has a greater value.

INTERVALs are first converted into appropriate units, meaning that all fields are converted into the units of the least significant field of either value, and these values are compared as NUMERICs.

Now that we understand how the individual elements of the row value constructor list are compared, we will examine how the entire lists are compared in terms of the results of the individual comparisons. We can call the first row value constructor RC1 and the second RC2. The rules are these:

- If all of the corresponding values are equal, then RC1 = RC2.

- Otherwise, both lists are traversed until the first difference or NULL is found among the corresponding values. If a difference is found, then those corresponding values are compared, and the truth value using any given comparison operator is the same as it would be using the same comparison operator on those two values. RC1 <> RC2 is TRUE if there are any differences in the corresponding non-NULL values.

- RC1 <> RC2 is FALSE if and only if RC1 = RC2 is TRUE.

- RC1 = RC2 is FALSE if and only if RC1 <> RC2 is TRUE.

- If either RC1 > RC2 or RC1 = RC2 is TRUE, then RC1 >= RC2 is TRUE.

- If either RC1 < RC2 or RC1 = RC2 is TRUE, then RC1 <= RC2 is TRUE.

- RC1 < RC2 is FALSE if and only if RC1 >= RC2 is TRUE.

- RC1 > RC2 is FALSE if and only if RC1 <= RC2 is TRUE.

- RC1 <= RC2 is FALSE if and only if RC1 > RC2 is TRUE.

- RC1 >= RC2 is FALSE if and only if RC1 < RC2 is TRUE.

- In any other case, the truth value of the comparison is UNKNOWN.

Some of the above may seem obvious, but it is useful for reference because of the subtleties of 3VL. For example, if the only difference between the RC1 and RC2 is the presence of NULLs in one or the other, then RC1 = RC2 is not TRUE; nor is it FALSE. It is UNKNOWN, as is RC1 <> RC2. Notice that this effect will be achieved even if both row value constructors have the NULLs only in corresponding values. NULL = NULL is UNKNOWN. For example, assuming a collating sequence that corresponds to alphabetical ordering, the first of the following comparison predicates would be TRUE, the second FALSE, and the third UNKNOWN:

```
('bat', 'raven') >= ('bat', 'cat')
('bat', 'beat')  >= ('cat', NULL)
('bat', NULL)    >= ('bat', 'man')
```

The BETWEEN Predicate

```
between predicate ::=
row value constructor [NOT] BETWEEN
  row value constructor AND row value constructor
```

NOTE The syntax for a row value constructor is shown under Row and Table Value Constructors.

BETWEEN predicates check to see whether the first row value constructor falls in an ascending range specified by the other two.

As with comparison predicates, the row value constructors must all have the same number of values, and the corresponding values must be comparable. We can call the first row value constructor RC1, the second RC2, and the third RC3.

```
RC1 BETWEEN RC2 AND RC3
```

is equivalent to

```
RC1 >= RC2 AND RC1 <= RC3
```

and

```
RC1 NOT BETWEEN RC2 AND RC3
```

is equivalent to

```
NOT (RC1 BETWEEN RC2 AND RC3)
```

(parentheses added for clarity). Notice that if RC1 BETWEEN RC2 AND RC3 is TRUE, this does not mean that RC1 BETWEEN RC3 AND RC2 is also TRUE. The first would be translated as

```
RC1 >= RC2 AND RC1 <= RC3
```

whereas the second would be translated as

```
RC1 >= RC3 AND RC1 <= RC2
```

These statements could both be TRUE only if RC1, RC2, and RC3 were all equal.

Here are some examples. The first of the following BETWEEN predicates would be TRUE, the second FALSE, and the third UNKNOWN.

```
(4, 6) BETWEEN (3, 9) AND (5, NULL)
(4, 6) BETWEEN (5, 3) AND (NULL, 9)
(4, 6) BETWEEN (3, 9) AND (NULL, 5)
```

The IN Predicate

```
in predicate ::=
row value constructor
[NOT] IN table subquery
| (value expression.,...)
```

NOTE The syntax for row value constructors is shown under Row and Table Value Constructors, and that for table subqueries is shown in Subqueries.

IN predicates determine whether the row value constructor is found in the set of values that either is specified directly or is produced by a table subquery. If the values are specified, it is equivalent to a table value constructor. The table subquery is a SELECT statement that produces zero or more rows of one or more columns each—in other words, a conventional table (see Subqueries in this section and SELECT in Part II for more information). In any case, the row value constructor preceding the word IN (the *match target*) is compared to the output rows of the table subquery or the row value constructors of the table value constructor, as the case may be. (In either case, call these the *specified rows*.) If the match target is equal to at least one of the specified rows according to the rules laid out in the Comparison Predicates section of this entry, then the truth value of the IN predicate is TRUE. If for every specified row (X) the match target <> X, then the truth value is FALSE. If a subquery is used and comes back empty (returns no rows) then the IN predicate is FALSE. If none of the foregoing conditions are met, the truth value is UNKNOWN. This happens when a partially NULL row matches in all of its non-NULL components.

For example, the first of the following IN predicates would be TRUE, the second FALSE, and the third UNKNOWN:

```
(4, 6) IN VALUES (3, 9), (5, NULL), (4, 6)
(4, 6) IN VALUES (3, 9), (5, NULL), (3, 6)
(4, 6) IN VALUES (3, 9), (5, 0), (NULL, 6)
```

Although the above examples are specified with row value constructors, subqueries that produce the same sets of rows would have the same effect.

Note that IN used with a subquery is equivalent to the quantified comparison predicate SOME used with an equals operator and the same subquery.

The LIKE Predicate

```
like predicate ::=
string value expression
[NOT] LIKE string value expression
  [ ESCAPE character ]
```

LIKE compares two strings, one of which can contain wildcards, to see if they match. These strings are value expressions of some string datatype and may be generated however value expressions may (see Value Expressions). The first string, the *match value*, is searched for substrings that are specified by the second, the *pattern*. The optional ESCAPE clause allows you to define an escape character as described below. All three expressions must be comparable as defined under Datatypes. Two wildcards may be used in the pattern:

- The underscore (_) stands for any single character in the match value.

- The percent sign (%) stands for any sequence of zero or more characters in the match value.

If you want to search for either of these wildcards as literals, you must use the ESCAPE clause to define an escape character. Whenever this character is used in the pattern, it must precede either the underscore or the percent sign and will indicate that the underscore or percent sign is to be interpreted literally, not as a wildcard.

The truth value of a LIKE predicate conforms to the following principles:

- If either the match value, pattern, or escape character is NULL, the truth value is UNKNOWN.

- If both the match value and the pattern are zero-length strings, the truth value is TRUE.

- Otherwise, if the match value can be subdivided into segments such that each equals (as defined under Comparison Predicates) a string in the pattern or is represented in the pattern by a wildcard, where the segments and wildcards are in the same sequence in the pattern as the matching segments in the match value, then LIKE is TRUE.

- If none of the above conditions hold, LIKE is FALSE.

No padding or truncating of the match value is done. If the pattern does not describe the entire match value, but really just a substring, you must place percent signs at the beginning and/or the end of the pattern to match (account for) the extraneous material in the match value. This implies that two strings that are equal according to the standards outlined under Comparison Predicates in this entry still may not be LIKE one another as defined here. The comparison predicate may pad the shorter string with blanks automatically, whereas LIKE will not match trailing blanks unless a trailing percent sign wildcard is used.

In the following examples, the first LIKE predicate is TRUE, the second FALSE, and the third UNKNOWN.

```
'Sherwood_Forest ' LIKE '%wood|_For%' ESCAPE '|'
'Sherwood_Forest ' LIKE '%wood|_Forest' ESCAPE '|'
'Sherwood_Forest ' LIKE '%wood|_For%' ESCAPE NULL
```

The comparison between the match value and the pattern must follow some collating sequence and coercibility attribute. These are based on the tables in the Collations entry as specified below.

If the escape character is not specified, then the collating sequence used is determined by Table III.4, taking the match value as comparand 1 and the pattern as comparand 2. Otherwise, let C1 be the coercibility attribute and collating sequence of the match value and C2 be the coercibility attribute and collating sequence of the pattern. Taking C1 as the operand 1 coercibility and C2 as the operand 2 coercibility, calculate the resulting collating sequence and coercibility according to Table III.3. Call this result C3. Now take C3 as the coercibility attribute and collating sequence of comparand 1 and the escape character—with its coercibility attribute and collating sequence—as comparand 2, and let Table III.4 determine the collating sequence and coercibility used in the LIKE predicate. Fun, eh?

The NULL Predicate

```
null predicate ::=
row value constructor IS [NOT] NULL
```

NOTE The syntax for a row value constructor is shown under Row and Table Value Constructors.

NULL predicates are designed specifically to check for the presence of NULL values. For this reason, they are never UNKNOWN—only TRUE or FALSE. If all of the values in the row value constructor are NULL, then IS NULL is TRUE. If they are all FALSE, then IS NOT NULL is TRUE. Notice that IS NOT NULL will not necessarily have the same value as NOT (IS NULL). This was not true in older SQL standards. There, the NULL predicate took a column reference where it now takes a row value constructor, and therefore *value* IS NOT NULL was the same as NOT (*value* IS NULL). This is no longer the case, unless the row value constructor happens to contain a single value. Table III.18 shows the truth table for the NULL predicate.

The expression column on the left indicates the number of values in the row value constructor and whether they are NULL, not NULL, all NULL, some NULL, or none NULL. The other columns show the appropriate truth values for variations of the NULL predicate to row value constructor R.

For example, the first and last of the following predicates are TRUE, and the second and third are FALSE:

```
(NULL, NULL) IS NULL
(NULL, 5) IS NULL
(NULL, 5) IS NOT NULL
 NOT ((NULL, 5) IS NULL)
```

TABLE III.18: Truth Table for the NULL Predicate

Expression	R IS NULL	R IS NOT NULL	NOT R NOT NULL	NOT R IS NOT NULL
1 value: NULL	TRUE	FALSE	FALSE	TRUE
1 value: NOT NULL	FALSE	TRUE	TRUE	FALSE
> 1 value: all NULL	TRUE	FALSE	FALSE	TRUE
> 1 value: some NULL	FALSE	FALSE	TRUE	TRUE
> 1 value: none NULL	FALSE	TRUE	TRUE	FALSE

Quantified Comparison Predicates

```
quantified comparison predicate ::=
row value constructor comp op { ANY | ALL | SOME }
  table subquery
```

NOTE The syntax for row value constructors is shown under Row and Table Value Constructors, and that for table subqueries is shown in Subqueries.

Quantified comparison predicates are a special type of comparison predicate that, rather than comparing two row value constructors, compares a row value constructor to the set of rows produced by a table subquery. The row value constructor (RC) is compared individually to each row from the subquery, but a single value is produced that describes the results of the entire set of comparisons. Either all of the comparisons were TRUE, some of them were, or none of them were. As in comparison predicates, RC and the subquery output must have the same number of columns, and corresponding values must be comparable. The rules for determining collating sequences and coercibility for character string datatypes are also the same as for comparison predicates. Simple single value expressions may also be used, which are treated like row constructors of only one column. In the earlier standards, only simple value expressions could be used.

The quantifier that precedes the comparison operator is one of three types: ANY, ALL, or SOME. ANY and SOME are synonymous, and we will use SOME to indicate either of them for the remainder of this discussion. The truth value result is determined as follows:

- Whether SOME or ALL is specified, if all of the comparisons between RC and each row produced by the subquery are TRUE, the result is TRUE.

- If the subquery returns zero rows and ALL is specified, the result is TRUE. If the subquery returns zero rows and SOME is specified, the result is FALSE.

- If ALL is specified and any of the comparisons between RC and the subquery rows are FALSE, then the result is FALSE.

- If SOME is specified and there is at least one comparison between RC and the subquery rows that is TRUE, the result is TRUE.

- If SOME is specified and every comparison between RC and the subquery rows is FALSE, the result is FALSE.

- In any case not covered by the preceding, the result is UNKNOWN.

ANY and ALL can be confusing in certain situations. For example, in ordinary English a value is normally considered greater than any of a set of values if it is greater than every member of the set. In SQL, that meaning would be expressed by > ALL. The expression > ANY would be true if RC were greater than at least one member of the set. SOME is probably a less-confusing term in this regard. The thing to remember is that you are looking at a group of comparisons between RC and each row returned by the subquery. Of this group, are ALL of the comparisons TRUE? Are SOME of the comparisons TRUE? Another point of confusion comes when using a zero-row subquery. Comparing a value to ANY (zero-row subquery) will result in a FALSE. Comparing a value to ALL (zero-row subquery) will result in a TRUE.

In the following examples, we show the rows produced by a subquery rather than the subquery itself. This, of course, is not the proper syntax, but it makes the predicate more readable.

Of the following SOME predicates, the first is TRUE, the second FALSE, and the third UNKNOWN:

```
(2100.00, 97) > ANY
(2500.00, 99
 18000.00, NULL
 2000.00, 118)

(2100.00, 97) = SOME
(2500.00, 97
 2100.00, NULL
 2000.00, 118)

(NULL, NULL) = SOME
(2500.00, 99
NULL, NULL
2000.00, NULL)
```

Of the following ALL predicates, again, the first is TRUE, the second FALSE, and the third UNKNOWN:

```
(2100.00, 97) > ALL
(2000.00, 97
1800.00, NULL
2000.00, 118)

(2100.00, 97) <> ALL
(2100.00, 77
```

```
2100.00, 97
NULL, 97)

(2100.00, 97) = ALL
(2100.00, 97
2100.00, NULL
2100.00, 97)
```

The EXISTS Predicate

```
exists predicate ::=
EXISTS table subquery
```

NOTE The syntax of the table subquery element is shown under Subqueries.

EXISTS is a predicate that takes a subquery as an argument and is TRUE if that subquery produces any rows and FALSE otherwise. Although predicates determine when subqueries produce rows, and most predicates can be TRUE, FALSE, or UNKNOWN, subqueries either produce rows or they do not. If the predicates are UNKNOWN, of course, they do not.

Normally, EXISTS is used with a correlated subquery. This is a subquery that has an outer reference, which is a reference to a value in some containing query. The subquery may have different results depending on this value and must be evaluated differently for each row of the containing query (see Subqueries). Therefore, a correlated subquery produces different answers for the different rows of the containing query, and EXISTS can also have different values for each such row. Otherwise, EXISTS would have the same value for every row of the query, which is not a very useful predicate.

Be careful in the presence of possible NULLs. If the predicate of the subquery is UNKNOWN, no row is produced, and EXISTS is FALSE. That might not be a problem, but if the predicate of the containing query is NOT EXISTS, this FALSE becomes TRUE, whereas UNKNOWN would stay UNKNOWN. This problem has been thoroughly analyzed by Chris Date, a leading relational theorist. A rule of thumb is that if the subquery in an EXISTS predicate tests a value that might be NULL, use the IS NULL predicate to find the NULLs and handle them appropriately. Many but not all EXISTS predicates can also be expressed as quantified predicates.

Since EXISTS uses correlated subqueries, clarity requires that examples use entire queries rather than the EXISTS predicates in isolation. The following example uses the Salespeople table as shown elsewhere in this book. For the sake of simplicity, we have built both the outer query and the subquery on the same table—this is not required by the EXISTS syntax. This query finds all rows with city values that are also present in some other row. This produces a list of salespeople with other salespeople in their cities (alerting us to territory conflicts). It will produce two rows of output for each such match (matching salesperson A to B and then matching B to A), so we specified DISTINCT.

```
SELECT DISTINCT *
FROM Salespeople outerquery
WHERE EXISTS
  (SELECT *
FROM Salespeople innerquery
WHERE innerquery.city = outerquery.city
    AND innerquery.snum <> outerquery.snum);
```

The innerquery.snum <> outerquery.snum predicate is necessary to prevent every row from being selected in a match with itself.

The UNIQUE Predicate

```
unique predicate ::=
UNIQUE table subquery
```

NOTE The syntax of the table subquery element is shown under Subqueries.

UNIQUE tests to see whether a subquery has produced any duplicate rows. It is either TRUE or FALSE never UNKNOWN. All of the rows from the subquery are compared as *row value constructor = row value constructor* comparison predicates. If this expression is TRUE for any combination of two subquery rows, UNIQUE is FALSE; otherwise, it is TRUE. This implies that if any NULLs are present in a row, it is automatically UNIQUE.

The following examples show the rows that would be produced by the subquery rather than the subquery itself. This is not the proper syntax, but it enhances readability. The first predicate is TRUE, and the second is FALSE.

```
UNIQUE (3, 7, NULL
3, 7, NULL
3, 7, 9)

UNIQUE (3, 7, NULL
3, 7, 9
3, 7, 9)
```

The MATCH Predicate

```
match predicate ::=
row value constructor MATCH [UNIQUE]
[PARTIAL | FULL] table subquery
```

NOTE The syntax for row value constructors is shown under Row and Table Value Constructors, and that for table subqueries is shown in Subqueries.

MATCH checks to see whether the row value constructor matches any of the rows produced by the subquery. It differs from IN in that it enables you to specify ways of handling partial matches, which are matches between partially NULL rows. Such matches are ignored by IN or the equivalent = ANY. The comparability and collating sequence of the row value constructor (RC) and the rows produced by the subquery follow the rules outlined earlier in this entry under Comparison Predicates.

MATCH behaves differently depending on whether PARTIAL, FULL, or neither is specified. "Neither" is its own case; there is no default. If PARTIAL is specified, then:

- If RC is entirely NULL, then MATCH is TRUE.

- Otherwise, if UNIQUE is not specified, and there is at least one row from the subquery that contains all the corresponding non-NULL values of RC, then MATCH is TRUE.

- Otherwise, if UNIQUE is specified, and there is only one row from the subquery that matches the non-NULL values of RC as described above, then MATCH is TRUE.

- Otherwise, MATCH is FALSE.

In the following examples, we show the rows produced by the subquery rather than the subquery itself. This is not the proper syntax, but it enhances readability. The first of the following predicates is TRUE, and the second is FALSE:

```
(34, NULL, 99) MATCH UNIQUE PARTIAL
(34, 87, 96
34, 87, 99
NULL, 87, 96)
```

```
(34, NULL, 99) MATCH UNIQUE PARTIAL
(34, 45, 99
34, 87, 99
NULL, 87, 96)
```

FULL essentially follows the same principles, except that if RC is partially NULL, it won't match anything. Specified more formally, the rules are:

- If RC is entirely NULL, then MATCH is TRUE.

- Otherwise, if RC contains any NULLs, then MATCH is FALSE.

- Otherwise, if UNIQUE is not specified, and there is at least one row from the subquery that equals RC (as defined under Comparison Predicates), then MATCH is TRUE.

- Otherwise, if UNIQUE is specified, and there is only one row from the subquery that equals RC, then MATCH is TRUE.

- Otherwise, MATCH is FALSE.

The first of the following predicates is TRUE, and the second is FALSE:

```
(NULL, NULL, NULL) MATCH UNIQUE FULL
(NULL, 88, 99
34, 88, 99
34, 88, 99)
```

```
(34, 88, 99) MATCH UNIQUE FULL
(34, 88, 99
34, 99, 88
34, NULL, 88
34, 88, 99)
```

If neither PARTIAL nor FULL is specified, the rules are as follows:

- If RC is partially or entirely NULL, then MATCH is TRUE.

- Otherwise, if UNIQUE is not specified, and there is at least one row from the subquery that equals RC (as defined under Comparison Predicates), then MATCH is TRUE.

- Otherwise, if UNIQUE is specified, and there is only one row from the subquery that equals RC, MATCH is TRUE.

- Otherwise, MATCH is FALSE.

The first of the following predicates is TRUE, and the second is FALSE:

```
(34, NULL, 99) MATCH
(34, 87, 96
34, 87, 103
NULL, 87, 34)

(34, 88, 99) MATCH UNIQUE
(34, 88, 99
NULL, 88, 99
34, 99, 88
34, 88, 99)
```

 NOTE If you specify neither PARTIAL nor FULL, be careful of NULLs. If there are any NULLs in your row value constructor (RC), they will match anything. You can prevent this by using CASE expressions to convert the NULLs to something else, like zeros or blank strings.

The OVERLAPS Predicate

```
overlaps predicate ::=
row value constructor OVERLAPS row value constructor
```

NOTE The syntax for a row value constructor is shown under Row and Table Value Constructors.

OVERLAPS is a specialized predicate for determining whether time periods overlap each other. The row value constructors will each have two elements, and the first of each will be DATETIME values with the same group of fields (see Datatypes). The second element of each row value constructor may be either a DATETIME or an INTERVAL datatype, and they do not have to be the same. If the second element is a DATETIME, it must have the same group of fields as the first element. If it is an INTERVAL, the fields in the INTERVAL must be such that it can be added to the DATETIME first element. The two row value constructors specify two periods of time. The first element of each is one boundary date, and the second, if a DATETIME type, is the other boundary date or, if an INTERVAL, is added to the first element to derive the second boundary date. If the INTERVAL is negative, the second boundary date will fall before the first; likewise if the second DATETIME specified chronologically precedes the first. In either case, call the chronologically earlier of the two boundary dates the start date and the later of the two the termination date. The start and termination dates derived from the first row value constructor are S1 and T1; those derived from the second are S2 and T2.

If the first element of either list is NULL, the other boundary date, however derived, becomes the start date, and NULL becomes the termination date. Note that, if the first element of a list is NULL and the second an INTERVAL, the start and termination dates will both be NULL, and the result of OVERLAPS will be UNKNOWN. If the second element is NULL, the first element is the start date and the termination date again is NULL.

Using the values derived from the preceding paragraphs, the following expression (a single predicate) is evaluated:

```
( S1 > S2 AND NOT ( S1 >= T2 AND T1 >= T2 ) )
OR
( S2 > S1 AND NOT ( S2 >= T1 AND T2 >= T1 ) )
OR
( S1 = S2 AND ( T1 <> T2 OR T1 = T2 ) )
```

Although complex, the effect of this fits with the intuitive sense of overlapping periods of time.

In the first of the following examples, OVERLAPS is TRUE; in the second, it is FALSE; and in the third, it is UNKNOWN:

```
(DATETIME '2001-11', INTERVAL '0004-01')
OVERLAPS (DATETIME '2001-11', DATETIME '2001-02')
```

```
(DATETIME '2001-11', INTERVAL '-0004-01')
OVERLAPS (DATETIME '2001-11', DATETIME '2001-02')

(DATETIME NULL, INTERVAL '0004-01')
OVERLAPS (DATETIME '2001-11', DATETIME '2001-02')
```

Conformance Levels

Intermediate	Implementations at this level are not required to support MATCH. Nor are they required to support value expressions other than value specifications (literals, host variables, parameters, or user value functions) in an enumerated list of values for IN.
Entry	Implementations at this level are not required to support UNIQUE or OVERLAPS. They may require that, in LIKE predicates, MATCH values be column references rather than general value expressions and that patterns and escape characters be value specifications. They may refuse to accept row value constructors for IS NULL—only references to single columns.

See Also Part II: SELECT, UPDATE, DELETE, and CREATE TABLE. Part III: Aggregate Functions, CAST Expressions, Datatypes, Constraints, Subqueries.

Row and Table Value Constructors
Structures That Define Sets of Values to Be Used in Expressions

Syntax

```
constructor element ::=
{ value expression }
| NULL
| DEFAULT

row value constructor ::=
constructor element
```

```
| (constructor element.,..)
|   row subquery

table value constructor ::=
VALUES row value constructor.,..
```

Usage

Row value constructors are groups of one or more value expressions in the specified sequence and are comparable to table rows, to which they can be compared in many predicates (see Predicates). If the row value constructor is a single element, the parentheses can be omitted.

A table value constructor is a group of row value constructors corresponding to a set of rows. Table value constructors are comparable to tables, including those resulting from queries. For example, you can have a query and exclude rows with certain values by using the EXCEPT operator and putting the values you want to exclude in a table value constructor following EXCEPT (see SELECT in Part II).

Row value constructors obey the following principles:

• NULL or DEFAULT can be specified only if the row value constructor (RC) is contained in a query that is producing rows for an INSERT statement. For NULL, however, many implementations may choose to disregard this restriction and support the specification of NULL in contexts other than INSERT as an extension of the standard.

• If a subquery is used, it must be a row subquery (see Subqueries). In other words, an error is produced if the results of the subquery contain more than one row.

• If a subquery is used and produces no rows, the RC is entirely NULL.

The following is an example of a row value constructor:

```
(24, NULL, 'Demetrious')
```

For a table value constructor, all the row value constructors must have the same number of values (including NULLs) and must align vertically (speaking logically, not visually) in columns of comparable values, so that the first, second, third, and so on columns of each match. The following is an example of a table value constructor:

```
VALUES
(24, NULL, 'Demetrious'),
(98, 77, 'Lamark'),
( 0, 444, NULL)
```

Conformance Levels

Intermediate — Implementations at this level may restrict row value constructors to single elements, unless they are contained in table value constructors. Such implementations also may be limited to using the table value constructor as a query expression to produce values to be inserted into a table (see INSERT in Part II), and the table constructors themselves may be restricted to a single row, in the form of a list even if it contains a single element. Effectively, these caveats emulate the structures used in SQL89.

Entry — Implementations at this level may disallow the specification of DEFAULT in row value constructors.

SQL89 — Implementations at this level need not support row or table value constructors.

See Also Part II: INSERT, SELECT. Part III: Predicates, Subqueries.

String Value Functions
Functions That Operate On and Produce Strings

Syntax

```
string value function ::=
{
{SUBSTRING (character value expression
  | bit value expression
```

```
      FROM start position
      [ FOR string length ] ) }
   | { {UPPER | LOWER (character value expression) }
   | { CONVERT (character value expression
         USING form-of-use conversion name)  }
   | { TRANSLATE (character value expression
         USING translation name)  }
   | {  TRIM ([ [LEADING | TRAILING | BOTH]
         [character value expression]
          FROM character value expression)    }
   }
   [COLLATE FROM collation name]
   [ ||  {string value expression | string value function} ]
```

Usage

String value functions operate on strings and produce strings.
The strings may be of a CHARACTER datatype or, for concatena-
tion (||) and SUBSTRING, a BIT datatype. The various functions
are described in the following paragraphs.

SUBSTRING extracts a substring from the character or bit value
expression, starting at the position indicated in the FROM clause
and running for the number of positions indicated in the FOR
clause or to the end of the value expression, whichever comes
first. If the FOR clause is omitted, it runs to the end of the value
expression by default. A *position* here is one character or bit in the
value expression, as appropriate. If the value expression, starting
position, or length is NULL, the result of the function is also NULL.
If the starting position exceeds the length of the string or if the
string length is zero, the result is a zero-length string. The datatype of the SUBSTRING result is a varying-length character or BIT
STRING with a maximum length equal to the length (if fixed) or
maximum length (if varying) of the value expression from which
the substring was extracted. If the value expression is a character
string, the collating sequence and coercibility of the result are as
determined by Table III.2 (see Collations), with the value expression being the single operand.

UPPER | LOWER converts the string to all uppercase or all lower-
case, respectively. Either of these operations can be referred to as a
fold. The character set of the result is that of the string, and the collating sequence and coercibility follow Table III.2 (see Collations).

CONVERT changes the string's form-of-use, the specification for the encodings used to represent the character repertoire internally—for example, the number of bits per character. The form-of-use used must be defined for the character repertoire of the string being converted. The result will have the Implicit coercibility attribute, and its collating sequence will be the default for its character repertoire (see Collations).

TRANSLATE changes the character set of the string. This differs from changing the form-of-use in that the character repertoire—the set of characters as represented visually, rather than just internally—may be changed. The translation must have already been defined by the implementation or with a CREATE TRANSLATION statement. It will consist of some one-to-one or many-to-one mapping of character elements from two (not necessarily distinct) repertoires. The result is a varying-length character string with an implementation-defined maximum length and the character repertoire of the target character set of the translation. If the string being translated is NULL, the result of the expression is still NULL.

TRIM removes occurrences of the specified character from the beginning and/or end of the string. By default, it removes blank spaces from both ends of the string. You may specify any single character in the repertoire of the string instead of blank, and you may just TRIM the characters from the beginning (LEADING) or end (TRAILING) of the string. Specifying BOTH is equivalent to the default and so is used only for clarity. The character being removed must have a length of one (no multiple-character sequences), and if either it or the value expression being trimmed is NULL, the result of the function is also NULL. The collating sequence and coercibility of the result follow Table III.2 (see Collations); the value expression being trimmed is considered that table's monadic operand.

The COLLATE FROM clause, if specified, imposes a different collation on the result of the string value function. The coercibility attribute in this case is Explicit (see Collations).

Concatenate (||) takes two strings—either of which can be directly expressed as a literal, be taken or derived from a column value, or be the result of one of the other functions—and appends the second to the first. It can append characters to character strings or bits to BIT strings but may not mix the two, nor may it mix character

repertoires. The collating sequence and coercibility of the result
follow Table III.3. The two strings being concatenated are the
two operands. If either of the strings being concatenated is NULL,
the result of the concatenation also is NULL. If both of the strings
are fixed-length, the result of the concatenation is fixed-length;
otherwise, it is varying-length. If the result of the concatenation
is varying-length and exceeds the implementation-defined maximum length for varying-length strings, and it cannot be shortened
sufficiently by eliminating trailing blanks (for character strings) or
zeros (for BIT strings) to fall within this length, an error is produced.
If it is fixed-length and exceeds the implementation-defined maximum, an error is produced without truncation being attempted.

Conformance Levels

Intermediate   Implementations at this level may disallow
the use of a COLLATE FROM clause, the use of
BIT strings, and/or the use of UPPER|LOWER,
TRANSLATE, or CONVERT.

Entry   Implementations at this level may disallow
SUBSTRING, TRIM, or concatenate (||).

See Also   Part II: CREATE CHARACTER SET, CREATE COLLATION,
CREATE TRANSLATION. Part III: Collations, Value Expressions.

Subqueries
Queries Used to Produce Values for Processing within Other Statements

Usage

Queries are SELECT statements, which are statements that extract
or derive data from tables and views (see Part II: SELECT). Subqueries are queries that produce data that is not the final output
of the statement but will be further processed within the statement. Subqueries can be used in the predicates of other queries
or of DELETE or UPDATE statements and may be used as well in
the FROM clauses of queries, in row value constructors, or in
value expressions. Wherever used, they are enclosed in parentheses. The fact that subqueries can be used in the predicates of

queries means that they can also be used within other subqueries to any level of nesting. There are three types of subqueries:

- Subqueries that can produce any number of rows are called *table subqueries*.

- Subqueries that can produce no more than one row, but may contain any number of column values in that row, are called *row subqueries*.

- Subqueries that can produce no more than one value are called *scalar subqueries*.

Since each of these three types is a more restricted case of its predecessor, each may be used wherever its predecessors may; scalar may be used as row subqueries (provided a row with a single value is acceptable in context) and row as table subqueries. Scalar subqueries are used in comparison predicates that are not quantified (in other words, do not use ANY, ALL, or SOME; see Predicates) and, in SQL92, may be used anywhere value expressions may unless explicitly excluded. Row subqueries may be used in row value constructors, and table subqueries are used in FROM clauses (see SELECT in Part II) and in those predicates other than simple comparison predicates that use subqueries.

The syntax for all three kinds of subqueries is the same. Row subqueries are distinguished from table subqueries by the effect; the predicate of the row subquery, combined possibly with the use of DISTINCT in the SELECT clause, must ensure that no more than one row is returned or else an error will be produced by the statement containing the subquery. In general, a row subquery should test for a primary key or unique value or use aggregate functions without specifying a GROUP BY clause. A scalar subquery is distinguished from a row subquery by only having one output column specified in the SELECT clause. However, it must still satisfy the same criteria for producing but a single row. A subquery with only one output column but multiple rows is still defined as a table subquery.

Often, a subquery contained in a predicate may refer to a value from the table(s) being tested in that containing predicate. This is called an *outer reference* and a subquery that employs it is a *correlated subquery*. An outer reference may have different values for each candidate row being evaluated by the containing predicate; therefore, the subquery must be evaluated independently for each such value. This is normally the case with the EXISTS predicate (see Predicates) and is not uncommon with other types of predicates. The containing predicate may contain the subquery at any level of nesting. It is possible that the name of some column referenced in a subquery may be the same as the name of a column referenced in the containing query or in some outer query in which the containing query is itself a subquery. By default, a column name applies to the matching table with the most local scope—that is to say, the table referenced in the current query or in the first containing query encountered as one moves out in levels of nesting. If the column name can match more than one table with the same scope, in other words, at the same nesting level, the name is ambiguous and must be qualified with a table or correlation name prefix (correlation names are temporary names for tables used for clarifying ambiguities and for convenience; see SELECT in Part II). Such prefixes also can be used to override the default interpretation and specify that a column name is to match a table at some level of nesting farther "outside" than would otherwise apply.

Conformance Levels

Entry   At this level, subqueries may prohibit the use of UNION, INTERSECT, and EXCEPT, and subqueries used in comparison predicates may prohibit the use of the GROUP BY or HAVING clauses, either directly in the subquery or in any views referenced by the subquery at any level of nesting.

See Also   Part II: CREATE CURSOR, CREATE VIEW, DELETE, INSERT, SELECT, UPDATE. Part III: Predicates, Row and Table Value Constructors.

Value Expressions
Specify a Value to Be Used in a Statement

Usage

Value expressions are used in SQL statements to produce values of various types for output or for further processing by the statement.

Provided they conform to the principles outlined in this entry, they may be any combination of literals (values that represent themselves), column references, aggregate functions, numeric or string value functions, CAST expressions, CASE expressions, user value functions, scalar subqueries, host variables possibly appended with indicator variables (in Embedded SQL), parameters possibly appended with indicator parameters (in the module language), and dynamic parameters (in Dynamic SQL). Complete value expressions may also be used as elements of value expressions, in which case parentheses to force an order of evaluation may be necessary.

Value expressions have datatypes, and all of the datatypes used to construct them (except for indicator parameters or variables, hereafter called *indicators* in this entry) must be comparable, and all operations performed must be suitable for those types (see Datatypes). The various value expressions categorized by datatype are as follows:

- Numeric value expressions are constructed from combinations of values of EXACT NUMERIC and APPROXIMATE NUMERIC datatypes.

- Character value expressions are constructed from combinations of values of CHARACTER and/or NATIONAL CHARACTER datatypes.

- Bit value expressions are constructed from combinations of values of the BIT datatypes.

- Datetime value expressions are constructed from combinations of DATETIME datatypes or from combinations of DATETIME and INTERVAL datatypes.

- Interval value expressions are constructed from combinations of INTERVAL datatypes.

- User value functions such as CURRENT_USER or SESSION_USER (see Authorization IDs) also are value expressions.

The various types of value expressions are described in the following sections.

Numeric Value Expressions

In numeric expressions, the expression is evaluated as a series of numeric values and monadic or dyadic (one-operand or two-operand) operations performed in a specified or implied order. The monadic operands are monadic plus (+) and monadic minus (-). The latter changes the sign of the operand, while the former does nothing but is allowed by the syntax. The dyadic operators are addition (+), subtraction (-), multiplication (*), and division (/). The order of evaluation can be controlled by parentheses. In the absence of these, numeric value functions (such as POSITION; see Numeric Value Functions) are evaluated before operations like multiplication (*) and division (/), and these are performed before addition (+) and subtraction (-). Beyond that, evaluation is left to right. The following principles hold:

- If any of the operands is NULL, the result of the expression also is NULL.

- The result of any dyadic operation with two EXACT NUMERIC operands is EXACT NUMERIC. The result of any dyadic operation with at least one APPROXIMATE NUMERIC operand is APPROXIMATE NUMERIC. In either case, the precision is implementation-defined.

- If the result of an addition or subtraction is EXACT NUMERIC, the scale is that of the larger of the two operands.

- If the result of a multiplication is EXACT NUMERIC, the scale is the sum of the scales of the two operands.

- If the result of a division is EXACT NUMERIC, the scale is implementation-defined.

- If the result of an operation other than division is EXACT NUMERIC, and that result cannot be precisely represented in the precision and scale specified, a range error is produced.

- If the result of a division operation is EXACT NUMERIC, that value may be rounded or truncated, implementation-defined, to fit into the given precision and scale. If leading significant digits must be lost for it to fit, however, an error is produced.

- If the result of an operation is APPROXIMATE NUMERIC, the scale does not apply (see Datatypes).

- If the result of an operation is APPROXIMATE NUMERIC, the exponent must fall within the implementation-defined maximum range or a range error is produced.

Character and Bit Value Expressions

In CHARACTER types, the values expressed may be literal strings set off with single quotes (apostrophes), column values, or string value functions. If they are literals, they optionally may be preceded by an underscore (_) followed without intervening characters by the name of the character set. If this character-set specification is omitted, the default for the session will apply. All the values expressed must be drawn from the same character repertoire (not necessarily the same set). Different character repertoires can be mixed only if there is a defined translation to convert some of them to the repertoire of the others (see CREATE TRANSLATION in Part II).

The other string types are preceded by an uppercase letter that identifies the type. This letter precedes the left quote that begins the string and does not itself go in quotes. The letter is N for NATIONAL CHARACTER types, B for BIT strings represented in binary form, and X for BIT strings represented in hexadecimal form (see Datatypes).

If multiple strings are specified with one or more intervening separators, they will be concatenated.

Datetime Value Expressions

Datetime value expressions consist of values of type DATETIME (see Datatypes), optionally incremented or decremented by values of type INTERVAL. The DATETIME values may be represented by datetime value functions such as CURRENT_DATE (see Datetime Value Functions) or by column references or literals. When a literal is used, it must be preceded by the name of the DATETIME datatype (DATE, TIME, or TIMESTAMP), followed by a separator, and it must be delimited by single quotes ('). If an INTERVAL modifier is given, it may be preceded by a plus (+) or minus (–) sign. Since the interval is itself signed, either of these may result in an increment or decrement of the DATETIME value. Naturally, the INTERVAL and DATETIME values must match according to the rules described under Datatypes. If either the DATETIME or INTERVAL value is NULL, the result of the expression is NULL.

The DATETIME value optionally may append an AT TIME ZONE clause, which may specify either a time zone or the keyword LOCAL. LOCAL indicates the session default and is also the default if the TIME ZONE clause is omitted. The TIME ZONE, if specified, may take a variable or parameter as an argument but without an appended indicator (see Parameters and Variables later in this entry), which means in effect that it cannot be NULL (since NULLs in variables and parameters can exist only with the use of indicators). It may also take a literal but not a column reference.

INTERVAL Value Expressions

An INTERVAL value expression consists of an INTERVAL value possibly modified by the addition or subtraction of another comparable INTERVAL value (all year-month INTERVALS are comparable, as are all day-time INTERVALS; see Datatypes) or by being multiplied or divided by a number. The INTERVAL value may be derived by subtracting two comparable DATETIME values, in which case the pair of DATETIME values must be parenthesized to force the order of evaluation, and an interval qualifier must be appended to indicate the fields that the resulting INTERVAL value should contain. If any of the DATETIME or INTERVAL values is NULL, the result of the expression is also NULL. If the INTERVAL value is a literal (rather than, say, a column reference or a variable), it must be preceded by the keyword INTERVAL and a separator and delimited with single quotes ('). The interval arithmetic to produce the resulting INTERVAL value is performed according to the principles outlined under "The INTERVAL Type" in Datatypes.

User Value Functions

Value expressions may also be user value functions. These are special built-in SQL variables with the following meanings:

• CURRENT_USER (or simply USER) indicates the Authorization ID under whose privileges SQL statements are currently being evaluated.

• SESSION_USER indicates the Authorization ID associated with the current SQL session.

- SYSTEM_USER indicates the user name associated with this session by the operating system.

All three of these can have the same value or they all can be different. They are explained in greater detail under Authorization IDs.

Parameters and Variables

Finally, value expressions may be variables, parameters, or dynamic parameters. All of these are used to pass values back and forth between the DBMS and the application. Variables are used in Embedded SQL, parameters in the module language, and dynamic parameters in Dynamic SQL (see Appendices A, B, and C, respectively). Variables and non-dynamic parameters (for the remainder of this discussion, *parameters* will mean non-dynamic parameters unless otherwise indicated) are prefixed with a colon (:) and generally may have integer variables or parameters called *indicators* appended to them. The indicators are set negative to indicate a NULL value, in which case the value of the variable or parameter is undefined for the purposes of the host language and NULL for the purposes of SQL. A positive indicator value occurs if a CHARACTER or BIT string is too long to fit in the variable or parameter. In this case, the value is truncated, and the indicator is set to the number of characters or bits, as appropriate, that were in the string prior to truncation. If this number is too great to be expressed in the precision of the indicator, an error is produced. In the absence of a NULL or truncated value, the indicator is set to zero.

Dynamic parameters are represented with question marks and may not be appended by indicators. Dynamic parameters can be described by descriptor items in lists created with an ALLOCATE DESCRIPTOR statement (see ALLOCATE DESCRIPTOR in Part II and Descriptor Areas in this part); each item has a number of fields, one of which is INDICATOR. That field can be used in the same way as the appended indicators for variables and parameters. In any case, variables, parameters, and dynamic parameters may be used to pass values in either direction between the DBMS and the application.

Conformance Levels

Intermediate   At this level, implementations are not required to support character set or collation specifications for CHARACTER literals, BIT STRING literals of either variety (binary or hexadecimal), or fractional seconds beyond six digits.

Entry   At this level, implementations are not required to support NATIONAL CHARACTER, DATETIME, or INTERVAL type expressions or to support empty strings or automatic or specified concatenation. CASE and CAST expressions may be excluded, as may scalar subqueries, except when the latter are used in a row value constructor for a comparison predicate (see Predicates, Row and Table Value Constructors).

See Also   Part II: ALLOCATE DESCRIPTOR, CREATE TRANSLA-TION, DELETE, INSERT, SELECT, UPDATE. Part III: Authorization IDs, CASE Expressions, CAST Expressions, Datatypes, Datetime Value Functions, Descriptor Areas, Numeric Value Functions, Predicates, Row and Table Value Constructors, String Value Functions. Appendices A, B, and C.

Part IV

Chapter 1
SQL99: An Overview

- The Structure of the Standard and the Levels of Conformance

- New Types of Data

- Extensions to SQL Statements

- Programmatic Extensions to SQL

- A Quick Overview of Object-Oriented Concepts

- Integrating Objects into the Relational World

SQL99, formerly known as SQL3 (just as SQL92 was formerly known as SQL2), is a new standard, which was approved by the ISO and by ANSI in 1999. This standard greatly extends SQL beyond its previous capabilities. In this chapter, we will show you how the whole standard works and how the various pieces fit together. We will also explain some of its more important features in detail.

First, we will discuss the standard itself and explain the various parts and conformance levels. Then, we will provide an overview of the new functionality, starting with the new datatypes and continuing with the extensions to common SQL statements. Next, we will give an overview of the programmatic extensions to SQL that are part of SQL99. Finally, we will discuss the integration of relational and object-oriented approaches to data, which is one of the most important features of the new standard and the approach that SQL99 takes to this problem. This approach is based on user-defined structured datatypes, which include methods as well as data, and on tables that can function as object classes.

The Structure of the Standard and Conformance Levels

The SQL92 standard was structured into three levels of conformance (Entry, Intermediate, and Full) so that implementers could
conform to it gradually. As it turns out, most implementers have
gotten stuck at Entry level because they are primarily interested in
focusing on proprietary features. Hence, SQL99 takes a different
approach. It uses a Core functionality that is a prerequisite for
any sort of conformance. This is a superset of Entry SQL92, so
implementations can go directly from Entry SQL92 to Core
SQL99. Beyond that functionality are several types of enhanced
conformance. Implementations that support Core can also support any, all, or none of the enhanced levels. Core conformance
also requires that the DBMS support either Embedded SQL or
directly coded modules.

The standard itself consists of several documents, which correspond to logical subdivisions of the standard. The main purpose
of this arrangement is to offer some hope of taming this beast.
These document divisions do not correspond directly to the conformance levels, which are specified below. Rather, some of these
modules were completed and published independently before the
standard itself, but they have since been incorporated into the
standard. The versions of these modules in the standard supersede
previously published versions. Let's take a brief look at the parts of
the standard:

SQL Framework   Provides the logical concepts that under-
lie the other parts of the standard.

SQL Foundation   Builds on the material in Framework
and specifies, for the more fundamental parts of the standard,
the actual nuts and bolts of the language, rather than just the
conceptual apparatus. Both Framework and Foundation are
utilized by the other parts, though neither corresponds directly
to Core SQL. Core SQL is rather a subset of Foundation and,
as such, is directly based on the material in Framework.

SQL/CLI (Call-Level Interface)   Specifies a standard
API (Application Programming Interface) through which SQL
operations can be called. This interface is adapted from the

old SQL Access Group standard that also forms the basis for the ODBC (Open Database Connectivity) standard, which is currently widely used in the industry. Because of their common pedigree, SQL/CLI and ODBC are already mostly the same, and, if you know ODBC, you should be able to write to a SQL/CLI interface with only minor modification. The general consensus is that SQL/CLI and ODBC should and will converge rather than diverge as time goes on.

SQL/PSM (Persistent Stored Modules) Refers to procedural extensions to SQL that make it computationally complete and therefore suitable for the development of full applications. More commonly, these extensions will be used to create more sophisticated standard operations that can be invoked by any application that can access the database. For example, SQL/PSM can be used to support *triggers*, which are modules of code automatically executed in response to specified changes in the data. Some proprietary products already do this, such as Oracle's PL/SQL.

SQL/Bindings Specifies how SQL is to be bound to various host languages, excluding Java, which is dealt with separately. This section is relevant to Embedded and Dynamic SQL. Although neither of those are new features of the language, various new features, such as multimedia and user-defined datatypes, require extensions to the interface between SQL and the host languages.

SQL/MM (Multimedia) This extends SQL to deal intelligently with large, complex, and sometimes streaming items of data, such as video, audio, and spatial data (for use in Global Positioning Systems or Virtual Reality applications).

SQL/OLB (Object Language Bindings) Part 0 (as they call it) of the SQLJ specification for embedding SQL in Java. Strictly speaking, this is a distinct standard based on Entry-level SQL92 and developed parallel to SQL99.

These documents, however, generally do not correspond to the levels of SQL99 conformance that are defined. Those levels are defined in terms of "packages" of related SQL functionality that an implementation must support to claim a particular variety of enhanced conformance. The standard also allows itself extensibility by explicitly stating that other groupings of SQL99 features may emerge. We show the types of enhanced conformance that are defined in the SQL99 standard itself in Table 1.1.

TABLE 1.1: SQL99 Conformance Levels

Conformance Level	Basic Functionality
Core	This level is explained in detail in Part IV Chapter 2.
Enhanced Datetime Facilities	This level indicates full support for DATETIME datatypes, including the INTERVAL datatype and TIME ZONE specification. Most of this level was also part of Full SQL92 conformance and is covered under "Datatypes" in Part III.
Enhanced Integrity Management	This level indicates support for advanced referential integrity features, including:
	Assertions (See "CREATE ASSERTION" in Part II.)
	Referential triggered actions ("CREATE TABLE" in Part II.)
	Triggers (Explained in this chapter.)
	Subqueries in CHECK constraints (See "CREATE TABLE" in Part II.)
Active Database	This level indicates support for triggers (explained later in this chapter).
OLAP Facilities	This level indicates support for the use of advanced query and table features, including:
	Full Outer Joins ("SELECT" in Part II.)
	Row and Table Value Constructors (See "Row and Table Value Constructors" Part III.)
	INTERSECT operator ("SELECT" in Part II)
PSM (Persistent Stored Modules)	This level refers to extensions to SQL to make it computationally complete by providing control-flow and such things. In this case, there is a one-to-one correspondence between the section of the standard and the enhancement conformance level, so that the mapping of SQL parts to conformance levels is neither orthogonal nor consistently non-orthogonal. An implementation has PSM-enhanced conformance if it supports Core SQL and everything in the SQL/PSM document. Among the elements of this document are:

Continued on next page

TABLE 1.1: SQL99 Conformance Levels (continued)

Conformance Level	Basic Functionality
PSM (Persistent Stored Modules)	Stored procedures and functions, including variables and flow-control statements (Explained in this chapter.)
	Overloading of procedures and functions (Explained in this chapter.)
	Additions to the standard INFORMATION_ SCHEMA to cover the new functionality
CLI (Call-Level Interface)	This level indicates support for SQL/CLI.
Basic Object Support	This level indicates support for the first level of object relational integration, which includes:
	Overloading of SQL-invoked external routines (Invocation of external routines from SQL is part of Core.)
	User-defined datatypes (UDTs)
	Reference datatypes
	Typed tables
	Arrays, including arrays of reference types and of UDTs
	Most of these items are explained in this chapter.
Enhanced Object Support	This is the second level of object relational support. It includes all of Basic Object Support with additions such as:
	Writing your own constructors
	Multiple inheritance, which means that a UDT can have more than one superclass

New Types of Data

As you have seen in this book, SQL has a variety of datatypes that it traditionally supports, including:

- Fixed-length and varying-length CHARACTER strings

- INTEGER, DECIMAL, and FLOATing point numbers

- DATEs and TIMEs

- BINARY data

SQL99 adds several new creatures to the mix. These include:

LOBs (Large Objects)   These are actually special cases of datatypes that SQL had already supported, but the pre-SQL99 versions were of comparatively modest size. New datatypes were needed to deal with items of data that could be much larger than what SQL supported previously. LOBs come in two delicious flavors:

- BLOBs (Binary Large Objects): These are large items of data that, being binary, can be anything but are intended primarily for multimedia data, such as audio, video, and graphics.

- CLOBs (Character Large Objects): These are similar to BLOBs but specifically represent large bodies of text. CLOBs are intended for use in such things as text databases.

Reference   More commonly known in programming as *handles*, these are variables that give the location of a value rather than expressing it directly. This location is not necessarily anything as literal as a memory address. These locations have to be meaningful across networks. Hence, they are some kind of reference that the DBMS can interpret and extract the value of as required. The idea is twofold: to enable coded references to items unknown at coding time, which is one of the traditional uses of pointers in programming, and to enable references to large values as an alternative to direct representation of them, so that they need not be shipped over the network or loaded into memory until and unless needed.

Boolean   Boolean datatypes are now supported. These differ from single-bit BINARY data because they are SQL Booleans: they can be unknown, as well as true or false.

Rows   A row can now be treated as a datatype.

Tables   A table can be a datatype. This is primarily done to make tables more like classes, so that the relational model can better support the object-oriented paradigm. Such tables are called *typed tables* and are based on user-defined datatypes (UDTs). We cover both UDTs and typed tables later in this chapter.

Arrays (a.k.a. collections)   An array is an ordered list of elements, where each element is of the same basic type, such as a DATE or an INTEGER. They are standard in many programming languages but are new to standard SQL primarily because, again, they violate the first normal form. Arrays will largely be used for technical or geographical databases.

UDTs (User-defined datatypes)   Users can now define their own datatypes by subclassing the given types or by creating new structured types that behave like objects in the OO world. Along with defining the type, the user can specify functions that can be applied to the type or methods that are included in it. These functions and methods can be used in SQL statements and the values they return referenced in predicates. We cover this subject later in this chapter.

Extensions to SQL Statements

Several familiar SQL statements have been extended in SQL99. In some cases, these statements duplicate advanced features of SQL92 that generally have not been implemented and in other cases they do not. Among the most important of these new features are:

The use of queries as named objects in SELECT statements

The ability to pattern tables after other tables (the LIKE clause of CREATE TABLE)

The ability to subclass and superclass tables

Recursive queries   Recursion is a basic programming concept and is such a favorite conceptual toy of nerds that it has been applied even to acronyms (GNU's Not Unix, WINE Is Not an Emulator). Essentially, a recursive operation is one defined in terms of itself. Such an operation proceeds by invoking variations on itself until some, generally trivial, case is found that can be solved without invoking a variation. Once this case is solved, all the variations based upon it also can be solved. If you don't understand recursion, refer to any general programming textbook. Recursive queries are, logically enough, queries that invoke variations on themselves. They are used chiefly for expounding circular relationships.

Regular expressions in predicates   Regular expressions are another standard programming trick that is new to SQL. A regular expression is a concise way to specify complex string operations for searches and other comparisons. Conceptually, they are similar to the wildcards used in LIKE, but much more complex. SQL supports them with a new predicate called SIM-ILAR. To find out about regular expressions, search the Web or Linux/Unix documentation for "grep."

The DISTINCT FROM predicate   This, of course, is distinct from DISTINCT as used in the SELECT clause of queries. DISTINCT FROM, the predicate, is equivalent to <>, save that it applies to entire rows rather than single values.

Programmatic Extensions to SQL

SQL99 extends SQL with programmatic capabilities. Most of these extensions are part of SQL/PSM, but some of them are included in Core SQL or in SQL/OLB. Various portions of this functionality are required for the Core, PSM, and Basic Object Support conformance levels. The basic problems that the programmatic extensions are designed to address are as follows:

To make SQL computationally complete   This is a fancy way of saying that SQL will be usable as a stand-alone application language. It will no longer need to be combined with another language, as with Embedded and Dynamic SQL, to create a complete program. This functionality is part of SQL/PSM, and some of it is also used for Basic Object Support. The extensions to achieve this fall into the following categories:

- Flow control: This creates a flow of conditional execution from one SQL statement to another. In other words, IF statements, loops, and such things.

- Procedures and functions: Sequences of SQL statements created with flow control can be named and called. Such sequences can include variables that are meaningful only from within them, i.e.; they have a local scope.

To enable SQL to function as a data repository for object-oriented (OO) languages, particularly Java
The main problem here is that OO languages combine data (instance variables) with the operations upon it (methods) in objects. These objects are the basic structural foundation of OO languages, just as tables are the basic structural foundation of SQL. Hence, a fully functional *data* repository for an OO language is also a *method* repository, which means it includes executable code. This is a completely different paradigm than SQL was designed to support. This is perhaps the most important part of the standard, so we will cover it later in this chapter.

To make SQL extensible   Extensibility is supported by enabling SQL to invoke programs written in other languages, such as Java or C. The term for this is *SQL-invoked external routines*, and the statements that implement it are CALL and RETURN. This is one of the more advanced parts of Core SQL, which we cover in Part IV, Chapter 2.

To enable SQL to deal with UDTs intelligently   We cover UDTs later in this chapter.

To allow you to create database triggers   *Triggers* are pieces of code stored in the database that are automatically executed whenever specified operations or changes to the data occur. These triggers are called *database triggers* to distinguish them from *application triggers*, which generally have the same function but reside within applications. Database triggers are generally better than application triggers for several reasons, most fundamentally because the specified operation will be performed regardless of which application, or which interactive user, effects the change to the database. Many implementers already support database triggers as a proprietary feature, and application triggers are an older approach that has for the most part been supplanted by database triggers. The referential triggered actions can be considered a special kind of database trigger, though they do not use the SQL99 trigger syntax. Triggers are part of SQL Foundation.

Persistent Stored Modules (SQL/PSM)

SQL/PSM is both a section of the SQL99 standard and an enhanced conformance level of that standard. Not unlike Oracle's PL/SQL, it is a programmatic extension of the SQL language that makes it computationally complete and therefore usable for creating applications. You need not use it for complete applications, however. It is fine, and in fact intended, that you use it for procedures and functions that encapsulate a series of SQL statements, including flow-control and variables that are meaningful within the procedure or function. It also interacts well with some features of Basic Object Support. If you are familiar with traditional procedural programming languages, SQL/PSM will actually make SQL into a more familiar creature than it perhaps has been. However, SQL/PSM is simpler and more elegant than SQL combined with procedural languages because it is designed around such SQL peculiarities as three-valued logic (see Predicates in Part III) and because it uses SQL datatypes directly.

One area of Core SQL99 that complements SQL/PSM particularly well is the invocation of external routines. This refers to the ability to invoke subprograms written in another language from a SQL database. The same SQL statements, CALL and RETURN, are used for invoking SQL routines as are used for external routines.

Since SQL/PSM introduces sequentiality into SQL, we need to introduce a new concept, that of the *SQL statement sequence*. This concept simply refers to a set of SQL statements executed sequentially, rather like a program fragment. Now that SQL is procedural, such sequences become basic units of work.

Let's take a look at the basic features of SQL/PSM:

SQL/PSM includes several flow-control statements of types familiar from other languages. The formal names for these are SQL-control statements, and they are of the following types:

> **CASE**   This statement conditionally executes one of several SQL sequences, depending on whether two values are equal or one is a WHEN clause. It is conceptually similar to, but actually distinct from, the CASE expression from SQL92, which can be used as a value expression (see Case Expressions in Part III).

IF   The old standby; it executes a sequence if a predicate is true. It includes ELSEIF and ELSE.

WHILE   Another favorite; it tests a predicate and repeats a sequence over and over until that predicate is false or unknown.

REPEAT   A variation on WHILE; it executes the sequence, then tests the predicate. Exits when the predicate is true (not false and not unknown). REPEAT ensures that the sequence is executed at least once, which WHILE does not do.

LOOP   Repeats a statement sequence until explicitly told to exit or until an error occurs.

FOR   A SQL-oriented variant on the old workhorse; it executes a statement for each row of a table.

As we mentioned, SQL/PSM introduces procedures and functions into SQL. These are like procedures and functions in other languages. They are subprograms that take input and possibly output parameters. Functions additionally return a value directly and so are used in the place of value expressions in SQL statements (see Value Expressions in Part III). Methods, which are part of Basic Object Support, are not required for PSM conformance but, if supported, are implemented as a special kind of function. The statements you use to create these things are CREATE PROCEDURE and CREATE FUNCTION (and, possibly, CREATE METHOD). There are also corresponding ALTER and DROP statements for these objects.

Another new feature is error handlers. Previously, SQL supported status parameters, but the actual error handling had to be done in another language. Now, you can have SQL itself react to detected errors.

Finally, there are variables. These stay in scope for the duration of the procedure, method, or function within which they are contained or for the entire "module." (The meaning of this term if modules are not directly supported, which they usually aren't, is implementation-defined. However, it probably means the entire application for Embedded or Dynamic SQL or the entire session for Interactive SQL.) Variables are created with the DECLARE statement and given values with the SET statement. They can be of any standard SQL datatype or, if UDTs are supported, can be UDTs, including structured UDTs. We provide example of UDT variables later in this chapter.

A Quick Overview of Object-Oriented Concepts

If you do not have a background in object-oriented (OO) programming, some of the terms and concepts used to explain this portion of SQL99 are likely to be confusing to you. Therefore, we are going to digress a moment to introduce a few basic OO concepts. If you know this material already, please feel free to skip ahead to the next subsection.

In the OO world, both data and operations upon it are combined and modeled as *objects*. You can do everything that can be done with an object by executing a method on the object. Data can reside in an object, and, if you want to retrieve or change some data that resides in the object, you execute a method on the object. The most important difference between these methods and the functions and procedures used in more traditional programming languages is that the methods are executed *by* the object itself in whatever manner the object sees fit. A program executes a procedure; the program finds in memory or storage the data on which it is supposed to operate, and it performs its operation. A method is more like a message sent to the object, which would itself do the executing. This is called *encapsulation*.

Each object, then, consists fundamentally of two things: the methods that it executes and the data that it holds (the latter are called *instance variables*). Objects fall into classes, and each object of a given class will have the same set of methods and the same instance variables, though not necessarily the same values in those variables. To create an object of a given class, you execute a special kind of method on the class called a *constructor*. This creates a new object of the given class. This process is called *instantiation*, and the new object is an *instance* of the class. Now the term *instance variable* may make more sense. An instance variable is a variable that can have different values for each instance of the class; it varies with the instance. The methods remain the same for all instances of a given class.

Any of the methods in an object can invoke other methods on other objects, which is how the control flow of the program is created. A method is invoked on some object and begins a cascade. Of course, the execution of methods is itself conditional, so that OO programs are computationally complete.

A class can be *subclassed*. This means that a new class, called the *subclass*, is created with the old class, called the *superclass*, as a starting point. All of the methods and instance variables of the old class are initially passed to the new. The new class can do either or both of two things:

- It can supplement the instance variables and methods it inherited with new ones.

- It can *override* the methods it inherited. This means that it defines a new method with the same name as, but a different implementation than, one of the methods it inherited. Since instance variables can be accessed only through methods, this technique can also be used to effectively change which instance variables the subclass has.

This brings us to another key concept of the OO world: polymorphism. *Polymorphism* refers to the fact that the same method executed on different objects, or with different parameters or context, need not do the same thing, though it is good programming practice for there to be some conceptual similarity among the various versions of the method (otherwise, it would be more logical to use different methods). For example, in the material world, the verb "to open" has a different meaning for doors than for jars, though the two meanings are not unrelated. In the OO world, "open" would be a method that is executed differently for door objects than for jar objects. Although polymorphism often reflects a method that has been inherited from a superclass and overridden, it need not. Any two objects can use methods with like names and different implementations, but the similarity of names should reflect a conceptual similarity, just as variable names, though in principle arbitrary, should have intelligible meaning where practicable.

Last, we come to the concept of an *interface*, which comes from the Java language. An interface is basically a way of dealing with the fact that there is, in principle, no easy way of telling which methods an object implements. An interface is a group of methods. Any object that supports that interface will have implementations of those methods. The declarations of the object classes indicate which interfaces they support. Unfortunately, they do not, in Java, have to support the entire interface. A single method will do. So, this is hardly a foolproof way to know that a given object supports a given method.

This overview was quick and dirty, but we hope it was sufficient for you to understand what follows. For more information, see a good book on object-oriented programming or a decent text on an OO language like Java or Smalltalk.

Integrating Objects into the Relational World

This section covers the Basic Object Support enhanced conformance level—not to be confused with the Enhanced Object Support enhanced conformance level, though I bet it will be. (The multiple meanings of "enhanced" in the standard will do little to enhance clarity.) Although support for SQL/PSM is not required for implementations that want to support Basic Object, certain SQL/PSM features are also features of Basic Object: basically procedures, functions, and variables.

One of the least enviable tasks of SQL99 was the integration of two different views of the world: the relational one and the object-oriented one. These two horses not only pull in different directions, but they are attached to different carts. Specifically, a key concept of the object-oriented world is *encapsulation*. Everything is an object, but each object is a "black box;" the contents of the object are invisible from outside. Likewise, data and the operations performed on it are both stuffed in that same black box.

Relational systems, on the other hand, do not marry data to the operations upon it and keep both the data and the operations visible, subject to security constraints. All data is stored in tables, and the same operations (the set of valid SQL statements) can be performed on all of it, provided the proper privileges are in place. Even though SQL does divide its data into "objects" called tables, these are hardly black boxes. Not only are the contents of the tables made visible by operations that have nothing to do with the tables per se, but the contents can be mixed from different tables in a completely ad-hoc fashion through the use of joins, subqueries, UNIONs, and similar operations.

One of the strengths of the object-oriented approach is flexibility: each object is its own little world with its own little rules. The relational model, however, makes a virtue of universality: all data is combinatorial fodder for the same relatively simple set of operations.

The fact of the matter is, though, that the relational data model has come to dominate the database field, while the object-oriented approach is becoming more and more important in programming, particularly in C++ and Java. Awkward or not, there are simply too many practical advantages to be gained by gluing an object head onto the relational body. Furthermore, the fact that the two approaches have contrary virtues does mean that a coherent combination of them can be very powerful. It could combine the diversity of the object approach with SQL's ability to efficiently pose general questions about the data regardless of which "object" holds it, which is hard to do in a purely object-oriented system. This, then, is one of the most onerous and valuable tasks to which the SQL99 committee set itself.

The approach that emerged has the following features:

- Users can define their own datatypes (UDTs). These datatypes can behave as objects in the OO sense. A UDT contains data fields (which would be called *instance variables* in the OO world) and methods. Certain basic methods are created automatically.

- A table can also be defined as a datatype. In fact, you do so by basing tables on UDTs. The main purpose of this is so that tables can be subclassed and hence behave more like objects.

- Methods are implemented as a special kind of function that is associated with an object.

- SQL procedures and functions can be *overloaded*. This means that there can be more than one version of the same routine, having the same name but different parameters.

- References and arrays, as described earlier, are part of Basic Object Functionality. This includes arrays of UDTs or of references and references to arrays or UDTs.

You create UDTs with the CREATE TYPE statement. UDTs fall into the following two categories:

Distinct UDTs   These are extensions of datatypes somewhat similar to SQL92 domains (see CREATE DOMAIN in Part II). A distinct UDT is based on a standard datatype. It cannot be a subclass or a superclass, and it cannot be instantiated. It does, however, have automatically generated constructor, mutator, and observer methods, all of which we explain later in this section.

Structured UDTs   These are similar to and are intended to emulate classes in the OO world.

UDTs work as follows:

- A UDT has one or more attributes. If it has more than one, it is a structured datatype; otherwise it is distinct. Strictly speaking, the term "attributes" does not apply to distinct types, but it is simpler for this discussion to speak as though it does. In any case, it is a somewhat unfortunate choice of term, because "attribute" is a more formal name for "column" in relational database theory, and the attributes of UDTs do not map to it precisely, save when UDTs are used as typed tables (explained below).

- Distinct types are considerably simpler than structured ones and do not serve quite the same purpose. They function as refinements of datatypes but do not support most of the functionality of objects. Most of the rest of this discussion applies to structured UDTs, which are more complex and interesting. A distinct UDT has these characteristics:

  - It is based on some standard datatype.

- It can neither be a subclass nor be subclassed (it is always FINAL).

- It cannot be instantiated.

- For structured UDTs, attributes correspond to instance variables.

- For structured UDTs, a declaration of whether the UDT is instantiable is included in the definition. If it is not, it cannot be directly instantiated. In that case, you must create subclasses of the UDT and instantiate those. This is a common OO feature known as an *abstract superclass*. The idea is that the abstract superclass provides a general definition for a category of objects, all of which will require more elaboration. Again, distinct UDTs are not instantiable by definition.

- An object contains a group of methods. If the datatype is instantiable, one constructor method is created automatically and named for the datatype. Other method types are mutator and observer. One of each of these is created automatically for each attribute. The observer is used to read the attribute value, and the mutator is used to change it. You can also explicitly place methods in classes, which can be implemented with SQL-invoked external routines (part of Core) or with SQL procedures and functions.

- Optionally, it is used as a superclass. This is a type from which the UDT is subclassed. This feature, of course, is provided to support inheritance. A UDT with no superclass is a *maximal superclass*; one with no subclasses is a *leaf class*. A UDT that cannot have subclasses is *final*; other ones are *not final*. The differences between a leaf class and a final class are twofold: a leaf class may just happen not to have subclasses at the moment, whereas a final class cannot have subclasses, and a leaf class does have a superclass, since it is part of a class hierarchy. A final class may simply be a class that is not involved in an inheritance hierarchy, and, in fact, all distinct types fall into this category. Multiple inheritance, which would complexify this simple tree structure, is a feature of Enhanced (rather than Basic) Object Support. Syntactically, subclasses are defined with an UNDER clause and require a new privilege that exists on UDTs, which is also called UNDER. A subclass inherits the attributes and methods of the superclass, which it may supplement and/or override.

- A distinct UDT can be used in a column. A structured UDT can be used in a column *or* be used as a table, with each attribute of the UDT becoming a column of the table. Tables generated from UDTs in this manner are called *typed tables* and have some special features that they inherit from the UDTs. For example, such tables can be subclassed. We explain this concept in greater detail later in this chapter.

NOTE For the sake of those of you who are familiar with object-oriented programming, we have adopted the standard terms "subclass" and "superclass" for UDTs. However, the SQL99 standard actually uses "subtype" and "supertype."

Creating Your Own Datatypes

A UDT is a database object and therefore resides in a schema like a table, collation, or view. To create a UDT, you use the CREATE TYPE statement; to destroy one, you use DROP TYPE. There is also an ALTER TYPE statement. Here is an example of CREATE TYPE:

```
CREATE TYPE persons AS
    fname          VARCHAR(20),
    lname          VARCHAR(20),
    address        VARCHAR(20),
    picture        BINARY
NOT INSTANTIABLE
NOT FINAL;
```

Since it has several attributes, this is a structured UDT. The reason we did not make this type final is that we intend to use it as a superclass; the reason we did not make it instantiable is that we intend to use it as an *abstract* superclass. We ended up creating Persons as a superclass of Students and Teachers, because some aspects of those two entities are common to both, and because both are logically subclasses of Persons. However, any person entered into that schema should not simply be a person; they should fall into a more specific role such as student or teacher. Persons is a class that should be instantiated only through its

subclasses. Hence, it is logical to make Persons an abstract superclass with Students and Teachers as subclasses.

Here, then, is how you would create a Students subclass of
Persons:

```
CREATE TYPE Students UNDER Persons AS
        gradelevel      INTEGER
        INSTANTIABLE
        NOT FINAL;
```

Now, we have an instantiable class. Note that we did not have
to list the fname, lname, etc. again, because they are inherited
from the superclass. If these were modified in the superclass, the
changes would automatically be reflected here as well.

To instantiate this class, then, we would use the constructor
method that is automatically created for us. Here is an example:

```
DECLARE stud1 student;
SET stud1 = student();
```

This statement makes use of the partial procedural feature set that
is a part of Basic Object Support (BOS), specifically the use of variables, which, under BOS, can be of UDT datatypes. The DECLARE
statement creates a variable to hold our new instance. The constructor for the UDT student is student(). Therefore, the SET statement
creates a new student object and stores it in the stud1 variable. We
could set the values in this object by using built-in mutator methods named for the attributes they affect. To wit:

```
SET stud1 = student.fname('Gerry');
SET stud1 = student.lname('Dustbin');
```

We are setting further components of the stud1 object. The mutators are student.fname() and student.lname(). Notice that we are
not setting a value in anything called "student," although the syntax
may give that appearance. The values are not part of the class "student," but of the instance, in this case, stud1. The term "student" is
simply telling in which UDT the fname and lname mutators are
located, just as schema names can prefix table names to indicate the
schema in which the table resides. Mutator methods are very simple:
they take a value expression and store it in the appropriate attribute.
Keep in mind that stud1 is currently working storage. To put this

information into the database, we would have to use an INSERT statement, like this:

```
INSERT INTO Studentlist
    VALUES(stud1.fname, stud1.lname);
```

Of course, we haven't seen that Studentlist table before. Did we just CREATE it as we normally would? We could do so, of course, but we could also base the table directly on the student UDT. We show how to do this in the next section.

Before we get into that, however, we should show you how to retrieve values from attributes. Just as a UDT automatically has a mutator to set the value of each attribute, it automatically has an observer method to retrieve that value. Like the mutator, the observer automatically takes the name of the attribute on which it works. How does the DBMS tell the difference between a mutator and an observer based on a given attribute? By looking at how the method is used, the DBMS can determine whether a value is being set or retrieved. Here is an example:

```
SELECT stud1.fname(), stud1.lname()
    FROM Studentlist;
```

The methods here are obviously observers simply because they fall in the SELECT clause of a query. The parentheses are part of the syntax requirements for methods.

Using UDTs as Tables (Typed Tables)

One of the interesting peculiarities of structured UDTs is that they can function either as column values or as entire tables. In the former case, they violate the first normal form, which will make them many enemies among relational purists. In any case, mapping UDTs to tables is a bit more logical, especially considering how both tables and classes can map to entities in the ER model, which is how we have been approaching it. When you make a table of a UDT, the following things happen:

- Each attribute becomes a column. This is logical because "attribute" is a more formal term for "column" in relational theory and because the two concepts are related. An attribute of a table or of a UDT is an atomic value that it stores. Nonetheless, UDT attributes are still peculiar from a relational viewpoint.

- Each row of the table corresponds to an instance of the UDT. Hence, the table is essentially the class, and the rows are the objects. This maps neatly to the ER model, where the entities represent logical classes that are instantiated.

- The object aspects of the UDT are retained, even though they do not fit into conventional SQL tables. That is to say:

  - The automatically defined constructor, mutator, and observer methods of the UDT become associated with the table and can still be executed upon it.

  - Any methods you specified directly as part of the UDT are also retained. Such methods are created as schema objects, just as procedures and functions are (in fact, in SQL99 methods are regarded as a special kind of function, though this is not necessarily the case in OO programming generally), but they are associated with UDTs.

The syntax to CREATE a typed table is rather simple:

```
CREATE TABLE Studentlist
    OF students;
```

This statement CREATEs the Studentlist table as described. You can also CREATE typed tables as subclasses of other typed tables. When you do so, each row of the subclass is also a row of the superclass, which is consistent with how subclasses work in the ER model.

Summary

In this chapter, we have quickly gone over the big picture of SQL99 and offered more detailed coverage of a couple of its more important features, particularly Persistent Stored Modules (PSM) and user-defined datatypes (UDTs). These two items extend SQL into the two prevailing programming paradigms in the world today: procedural and object-oriented, respectively. We have given you some idea of the conceptual and practical difficulties inherent in this, especially in the case of the object-oriented (OO) material. We have also provided a quick and dirty introduction to OO concepts, in case this material was new to you.

Chapter 2
Core SQL99

Core SQL99 is that portion of the SQL99 standard that is intended to act as a basis for the rest of it. Implementations claiming any sort of SQL99 conformance must support Core SQL99 and may optionally support one of the enhanced conformance levels outlined in the previous chapter. For the sake of brevity, in this chapter we will generally refer to Core SQL99 simply as "Core." This chapter will show you how to use Core, which will apply to any SQL99 system.

What Is Core?

For the most part, Core consists of modest extensions to Entry SQL92, many of which were part of the more advanced portions of SQL92 anyway. However, it does move SQL into some new areas for supporting the enhanced levels as well. The major new areas of functionality in Core are as follows:

LOBs (Large Objects) These are very large data items, either binary or text string.

External SQL-invoked routines These are procedures or functions in other languages that can be directly called from SQL, greatly extending the functionality of the DBMS.

Distinct datatypes These are the simpler of the two types of user-defined datatypes (UDTs). They are atomic and are basically specializations of existing datatypes.

We'll expand each of these areas in the following sections.

LOBs

As we explained in the previous chapter, LOBs come in two flavors: binary (Binary Large Objects, or BLOBs) and character text string (Character Large Objects, or CLOBs). Both of these types address how to deal with data items that are too large to practically manipulate in the same way as the data items with which databases traditionally work. In both cases, the solution is to treat such obese data items as values in columns like you would other SQL data items but to implement them differently.

BLOBs and CLOBs are quite similar in how they work, but the intended uses are different. BLOBs are intended chiefly for what has come to be called *multimedia*—graphics, audio, video, and the like. They are also useful in many scientific and engineering applications. CLOBs are basically intended for dealing with large bodies of text, such as Web pages, rather than the simple text values for which relational databases were designed.

Never use a LOB as a primary key because it would be far too inefficient. Create some short number instead.

Locators

One of the key differences between LOBs and other datatypes is the use of objects called *locators* that access LOBs by reference. This means that whenever you pass a LOB through a parameter or variable of Embedded SQL, Dynamic SQL, the module language, or a SQL-invoked routine (explained later in this chapter), you can use a four-byte integer to retrieve the LOB later, when and where you actually need to use it, rather than retrieving the value directly whenever referenced. Locators are handy for the following reasons:

- Not all languages can handle LOBs stored directly in variables.

- Most often, the DBMS is on a different machine than the application that accesses it. Sending LOBs across the network can bog down everyone using the network, so it is not something to do until and unless it is necessary.

- Even if they are on the same machine, the DBMS generally has one area of allocated working memory, the application another, and the output (say a page dynamically generated and sent through a Web server) possibly a third. This could lead to the same gargantuan LOB being replicated in memory more than once.

Locators deal with these problems by passing to the host language references to the LOBs, rather than passing the LOBs themselves. A locator is a variable in the host language that the DBMS knows to treat differently than other variables. Specifically, it stores a four-byte integer in the variable that acts as a unique identifier for the LOB the locator represents. Hence, a locator is a sort of pointer, but with some rather nifty features that make it easier to use than pointers in most languages. Locators have the following features:

- Locators operate transparently. You need not perform some special operation to go from the pointer to the value it indicates. The application determines based on the context whether it needs the actual value or merely a reference to it and behaves accordingly.

- Locators are typed to match the datatypes to which they point. There are BLOB locators, CLOB locators, and NCLOB (national language support CLOB) locators, as well as UDT and array locators, for products that support those advanced SQL99 features (not part of Core).

- Locators are declared in host programs like other variables but are followed by the keywords AS LOCATOR. They are of the datatype that corresponds to SQL INTEGER or EXACT NUMERIC.

- Locators are valid until the end of the transaction. These are *non-holdable* locators. SQL99 also specifies *holdable* locators that can remain valid throughout a session, but these are not part of Core.

- Locators are not valid across sessions, so there is no point in storing them.

Here is an example of a locator declaration. This declaration, of course, goes in the code of the host language, in this case Pascal:

```
var
EXEC SQL BEGIN SQL DECLARE SECTION;
picture_handle: integer AS LOCATOR;
EXEC SQL END SQL DECLARE SECTION;
```

Now that `picture_handle` exists, you can use it to represent a LOB. Let's suppose we have added a snapshot column to the Salespeople table that contains a digitized photograph of each employee. We could do the following:

```
EXEC SQL SELECT snapshot
     INTO :picture_handle
     FROM Salespeople
     WHERE snum = 1003;
```

The locator `picture_handle` now contains a number that will be used to retrieve the actual value of the snapshot for salesperson 1003 when the time comes. How precisely this is achieved is an implementation-defined matter. When `picture_handle` has such a value, it is considered *valid*. When it does not, it is *invalid*. All locators automatically become invalid at the end of the current transaction.

NOTE There are three functions in SQL/CLI that are designed for use with locators: SQLGetLength(), SQLGETPOSITION(), and, SQLGETSUBSTRING(). Since SQL/CLI is not part of Core, we will not discuss it in this chapter. We will mention, however, that these three functions, unlike the bulk of SQL/CLI, are not included in ODBC because the latter is not designed with locators in mind.

Using BLOBs

As we mentioned, BLOBs are simply binary data items that can be quite large and can be referenced by locators. BLOBs can be anything, but they will probably be used primarily for large, complex items of data such as graphics, video, and audio—in other words, those datatypes commonly called *multimedia* in the software world. In the SQL99 standard, BLOBs are formally called Binary Large Objects or Binary Strings. Binary Strings are distinct from Bit Strings. The latter term refers to the datatype Bit. Bit Strings are not required to be extraordinarily large as BLOBS are, and there is nothing unconventional in how they are handled. They are part of SQL92 and are appropriate for smaller binary data items.

Whenever you need to refer to a BLOB or other binary data, you do it in hexadecimal (hex) notation. As you may know, hex is a base 16 number system that is used as a more concise way to express binary numbers. There are 16 possible values for each digit, which is the same number of values that four bits can express. Therefore, each hex digit represents four bits. The 16 digits are the numbers 0-9 and the letters a-f. Further information on hex is beyond the scope of this book; see any standard programming text if you need more information. You write hex numbers in SQL as shown here:

```
X 'aa9073f9c79bbe900'
```

This is a hex literal. The uppercase X is necessary to denote that what follows is hex rather than conventional text characters, which, of course, are also enclosed in single quotes. You can also break hex literals across lines, like this:

```
X 'aa9073f9c79bbe900'
  '89e9a6cc45d7d990dca257a'
```

The DBMS automatically concatenates both of these lines into a single hex number. The separate lines are independently bracketed in single quotes, but only the first takes an X argument. The separator between the two parts of the number has to be a newline, rather than just a body of white space, even though, for most other purposes, newlines are simply equivalent to any other white space.

Here is the text to add a snapshot column to the Salespeople table:

```
ALTER TABLE
    ADD COLUMN snapshot BLOB(500K);
```

or

```
ALTER TABLE
    ADD COLUMN snapshot BINARY LARGE OBJECT(500K);
```

This is much the same as adding any other type of column: BLOB (or BINARY LARGE OBJECT) is the datatype and 500K is the length. Although strictly speaking an implementation matter, the length will probably be the maximum rather than the allocated length. If a given snapshot is only 200K, the value won't be padded to 500K. Length functions differently in the VARCHAR datatype than in the CHAR datatype, for example. Length can either be in bytes (the default), kilobytes (expressed as K), megabytes (expressed as M), or gigabytes (expressed as G). (Contrary to the popular misconception, K, M, and G do not correspond to a thousand, a million, and a billion bytes, respectively, because these are not round numbers in the binary world. Rather, they indicate 1,024, 1,048,576, and 1,073,741,824 bytes, respectively, because these numbers are even powers of two.) If the length is omitted, some implementation-defined default will apply.

The operations you can perform on BLOBs are somewhat restricted. Many of the operations you would use for other datatypes are simply not meaningful. For example, BLOBs are not sortable. It makes no sense to say that one BLOB is less than another. Therefore, the only comparison operators you can apply to BLOBs are = and <>. To be =, two BLOBs must be the exact same length; if one is zero-padded and the other is not, the two are not equal. This is because a large set of zeros could well be meaningful in a BLOB in most raster (pixel map) graphics formats; it would indicate a field of black so it cannot be assumed to be padding. Keep this in mind if you write any code that manipulates BLOB data directly.

BLOBs can use the concatenation and substring operators that have been available for strings since SQL92. We describe these operators in Part III under String Value Functions. You can also use a function called LENGTH to determine the size of a BLOB. You will do this frequently while working with a BLOB as a locator so that you know how much data you will be dealing with before you actually retrieve it.

These additional principles apply to BLOBs:

- They cannot be produced by CASE expressions. This functionality is supported at the Extended LOB Support level but not at Core. For more information on this topic, see Case Expressions in Part III.

- They can use most of the functionality of character strings; for example, most string value functions apply, as does the LIKE predicate. Not all of this is required for Core, however.

- They cannot be cast to or from other datatypes with CAST expressions (see Cast Expressions in Part III).

- If any of a group of concatenated BLOBs is NULL, the resulting BLOB is NULL.

Using CLOBs and NCLOBs

There are actually two kinds of CLOBs: CLOBs and NCLOBs. The latter are national language support (NLS) CLOBs. The difference between CLOBs and NCLOBs is precisely the same as that between the CHAR and NCHAR datatypes.

CLOBs are intended primarily for large bodies of text. Picture an online library. What would a data item for such a library be? A page? A book? Clearly not a word. A body of text is something you need to treat as a whole while also being able to independently treat its parts if desired. Even a Boolean search of the sort that Web search engines provide would be complicated and extremely inefficient to implement with LIKE. Hence, large bodies of text form a new category of single items—those that also have components that need to be independently treated. CLOBs also may have uses beyond these relatively obvious ones. For example, VRML (Virtual Reality Modeling Language) is ASCII-based, and VRML components could be treated as CLOBs. Likewise, many potential scientific and technical applications use forms of data that can be expressed as CLOBs. Because it is difficult to generalize about what CLOBs may be used for or how they will be structured, there is little direct functionality in Core for directly manipulating the internals of CLOBs. That will have to be left to the implementation, the application, the user, or to the external routines described elsewhere in this chapter.

For the most part, the rules concerning CLOBs are the same as those for BLOBs, described in the previous section. The main differences are as follows:

• Unlike BLOBs, CLOBs are sortable. You can compare them in terms of inequalities, such as < or > =. In fact, like other text datatypes, CLOBs have collations and can have translations. For more information on these items, see Collations in Part III.

• Datatypes other than BLOBs can be cast as CLOBs, although CLOBs cannot be cast as other datatypes. Other datatypes can be cast neither to nor from BLOBs. For more on datatype casting, see Cast Expressions in Part III.

• CLOBs are a special kind of text datatype, and therefore the special attributes and functions associated with text datatypes are available. For example, CLOBs have character sets and collations and can have translations. You can use string value functions on them.

Let's suppose we wanted to keep our salespeople's resumes in the Salespeople table. Here some variations on the statement to add the resume column:

```
ALTER TABLE Salespeople ADD COLUMN resume CLOB(20K);
ALTER TABLE Salespeople ADD COLUMN resume NCLOB(20K);
ALTER TABLE Salespeople
     ADD COLUMN resume CHARACTER LARGE OBJECT(20K);
ALTER TABLE Salespeople
     ADD COLUMN resume NATIONAL CHARACTER LARGE
OBJECT(20K);
```

The national character versions, of course, will have a different character set.

External SQL-Invoked Routines

Another of the important Core SQL extensions is the ability to
invoke from SQL routines written in other languages, such as C,
Java, Perl, and so on. Core SQL provides a way for you to do this
by specifying routines as SQL objects that are essentially wrappers
for routines written in another language. The wrapper provides an
interface from SQL to the other language, so that the routine can
operate as part of SQL despite the fact that it is not written that
way. The specification provided in the standard for this is necessarily somewhat incomplete because platform- and language-specific issues inevitably come into play. Since the DBMS cannot itself
execute these external routines, it must pass execution elsewhere
to do so. Also, these routines will not be stored as data in the DBMS,
so there must be some way to specify where they are, such as in a
shared (or dynamic linked) library. These are implementation-
defined matters.

Nonetheless, Core SQL is relatively sophisticated in the support
it does provide. In part, this is because the syntax for creating and
invoking external routines is the same as that for SQL procedures
and functions. However, the latter are not part of Core but are
instead part of the Persistent Stored Modules (PSM) enhanced conformance level. Other than the actual content of the procedure or
function, the syntax for creating and executing SQL and external
routines is mostly the same.

External routines can be functions, procedures, or methods.
Methods are considered a special case of functions and are only
relevant if the DBMS supports abstract UDTs, which are not part
of Core (for more on abstract UDTs, see Part IV, Chapter 1). The
difference between functions and procedures is the standard one
in programming: functions return a value and are therefore used
as value expressions, whereas procedures simply do something
and are therefore used as statements. Procedures can also return
one or more values through output parameters but not directly
as functions do. Methods are functions whose return value is an
object (a structured UDT).

External routines are objects in a schema, just like tables and
views. The actual code will generally reside elsewhere (strictly

speaking, this is an implementation matter), but the wrapper will
be a database object. There are a number of corollaries to this fact:

- You can create, alter, and drop SQL-invoked routines, using
  the CREATE, ALTER, and DROP PROCEDURE or FUNCTION
  statements, respectively, and the DROP ROUTINE statement,
  which drops either a procedure or a function.

- The use of a routine is controlled by an EXECUTE privilege on
  the routine. You automatically have the EXECUTE privilege
  on any routines you create and can GRANT it to and REVOKE
  it from others at will.

- Routines can be created as part of a CREATE SCHEMA statement but only if they are to be part of the schema being created (for more on CREATE SCHEMA, see CREATE SCHEMA
  in Part II).

- A function can take only input parameters. A procedure can
  take input (IN), output (OUT), or combination (INOUT) parameters. Therefore, a function can produce only one value, the
  return value, while a procedure can produce as many as you
  like, one for each output or INOUT parameter. Actually, one of
  the input parameters to the function can be an INOUT parameter, in which case its final value will be the return value of the
  function. This enables you to have the effect of functions for
  routines written in languages that do not support them directly.

- The return values for functions and the parameter values for
  functions and procedures are SQL datatypes. Conversion to
  the host-language datatypes is handled just as it is for Embedded SQL (see Appendix A).

- The standard gotchas from Embedded SQL apply. Specifically,
  this means you can either use or not use indicator variables to
  indicate NULLs or string truncation. This is a parameter to the
  CREATE statement, as we shall see.

- If you are using LOBs, you can have the routine return locators.

- The host languages you can use are implementation-defined.
  The standard supports all of those supported for Embedded
  SQL. Java, as specified in SQLJ, will be a common extension,
  as perhaps will be Perl.

- You can use Embedded SQL statements in the external routine, but that complicates matters a lot because you then have to connect to a database from the external routine, which will be independent of the database connection from which you are calling the routine. Doing so is asking for trouble and usually will not achieve anything you could not achieve another way.

So now let's look at some examples of all this in action. First, here is the syntax of the CREATE PROCEDURE and CREATE FUNCTION statements as these are implemented in Core SQL. We omit portions of the syntax relevant only to non-Core features or to external routines that contain SQL:

```
{CREATE PROCEDURE} | {CREATE FUNCTION} routine_name
    ([parameter_declaration.,..])
    [RETURNS datatype [CAST FROM datatype [AS LOCATOR]]
    LANGUAGE language_specification
    [PARAMETER STYLE {SQL | GENERAL}]
    [DETERMINISTIC | NOT DETERMINISTIC]
    [{RETURN NULL ON NULL INPUT} | {CALL ON NULL INPUT}]
    EXTERNAL [NAME external_routine_name]
    [PARAMETER STYLE {SQL | GENERAL}];
parameter_declaration ::=
    [ IN | OUT | INOUT ]
    [ SQL_parameter_name ]
    datatype [AS LOCATOR]
```

The following sections explain the components of the above statements.

Routine Name

The routine_name is a SQL identifier. Since Core does not require support for overloading (having multiple routines with the same name), it may have to be unique for all routines within the schema. Otherwise, the semantics of overloading will be implementation-defined (for Core, though not for more advanced levels of conformance).

Parameter List

Next comes a comma-separated list of parameters. As the syntax diagram above shows, the list must be present, but it may be empty, which is expressed as an empty pair of parentheses.

Each parameter has a mode, either IN, OUT, or INOUT. The mode indicates whether parameter is to pass a value to the routine (IN), receive a value from it (OUT), or both (INOUT). The mode applies only to procedures; the mode of all parameters to functions is IN. For procedures, it is optional for each parameter and the default for any parameters not specified is IN. We mentioned earlier that a function could take an INOUT parameter. This is true, but you do not declare the INOUT parameter as such. Rather, you set one (and only one) of the parameters in the function in the body and that value becomes the INOUT parameter and the RETURN value of the function. Naturally, the datatype of that parameter must either be the same as the datatype the function returns, as specified by the RETURNS clause, or be CAST to that datatype in the RETURNS clause.

The *SQL_parameter_name* is an optional name that you can use to refer to the parameter within the routine. The reason the name is optional is that parameters are matched to references in the routine on the basis of the order in which they occur. The first parameter in the list gets assigned to the first target available, the second to the second, and so on. The name is merely a convenience to help you keep the parameters straight.

Finally, you specify the datatype of the parameter. This will map to the datatype of the host-language routine according to the rules for Embedded SQL, which are given in Appendix A; for Java, it will map according to the rules for Embedded SQLJ. If you wish the parameter to be a locator, of course, you can specify AS LOCATOR.

Returns

The RETURNS clause applies only to functions. It specifies the datatype the function returns, which may be CAST from another datatype. The CAST follows the principles given under Cast Expressions in Part III. You generally use it to convert from a SQL datatype that the host language can support to one it cannot. Again, you can include an AS LOCATOR clause to have the function return a locator.

Language

The LANGUAGE clause simply specifies the host language. The Core SQL supported languages are the same as those supported for Embedded SQL (Appendix A). The SQL/PSM enhanced level adds SQL itself as a supported language. Java is a common addition and, if supported, is almost bound to follow the principles of Embedded SQLJ. There can be but one language clause and one language. The host language may be able to call subroutines in still other languages (as Java can, for example), but that is of no concern to SQL. It pays attention to only the language it calls directly. By the way, the language the standard supports is called C. If you are using C++, you will still refer to it as C in the LANGUAGE clause, unless your implementation extends the standard by recognizing C++ as such.

In theory, this clause is optional. However, the default is SQL, which is not part of Core. So, for Core SQL, this clause is mandatory.

Parameter Style

If the PARAMETER STYLE is SQL, then you can append indicators to the variables that match the parameters in the host-language routine, and the DBMS will set and use them appropriately. Your DBMS may also have the routine set the current value of SQLSTATE, so as to provide you with status information. If the PARAMETER STYLE is GENERAL, you're just passing values around. In this case, you have to be careful of NULLs; although the ON NULL INPUT clause (described below) gives you an alternative way to deal with these.

You can specify the PARAMETER STYLE here or as part of the EXTERNAL clause. It does not matter which you choose, but it must be one or the other, not both.

Deterministic or Non-deterministic

The notion of DETERMINISTIC and NON-DETERMINISTIC routines is based on that of deterministic and possibly non-deterministic queries (see SELECT in Part II). The general idea is that a deterministic query or routine is guaranteed to always provide the same answer given the same inputs and the same current data, whereas a non-deterministic one has no such guarantee. Most queries are deterministic (again, the exceptions are outlined under SELECT in Part II). How *determinism* will be determined when applied to external routines is implementation-defined, but the general principle is that a routine that will always give the same output provided it has the same input parameters is deterministic and other routines are non-deterministic. You're a bit on your own here: the DBMS has no way of verifying whether the option you choose is, in fact, correct, since this could depend on host-language logic. The default is non-deterministic because that is the safest bet. If you rely on the routine being deterministic when it is not, you could get programming or data-consistency errors, whereas the reverse is likely to be only an inconvenience.

On NULL Input

The question is what to do when one of the input parameters is NULL. The host language cannot necessarily handle SQL NULLs. In fact, it surely cannot, unless you have used indicator variables in the routine and specified the SQL PARAMETER STYLE (see above). Therefore, the best way to deal with NULLs—at least for functions, which must return a value—is to have the function itself return NULL. This is what RETURN NULL ON NULL INPUT does. The response is immediate, since the function is not actually even called. CALL ON NULL INPUT, the default, calls the function as normal and hopes for the best.

External

The EXTERNAL clause specifies that we are dealing with an external, not a SQL, routine. Since only external routines are part of Core, this is a requirement as far as we are concerned in this chapter. The rest of the statement is part of the EXTERNAL clause and therefore also applies only to external routines. The NAME, as indicated, is optional. The binding of the external routine to its SQL wrapper is implementation-defined, so it may or may not rely upon you supplying a name here, and that name may or may not involve some entire path.

Parameter Style

This clause has the same meaning as the previous PARAMETER STYLE above. You may specify it here or there, but not in both places.

Now that we've shown you the pieces, let's see some examples:

```
CREATE PROCEDURE Calculate_payment
    (IN total_balance DEC, IN months_to_pay INT, OUT
payment DEC)
    LANGUAGE C
    PARAMETER STYLE SQL
    CALL ON NULL INPUT
    EXTERNAL NAME paycalc;
```

This creates a SQL wrapper called Calculate_payment for a C procedure called paycalc. How the program or library containing paycalc is bound to the DBMS is an implementation-defined matter. This procedure takes the input parameters total_balance and months_to_pay and stores the result of its calculations in the output parameter payment. The CALL ON NULL INPUT goes logically with the SQL PARAMETER STYLE; we can go ahead and call the procedure because we have a way of handling the NULLs. While no relationship is necessary between the PARAMETER STYLE and the ON NULL INPUT clause, when you have to use a GENERAL PARAMETER STYLE you often use RETURN NULL ON NULL INPUT. A GENERAL PARAMETER STYLE might be mandatory if you were invoking a procedure from a library that you were not free to modify.

So how do you invoke this thing? With a CALL statement. Luckily, the CALL statement is considerably simpler than CREATE PROCEDURE. Here is an example:

```
exec sql CALL Calculate_payment(:total_amount,
    :number_of_months, :monthly_payment);
```

Distinct User-Defined Datatypes (UDTs)

As we explained in Part IV, Chapter 1, user-defined datatypes (UDTs) fall into two categories: distinct and structured. Since only the former are part of Core, we discuss only the former here, though we summarized the latter in Part IV, Chapter 1.

Distinct UDTs are distinctly less sexy than the structured type. Simply put, a *distinct UDT* is a renamed conventional datatype that restricts possible comparisons. A data item of a given distinct UDT (hereafter, *distinct type*) can be compared only to other items of the same distinct type, not to anything else that happens to be of the same original datatype.

To see the logic of this, let's think a bit about domains. Domains are part of Intermediate SQL92 and are also part of SQL99, though not of Core. Nonetheless, distinct types and domains complement each other. However, the idea of a domain in database theory, as strongly advocated by Ted Codd, the father of relational database, is somewhat different from that found in the standard. In theory, a *domain* denotes a set of values within which, and only within which, direct comparisons make sense. For example, it makes no sense to compare social security numbers and telephone numbers, even though both are numbers and could be of the same datatype: they are in different domains.

A *domain* in the standard, however, is something slightly different. It is a conventional datatype combined with one or more of the following:

- One or more constraints
- A default value
- A collation

All of the above are optional for any given domain, though it would be senseless to have a domain that did not include at least one of them (for more information on domains, see CREATE DOMAIN in Part II). Thus, you could create a `marital_status` domain based on the CHAR datatype. This domain could be restricted to the values 'S', 'M', and 'D', with a default of 'S' and no collation (which would mean the collation of the underlying datatype applies by default). You probably would not do this for only one marital status column, of course, but you would if you had a huge number of such columns in various tables and wanted to standardize the possible values and the default across all of them. What you do is use the domain in place of the datatype in all CREATE TABLE statements that have such columns. Then you do not need to code the constraint and the default separately and can be assured that they will be the same for all `marital_status` columns. This is very practical, but it does not restrict comparisons as Codd's domains would. Values in the domain `marital_status` could still be compared in queries to any other text string, such as names, even though the comparison would make no sense. Domains as the SQL standards have defined them do not provide the particular type of integrity protection that Codd sought.

Therefore, the standards committee came up with distinct types, which pretty much do what Codd wanted for domains. Social security numbers (SSNs) could be one distinct type and telephone numbers another. Both could be based on the INTEGER datatype, but attempts to compare SSNs to phone numbers would produce an error. That's the idea. Such a comparison indicates that you are doing something wrong, so the error helps you find the mistake. However, distinct types do not do what SQL92 domains do, which is to standardize constraints and so on. So, if you have an implementation that supports both Core and domains, you can combine them by creating a distinct type and then creating domains based upon the distinct type. You do not *have* to do this, however. Domains and distinct types exist independently of one another, so you can use either, both, or neither, as suits you.

Now that you understand the rationale, here is an example of how to create a distinct type:

```
CREATE TYPE phone_number AS INTEGER(10) FINAL;
CREATE TYPE ssn AS INTEGER(9) FINAL;
CREATE TABLE Student
  (studnum      INTEGER(10) NOT NULL PRIMARY KEY,
   phone_num    phone_number,
   ssn_num      ssn);
```

That's it! The distinct type definition doesn't change the meaning or possible values of the datatype at all; it just restricts comparisons. Since these are both based on INTEGERs, they would have to be strict numbers—no dashes or parentheses. The FINAL argument is a required part of the CREATE TYPE syntax, though it is really more meaningful for structured types. It means the datatype being created cannot be subclassed further, which is always true for distinct types, since they are not subclassed in the first place. While you could consider a distinct type to be a subclass of the base datatype in some logical sense, it is not a subclass according to how that term is used in standard SQL. It is also true, however, that you cannot base distinct types on other distinct types, forming a hierarchy. In this sense, you could say that every distinct type is indeed FINAL.

If you do decide you want to compare a distinct type to some other type, you can always cast it as another datatype in the SQL statement wherein you want to make the comparison. These casts follow the rules laid down in the Part III of this reference under Cast Expressions. The valid casts of the distinct type are the same as those of the datatype on which it is based.

A distinct type is an object in a schema, just like a table, or, for that matter, a domain. Although you cannot alter it (what would you change?), you can drop it thusly:

```
DROP TYPE phone_number;
```

Also, like other schema objects, a distinct type is preceded by the schema name if referenced from outside the schema. A USAGE privilege is associated with each distinct type, and anyone who wishes to CREATE a TABLE with a column of that type must have the privilege. The creator of the type, of course, automatically has the USAGE privilege with the GRANT OPTION. For more on privileges, see GRANT in Part II.

Summary

You have now seen how the most important parts of Core SQL99 work. Core enables you to deal with multimedia data transparently without most of the difficulty that usually comes from trying to move such unwieldy data items around. It lets you create your own datatypes, which are subtypes of the regular datatypes and which preserve operational integrity by prohibiting certain kinds of illogical comparisons.

Core also lets you invoke host-language routines from within SQL. This capacity somewhat changes the function of the database. Now it becomes not only a repository of data, but also an effective repository of code related to that data, from which it can, to a degree, dynamically construct applications. This capacity is furthered in the PSM and Object Support enhanced conformance levels, which, between them, turn the DBMS into an engine, in effect, for dynamically deriving and executing entire applications in response to changes in the data.

Appendix A

Mapping SQL to Other Languages

- Ada

- C

- COBOL

- Fortran

- MUMPS

- Pascal

This appendix presents a detailed description of those attributes of Embedded SQL that are specific to various host languages. Material in this appendix is also relevant to Dynamic SQL. SQL86 did not officially include Embedded SQL but provided annexes specifying syntax and semantics for using Embedded SQL in COBOL, Fortran, Pascal, and PL/I. SQL92 made these official and added C, Ada, and MUMPS to the list of supported languages. SQLJ adds Java. SQLJ Java support is unorthodox due to the unconventional nature of Java itself. For example, SQLJ relies on Java's capability to catch exceptions for error handling rather than using Embedded SQL's WHENEVER clause. Since it does not fit the mold, SQLJ is not covered in this appendix.

In the next sections, we describe the language-specific definitions for the following:

- The syntax of Embedded SQL variable declarations in the various standard-supported languages.

- The host-language elements that correspond to the following special SQL tokens:

  SQLprefix   This is the string, usually some variation on EXEC SQL, that informs the precompiler that the statement that follows is a SQL, not a conventional host-language, statement.

  SQLterm   This is the SQL statement terminator. In Interactive SQL, it is the semi-colon (;), but in Embedded or Dynamic SQL, it depends on the host language.

  Target   This is the item that can serve as a legitimate target for a GOTO executed within SQL (for example, with a WHENEVER clause).

- The host-language datatypes that are equivalent to the standard SQL datatypes. Note that the SQL types DATE, TIME, TIME-STAMP, and INTERVAL have no equivalent in any of these languages. Other datatypes may or may not have equivalents in a given language. You can use CAST expressions to convert unsupported datatypes to character strings (see CAST Expressions in Part III).

Ada

Table A.1 shows the standard SQL syntax elements in Ada. The datatypes in Ada that map to SQL datatypes are shown in Table A.2.

TABLE A.1: SQL Syntax Elements in Ada

Standard Element	In Ada
SQL prefix	EXEC SQL
SQL term	;
target	label_name

Variable Declaration Syntax

```
Ada variable definition ::=
Ada host identifier.,... : Ada type spec
[:= character representation...]
```

The host identifier is the variable name, the type spec is one of those outlined below, and the := character representation sequence is an optional initial value. Ada text, once precompiled, will conform to the Ada standard ISO/IEC 8652. The precompiler will convert variations in Ada syntax that are allowed for Embedded SQL; other variations, of course, are errors. An Embedded SQL statement may be used wherever an Ada statement may be used, and it may be prefixed by a label.

An Ada variable definition must be specified within the scope of Ada WITH and USE clauses that specify the following:

```
with SQL_STANDARD;
use SQL_STANDARD;
use SQL_STANDARD.CHARACTER_SET;
```

This will import the following built-in SQL standard type declarations:

```
SQL_STANDARD.CHAR [CHARACTER SET [IS] character set name]
(1..length)
SQL_STANDARD.BIT (1..length)
SQL_STANDARD.SMALLINT
SQL_STANDARD.INT
SQL_STANDARD.REAL
SQL_STANDARD.DOUBLE_PRECISION
SQL_STANDARD.SQLCODE_TYPE
SQL_STANDARD.SQLSTATE_TYPE
SQL_STANDARD.INDICATOR_TYPE
```

TABLE A.2: SQL Datatypes in Ada

SQL Type	Ada Equivalent
CHAR(length)	CHAR (1..length)
BIT(length)	BIT (1..length)
SMALLINT	SMALLINT
INT	INT
REAL	REAL
DOUBLE PRECISION	DOUBLE_PRECISION
type of SQLCODE	SQLCODE_TYPE or INTEGER
type of SQLSTATE	SQLSTATE_TYPE or CHAR(5)
type of indicator	INDICATOR_TYPE

If a character set is specified, the length is given in characters but will be converted by the precompiler to octets (bytes). If a character set is not specified, the implementation default will apply. The character set need not be supported by products claiming less than Intermediate SQL92 conformance, including those claiming Core SQL99 conformance, which requires slightly more than Entry SQL92.

C/C++

Table A.3 shows the standard SQL syntax elements in C/C++. The datatypes in C/C++ that map to SQL datatypes are shown in Table A.4.

TABLE A.3: SQL Syntax Elements in C/C++

Standard Element	In C
SQL prefix	EXEC SQL
SQL term	;
target	label

Variable Declaration Syntax

```
C variable definition ::=
[auto | extern | static]
[const | volatile]
C numeric variable
| C character variable
| C derived variable;
C numeric variable ::=
{ long | short | float | double }
{ C host identifier [initial value] }.,..
C character variable ::=
char [CHARACTER SET [IS] character set name]
{ C host identifier {length} [initial value] }.,..
C derived variable ::=
{ VARCHAR [CHARACTER SET [IS] character set name]
{ C host identifier {length}
[ = character representation... ]}.,..}
| { BIT {C host identifier {length}
[ = character representation... ]}.,..}
```

For the purposes of Embedded and Dynamic SQL, C++ is treated like regular C. The C host identifier is the variable name, the length is the fixed or maximum varying length of the string, and the character representation sequence is an optional initial value. The character set need not be supported by products claiming less than Intermediate SQL92 conformance, including those claiming Core SQL99 conformance, which requires only slightly more than Entry SQL92.

Once precompiled, the C text must conform to the C standard ISO/IEC 9899. SQL statements may be used within a function block wherever C statements may; if a C statement used in that location can be prefixed by a label, the SQL statement can also be so prefixed. The compiler will convert BIT and VARCHAR datatypes to C char equivalents. For CHARACTER types, the length given is in characters and will be converted to the octet (byte) length. It will be at least one character longer than the fixed-length or maximum varying length of the SQL data value that will be assigned to it, as it will include a null character as a string terminator (a C convention not to be confused with SQL NULLs). The length will therefore be greater than 1, since the length of a one-character string would be 2. For BIT types, the length given is the bit length and will be converted to the C character length. The SQL keywords (BIT, CHARACTER, SET, and so on) used in the C syntax may be uppercase or lowercase.

Table A.4 shows the C equivalents for standard SQL datatypes and the datatypes for status and indicator variables. If neither of the status variables is declared, SQLCODE will be created automatically.

TABLE A.4: SQL Datatypes in C/C++

SQL Datatype	C Equivalent
CHAR (length)	char length
VARCHAR (length)	char length
BIT (length)	char length
INTEGER	long
SMALLINT	short
REAL	float

Continued on next page

TABLE A.4: SQL Datatypes in C/C++ (continued)

SQL Datatype	C Equivalent
DOUBLE PRECISION	double
type of SQLCODE	long
type of SQLSTATE	char 6
type of indicators	short or long

COBOL

Table A.5 shows the standard SQL syntax elements in COBOL. The datatypes in COBOL that map to SQL datatypes are shown in Table A.6.

TABLE A.5: SQL Syntax Elements in COBOL

Standard Element	In COBOL
SQL prefix	EXEC SQL
SQL term	END-EXEC
target	section-name or unqualified paragraph name

Variable Declaration Syntax

```
COBOL variable definition ::=
{01|77} COBOL host identifier  COBOL type spec
[ character representation... ] .

COBOL type spec ::=
COBOL character type
| COBOL bit type
| COBOL numeric type
| COBOL integer type

COBOL character type ::=
[ CHARACTER SET [IS] character set name ]
{ PIC | PICTURE } [IS] { X [(length)] }...

COBOL bit type ::=
{ PIC | PICTURE } [IS] { B [(length)] }...
```

```
COBOL numeric type ::=
{ PIC | PICTURE } [IS]
S { {9 [(length)]}... [ V [{9 [(length)]}...] ]
| V {9 [(length)]}... }
[ USAGE [IS] ] DISPLAY SIGN LEADING SEPARATE

COBOL integer type ::=
COBOL computational integer
| COBOL binary integer

COBOL computational integer ::=
{ PIC | PICTURE } [IS] S{9 [(length)]}...
[ USAGE [IS] ] { COMP | COMPUTATIONAL }

COBOL binary integer ::=
{ PIC | PICTURE } [IS] S{9 [(length)]}...
[ USAGE [IS] ] BINARY
```

Once precompiled, the COBOL text must conform to the COBOL standard ISO 1989. A SQL statement may be inserted in the Procedure Division wherever a COBOL statement may: if a COBOL statement in the same location could be immediately preceded by a paragraph name, then the SQL statement can also be so preceded. For the COBOL bit type, the length given is the bit length, which will be converted automatically to the character length, and the 'B' will be changed automatically to 'X'. For the COBOL character type, the length is given in characters and will be converted automatically to the length in octets (bytes). The character set need not be supported by products claiming less than Intermediate SQL92 conformance, including those claiming Core SQL99 conformance, which requires only slightly more than Entry SQL92.

TABLE A.6: SQL Datatypes in COBOL

SQL Datatype	COBOL Equivalent
INTEGER	COBOL binary integer
SMALLINT	COBOL binary integer
CHAR	COBOL character type
BIT	COBOL binary type
NUMERIC	COBOL numeric type

Continued on next page

TABLE A.6: SQL Datatypes in COBOL (continued)

SQL Datatype	COBOL Equivalent
type of SQLCODE	COBOL computational integer
type of SQLSTATE	COBOL character type
type of indicators	COBOL binary integer

Fortran

Table A.7 shows the standard SQL syntax elements in Fortran. The datatypes in Fortran that map to SQL datatypes are shown in Table A.8.

TABLE A.7: SQL Syntax Elements in Fortran

Standard Element	In Fortran
SQL prefix	EXEC SQL
SQL term	none
target	unsigned integer (must be the label of a statement that appears in the same program unit as the WHENEVER clause)

Variable Declaration Syntax

```
Fortran variable definition ::=
Fortran type spec
Fortran host identifier.,...

Fortran type spec ::=
{ CHARACTER [ * length]
[CHARACTER SET [IS] character set name] }
| {BIT [ * length]}
| INTEGER
| REAL
| DOUBLE PRECISION
```

After precompilation, the Fortran text must conform to the Fortran standard ISO/IEC 1539. A SQL statement may be used wherever a Fortran statement could be used. If the SQL statement immediately precedes an executable Fortran statement, it may not be preceded by a Fortran statement number; otherwise, if a Fortran statement used in the same place could have a statement number, the SQL statement may have one. The host identifier is a valid Fortran variable name with all blank spaces removed. The length of Fortran character types will be expressed in characters and converted to octets (bytes); that of Fortran bit types will be expressed in bits and converted to characters, and the type will be converted to character. The character set need not be supported by products claiming less than Intermediate SQL92 conformance, including those claiming Core SQL99 conformance, which requires only slightly more than Entry SQL92.

TABLE A.8: SQL Datatypes in Fortran

SQL Datatype	Fortran Equivalent
INTEGER	INTEGER
SMALLINT	INTEGER
CHAR	CHARACTER
VARCHAR	CHARACTER
BIT	CHARACTER
REAL	REAL
DOUBLE PRECISION	DOUBLE PRECISION
type of SQLCOD	INTEGER
type of SQLSTA	CHARACTER
type of indicator	INTEGER

MUMPS

Table A.9 shows the standard SQL syntax elements in MUMPS. The datatypes in MUMPS that map to SQL datatypes are shown in Table A.10.

TABLE A.9: SQL Syntax Elements in MUMPS

Standard Element	In MUMPS
SQL prefix	&SQL(
SQL term	)
target	statement label

Variable Declaration Syntax

```
MUMPS variable definition ::=
{ MUMPS numeric variable | MUMPS character variable };
MUMPS character variable ::=
VARCHAR { MUMPS host identifier (length) }.,..

MUMPS numeric variable ::=
{ INT
| { DEC [ ( precision [ , scale ] ) ] }
| REAL }
MUMPS host identifier.,..
```

After precompilation, the MUMPS text must conform to the MUMPS standard ISO/IEC 11756. A SQL statement may be specified wherever a MUMPS statement may be used.

TABLE A.10: SQL Datatypes in MUMPS

SQL Datatype	MUMPS Equivalent
CHAR	VARCHAR
VARCHAR	VARCHAR
INTEGER	INT
DECIMAL	DEC
REAL	REAL
type of SQLCODE	INTEGER
type of SQLSTATE	VARCHAR (5)
type of indicator	INT

Pascal

Table A.11 shows the standard syntax elements in Pascal. The datatypes in Pascal that map to SQL datatypes are shown in Table A.12.

TABLE A.11: SQL Syntax Elements in Pascal

Standard Element	In Pascal
SQL prefix	EXEC SQL
SQL term	;
target	unsigned integer (must correspond to a valid label)

Variable Declaration Syntax

NOTE In Pascal, brackets ([and]) are part of the syntax of variable declarations. They are also one of the conventions we use in this book to create syntax diagrams. In the following diagram, the expressions *left bracket* and *right bracket* indicate that brackets are literally to be used in the Pascal statement. Brackets shown directly ([and]) enclose an optional portion of the statement as usual.

```
Pascal variable definition ::=
Pascal host identifier.,.. : type spec;

type spec ::=
{ PACKED ARRAY left bracket 1..length  right bracket
OF CHAR
[CHARACTER SET [IS] character set name] }
| { PACKED ARRAY left bracket 1..length  right bracket
OF BIT }
| INTEGER
| REAL
| { CHAR [CHARACTER SET [IS] character set name] }
| BIT
```

After precompilation, the Pascal text must conform to one of the following Pascal standards: ISO 7185 or ISO/IEC 10206. A SQL statement may be used anywhere a Pascal statement may and may be prefixed with a label. The following conversions are performed during precompilation:

If a CHARACTER SET is specified, that reference is deleted from the source code, and the length specified, which was measured in characters, is converted to the length in octets (bytes). The character set need not be supported by products claiming less than Intermediate SQL92 conformance, including those claiming Core SQL99 conformance, which requires only slightly more than Entry SQL92.

If a CHAR declaration specifies a character set, and the form-of-use of that character set allocates more than one octet (byte) per character, the declaration is converted to a PACKED ARRAY OF CHAR.

The BIT and PACKED ARRAY OF BIT types are converted to CHAR and PACKED ARRAY OF CHAR, respectively. Only the most significant bit of the CHAR can have a nonzero value, and for the PACKED ARRAY, the bits are effectively concatenated.

TABLE A.12: SQL Datatypes in Pascal

SQL Datatype	Pascal Equivalent
CHAR (length)	PACKED ARRAY [1..length] OF CHAR
VARCHAR (length)	PACKED ARRAY [1..length] OF CHAR
CHAR (1)	CHAR
BIT (length)	PACKED ARRAY [1..length] OF BIT
BIT VARYING (length)	PACKED ARRAY [1..length] OF BIT
BIT (1)	BIT
INTEGER	INTEGER
REAL	REAL
type of SQLCODE	INTEGER
type of SQLSTATE	PACKED ARRAY [1..5] OF CHAR
type of indicators	INTEGER

PL/I

Table A.13 shows the standard SQL syntax elements in PL/I. The datatypes in PL/I that map to SQL datatypes are shown in Table A.14.

TABLE A.13: SQL Syntax Elements in PL/I

Standard Element	In PL/I
SQL prefix	EXEC SQL
SQL term	;
target	label constant or PL/I label variable

Variable Declaration Syntax

```
PL/I variable definition ::=
{DCL | DECLARE}
{ PL/I host identifier
| (PL/I host identifier.,..) }
type spec [ character representation...] ;

type spec ::=
{ { CHAR | CHARACTER } [VARYING] (length)
[CHARACTER SET [IS] character set name] }
| { BIT [VARYING] (length) }
| { type fixed decimal ( precision [ , scale ] ) }
| { type fixed binary [ ( precision ) ] }
| { type float binary ( precision ) }

type fixed decimal ::=
{ DEC | DECIMAL } FIXED
| FIXED { DEC | DECIMAL }

type fixed binary ::=
{ BIN | BINARY } FIXED
| FIXED { BIN | BINARY }

type float binary ::=
{ BIN | BINARY } FLOAT
| FLOAT { BIN | BINARY }
```

After precompilation, the PL/I text must conform to the PL/I standard ISO 6160. A SQL statement may be placed anywhere within a procedure block that a PL/I statement may be; if the latter could take a label prefix, the former also could be immediately prefixed by a label. The PL/I host identifier is any valid PL/I variable name. The variable must be of a simple scalar type, not an array or structure. If a CHARACTER SET is specified, the reference will be deleted. The length given, which is the length in characters, will be replaced by the length in octets (bytes). The character set need not be supported by products claiming less than Intermediate SQL92 conformance, including those claiming Core SQL99 conformance, which requires only slightly more than Entry SQL92. The character representation sequence allows you to specify an initial value in the ordinary PL/I syntax.

TABLE A.14: SQL Datatypes in PL/I

SQL Datatype	PL/I Equivalent
CHAR (length)	CHAR (length)
VARCHAR (length)	CHAR VARYING (length)
BIT (length)	BIT (length)
BIT VARYING (length)	BIT VARYING (length)
INTEGER	FIXED BINARY
SMALLINT	FIXED BINARY
DECIMAL (precision, scale)	FIXED DECIMAL (precision, scale)
FLOAT (precision)	FLOAT BINARY (precision)
type of SQLCODE	FIXED BINARY (PP), where PP equals the implementation-defined precision for SQLCODE
type of SQLSTATE	CHAR (5)
type of indicator	FIXED BINARY

Appendix B

Specification of the Module Language

- Overview

- Syntax

The module language is the paradigm used in the various ANSI/ISO standards to explain the semantics of SQL. There is no requirement that it is manifested as such by implementers, but its effects are to be emulated. Embedded SQL is the more common approach to fixed-code SQL, but Embedded SQL, in effect, is supposed to generate modules. In fact, it does generate modules, though the modules themselves need not conform to the module language syntax; they merely need produce the desired effect. Dynamic SQL, too, effectively operates as the generation of statements from within modules.

Overview

It is important to be able to refer to the semantics of the module language, even if your implementation does not directly support it (some do, but most do not). In particular, objects such as declared local temporary tables and Dynamic SQL descriptor areas with local scopes, when used in Embedded or Dynamic SQL have their visibility restricted to some implementation-defined area that corresponds to a module. Embedded SQL programs produce compilation units, which have an implementation-defined many-to-many link to (implied or actual) modules. Dynamic SQL statements also have an implementation-defined association with modules.

Also, either static or dynamic applications can be associated with Authorization IDs. This enables those applications to run under "definer's rights," where the privileges are associated with the application rather than the user executing it. When this happens, it will be as though these privileges were granted to the modules. Besides this, the module approach seems to harmonize better with the object-oriented philosophy of programming than does Embedded SQL and may therefore become more widely implemented as such in the future.

Syntax

Modules are groups of SQL cursor declarations and procedures called as subprograms by applications. The syntax is as follows:

```
module ::=
MODULE [ module name ]
[NAMES ARE character set name]
LANGUAGE {Ada | C | COBOL | Fortran | MUMPS | Pascal | PL/I}
module authorization clause
[ declare local temporary table statement... ]
{declare cursor statement | procedure}...
module authorization clause ::=
{ SCHEMA schema name }
| { AUTHORIZATION module Authorization ID }
| { SCHEMA schema name
AUTHORIZATION module Authorization ID}
```

If the module name is omitted, the module is unnamed. Any number of unnamed modules may exist, and they will be linked to the application's compilation units in an implementation-defined manner. If the module is named, its name must be unique. If the NAMES ARE clause is omitted, an implementation-defined default character set whose repertoire includes all the characters necessary to express the SQL language will apply.

The LANGUAGE Clause

The LANGUAGE clause identifies the host language from which the module is called. Although this clause is not optional in the standard, if the program calling the module is not actually written in the specified language, the effect is implementation-dependent. This gives implementations some leeway to call modules from, for example, proprietary 4GLs and to specify some language whose parameter-passing procedures they wish to conform to, or to have single modules that can be called from multiple languages.

Ada

If the LANGUAGE clause specifies Ada, then the module must be named, and its name must be a valid Ada library unit name. The implementation will generate the source code of the Ada library unit package specification. An Ada package named SQL_STAN-DARD will be included and will define SQL equivalent datatypes for Ada, as well as the possible standard SQLSTATE values. The parameter mode of input parameters is in, that of output parameters is out, and that of parameters serving both functions is in/out.

C

The datatype of all numeric types will be pointer to the corresponding C type. That is to say, SQL INTEGER (including SQL-CODE) is pointer to long, SQL SMALLINT is pointer to short, SQL REAL is pointer to float, and SQL DOUBLE PRECISION is pointer to double. CHARACTER string types are passed directly as C char, and to avoid truncation they must have lengths one octet (byte) longer than the maximum length of the corresponding SQL value to allow for the string terminator. If the string terminator occurs for some reason in the middle of the string, the rest of the string will be lost. BIT string types are passed to the host program as C char with a length not less than the bit length (BL) of the value divided by the implementation-defined bit length of C characters (CL) plus one. That is to say, it is at least BL / (CL + 1). C char values that are passed to BIT input parameters are automatically cast as SQL BIT by the DBMS.

COBOL

For CHARACTER datatypes, the corresponding COBOL type is alphanumeric with the same octet (byte) length; for BIT strings it is the same, except that the length is the bit length divided by the number of bits per character in COBOL (implementation-defined). The casting of SQL BIT as COBOL alphanumeric and vice versa is done automatically. If the datatype is NUMERIC, call the precision P and the scale S. The COBOL type is COBOL USAGE DISPLAY SIGN LEADING SEPARATE with one of the following PICTUREs:

If scale is equal to precision, then use a PICTURE with an S followed by a V followed by P 9s. For example, COBOL PICTURE SV9999 represents a scale of 4 and a precision of 4, or numbers such as 0.9999.

If scale and precision are different, then use a PICTURE with an S followed by (P-S) 9s, followed by a V followed by P 9s. For example, COBOL PICTURE S999V99 represents numbers of the form 999.99 for a precision of 2 and a scale of 5.

If the datatype is INTEGER, the equivalent is COBOL PICTURE S9(PI) USAGE BINARY, where PI is some implementation-defined precision (number of digits). SMALLINT is the same as INTEGER, except that the precision may be less.

Fortran

The rules here are the same as listed in Appendix A. The casting of SQL BIT types as Fortran CHARACTER and vice versa is done automatically.

MUMPS

The possible SQL datatypes are CHARACTER, VARCHAR, INTEGER, DECIMAL, and REAL. All of these are passed to and from the host program as MUMPS VARCHAR and converted automatically.

Pascal

The argument mode of all parameters will be VAR. Conversion between SQL BIT and Pascal PACKED ARRAY OF CHAR and vice versa is performed automatically.

PL/I

The rules here are the same as listed in Appendix A.

The Schema Name

The schema name specifies the default schema name to be effectively applied to all object names referenced in the module that
do not have another schema name prefixed. If the schema name
is omitted, the module Authorization ID will be the schema name.
This is primarily for compatibility with the SQL89 standard, which
assumed a one-to-one correspondence of this sort between modules with schemata. If the schema name is not prefixed with a catalog name, some implementation-defined default will apply. This
catalog name, whether specified or defaulted to, will be the default
catalog name for all schema names in the module that are not
prefixed with some other catalog name.

The Module Authorization ID

The module Authorization ID determines the privileges under which
the SQL statements in the module are executed (see GRANT in Part
II). The privileges necessary to access the module—and thus the privileges it contains, if any—are implementation-defined. If the module
Authorization ID is omitted, the SQL statements will operate under
the privileges of the user calling the procedures in the module (the
SESSION_USER; see Authorization in Part III). These are also the privileges that apply in the 86 and 89 standards, wherein the module
Authorization ID simply identifies the default schema. In other
words, if the name is omitted, it is invoker's rights. Otherwise, it is
definer's rights.

Procedures

A procedure is a named object in the module containing a list
of parameters and a SQL statement. A module may contain any
number of temporary table declarations, cursor declarations, and
procedures, in accordance with the following principles:

* All DECLARE LOCAL TEMPORARY TABLE statements precede
  all cursor declarations and procedures.

* When referred to in other statements in the module, all declared
  local temporary tables shall be prefixed by the keyword MOD-
  ULE in the same manner as other tables could be prefixed by a
  schema name.

- All cursors must be declared or allocated (applies only to Dynamic SQL) before they are referenced in a procedure.

- For each cursor declared in the module, there shall be one and only one procedure containing an OPEN statement that identifies that cursor.

Syntax

The syntax for procedures is as follows:

```
procedure ::=
PROCEDURE procedure name
(parameter declaration.,..)
| {parameter declaration...};
  SQL procedure statement;

parameter declaration ::=
{ parameter name   datatype }
  | status parameter

status parameter ::=
SQLCODE | SQLSTATE

list of possible SQL procedure statements ::=
ALLOCATE DESCRIPTOR, ALLOCATE CURSOR, ALTER TABLE, ALTER
DOMAIN, CLOSE CURSOR, COMMIT, CONNECT, CREATE ASSERTION,
CREATE SCHEMA, CREATE VIEW, CREATE DOMAIN, CREATE CHARACTER
SET, CREATE COLLATION, CREATE TRANSLATION, CREATE TABLE,
DEALLOCATE PREPARE, DEALLOCATE DESCRIPTOR, DELETE, DESCRIBE,
DISCONNECT, DROP SCHEMA, DROP DOMAIN, DROP CHARACTER SET,
DROP COLLATION, DROP VIEW, DROP TRANSLATION, DROP TABLE, DROP
ASSERTION, EXECUTE, EXECUTE IMMEDIATE, FETCH, GET DESCRIPTOR,
GET DIAGNOSTICS, GRANT, INSERT, OPEN CURSOR, PREPARE, REVOKE,
ROLLBACK, SELECT (only single-row version using INTO clause),
SET CONNECTION, SET CATALOG, SET DESCRIPTOR, SET SESSION
AUTHORIZATION, SET SCHEMA, SET LOCAL TIME ZONE, SET NAMES,
SET TRANSACTION, SET CONSTRAINTS MODE, UPDATE
```

NOTE The option to list the parameters without enclosing parentheses and separating commas is a deprecated feature of SQL92 supported for compatibility with the 89 standard. Support for this syntax may disappear in the future, so it is better to use the parenthesized syntax if your implementation gives you this choice.

Each procedure contains one and only one SQL statement. The procedure is to be called from a host program currently linked (in an implementation-defined manner) to the containing module. If the procedure does not conform to the syntax for subprogram calls in the host language, the effect is implementation-dependent. The calling program must, however, supply all parameters listed. If the datatypes passed to the procedure are not comparable to those of the parameters in the SQL statement, the DBMS will attempt to use a CAST expression to convert them. If the needed conversion is disallowed for a CAST expression (see CAST Expressions in Part III), the procedure call produces an error. If the CAST is legal but produces values outside the acceptable range, the effect is implementation-defined.

The procedure name has to be unique within the containing module. It is possible that the program calling the procedure may be linked simultaneously to other modules that contain procedures of the same name as the present procedure. How this is resolved is implementation-defined. The parameter names listed in a given procedure must all be distinct, and the list must include every parameter in the SQL statement contained in the procedure. When used in the SQL statement, these parameters will have the same names but be preceded by colons (:), unless they are used in dynamically generated statements, in which case they will be represented by question marks (?) and associated with the procedure call parameters on the basis of their sequence in the text of the SQL statement (see Appendix C). In addition, one or both status parameters must be specified, but neither may be specified more than once. These are used by the DBMS to store information about the execution of the statement and are not directly referenced therein. SQLSTATE is the preferred status parameter, SQLCODE being a deprecated feature supported for compatibility with the previous standards. The standard values for the status parameters are given in Appendix F; the datatypes for them in various host languages are listed in Appendix A under the various language headings.

Indicator parameters may also be included and should be for parameters that may possibly be NULL. The datatype of these is the host-language equivalent of SQL INTEGER, as given in Appendix A. They operate just as indicator variables do in Embedded SQL. An indicator parameter follows another parameter (called its *associated parameter*) with no separator other than the optional word INDICATOR. If the indicator parameter has a negative value, the associated parameter is NULL, and its actual value is ignored. This applies to both input and output parameters (explained below). If the associated parameter stores the value of a CHARACTER or BIT string type that has had to be truncated to fit in the parameter, the indicator parameter is set to the length of the string prior to truncation, in characters or bits as appropriate, so that you know how much data you lost. If this number cannot be expressed in the number of digits in the indicator, an error is produced. (You lost a whole lot of data there.) In the absence of truncation or NULLs, the indicator is set to zero.

Parameters can be input parameters, output parameters, or both, as determined by the following principles:

- Status parameters are output parameters and only output parameters.

- Target specifications are output parameters. These are parameters used in the INTO clauses of SELECT and FETCH statements to store values. In Dynamic SQL, target specifications are also used in the GET DESCRIPTOR statement to store descriptor values. Also in Dynamic SQL, SELECT and FETCH statements may be dynamically generated, in which case they will actually be executed with EXECUTE or EXECUTE IMMEDIATE statements, and output parameters will be used in the latter statements to store the produced values.

- Parameters that are used to supply values for statements are input parameters. The same parameter may be used for input and output but must already have a value when used for input.

- Indicator parameters take their input and/or output status from the parameter with which they are associated.

If a session is not active at the time a procedure is called and there is some default connection, the connection is performed and a session begun automatically. Otherwise, the first procedure in a session must contain a CONNECT statement. Rules for modules that apply to specific host languages are described in the following sections. Unless otherwise indicated in these sections, datatype compatibility between host parameters and the SQL values they will contain are the same as for Embedded SQL variables (outlined in Appendix A).

Appendix C

Specification of Dynamic SQL

In Dynamic SQL, applications have the capability to generate SQL statements on the fly in reaction to events. How to determine the exact SQL statements needed at any point in time and generate the appropriate code is the application's responsibility. Once the code is generated, however, it is stored in a variable and then converted to SQL. If the statement is to be executed only once, it can be converted and executed in one step with the EXECUTE IMMEDIATE statement; otherwise, it can be readied for execution using a PREPARE statement and executed repeatedly as desired with an EXECUTE statement. The queries in dynamically generated cursors are also readied with a PREPARE statement. Once the statement is prepared, the cursor is created with a DECLARE CURSOR or an ALLOCATE CURSOR statement. The difference between the two is that in the ALLOCATE CURSOR statement, the name the cursor will be given is also a string variable that will have been given a value by the application. This frees the application's programmer from having to know when writing the application how many cursors it will need at one time. For more details on any of the statements just mentioned, consult the relevant entries in Part II.

Whenever a dynamically generated statement references values to be passed to or from the application, it can use a dynamic parameter, which is represented with a simple question mark (?). These will be matched, on a simple ordinal basis, to the parameters passed to the USING (for input) and/or INTO (for output) clauses of the statement that assigns or retrieves values, which will be EXECUTE, OPEN CURSOR, or FETCH. (Hereafter, we will refer to any of these statements as "the execution statement.") The first question mark will stand for the first parameter specified in the execution statement, the second question mark for the second parameter specified, and so on. If the datatype of the dynamic parameter does not match the corresponding host-language parameter, the DBMS will attempt to effect a conversion as specified in CAST Expressions in Part III. If the datatype conversion is disallowed, the statement will produce an error. Otherwise, all will proceed normally.

An application may create a descriptor area to provide information about the parameters of dynamically generated statements and/or to pass or receive values. This area will contain a number of items, each of which provides information for a single dynamic parameter. Because a descriptor area used for input parameters will be placed in a USING clause, while one used for output parameters will be placed in an INTO clause, you would not normally use the same descriptor area for both input and output. You could do so only if all of the parameters were both input and output parameters. Therefore, a given statement will have zero to two descriptor areas: one for input, one for output, both, or neither. The number of items in each area should equal the number of dynamic input parameters or of dynamic output parameters in the statement, as appropriate.

You can pass values to and from the dynamic parameters in the statements using either the descriptor areas or host-language variables. Regardless of which you choose, you pass input parameters with the USING clause and output with the INTO clause. You can use a descriptor area for one of these clauses and variables for the other if you like, but each clause will be entirely one or the other.

To pass data values through the descriptor area rather than through host language parameters, use the pair of fields labeled DATA and INDICATOR. To input values, you set these fields with SET DESCRIPTOR. To retrieve values, use GET DESCRIPTOR. The DATA field contains the value passed from or to the dynamic parameter. The INDICATOR field is set to a negative value to indicate that the DATA value is actually NULL and that the content of the DATA field is to be ignored—in other words, it functions just as an indicator parameter (in the module language) or indicator variable (in Embedded SQL) would. For more information on these matters, refer to "Descriptor Areas" in Part III, and to the following statements in Part II: ALLOCATE CURSOR, ALLOCATE DESCRIPTOR, DEALLOCATE DESCRIPTOR, DESCRIBE, EXECUTE, EXECUTE IMMEDIATE, GET DESCRIPTOR, PREPARE, and SET DESCRIPTOR.

Appendix D

SQL Linguistic Definitions and Conventions

- Identifiers

- SQL Keywords

This appendix provides details on the linguistic elements used to specify the SQL language. Essentially, SQL statements consist of a series of tokens broken up by separators. The separators are spaces (however that character is defined for the implementation's SQL_TEXT character set), newlines (also implementation-defined), and comments. Other white space characters such as tabs may also be separators. This is implementation-defined. Comments begin with two or more minus signs in sequence and end with a newline. As in most languages, comments are for explanatory text and have no effect other than that of being separators.

The tokens are keywords, identifiers, value expressions, operators, and parenthesized or bracketed expressions—essentially any element delimited by separators that may appear in a SQL statement. Statements in Interactive SQL or the module language are terminated with semicolons (;). In Embedded SQL, the statement terminator depends on the host language used but is also usually the semicolon, and in Dynamic SQL no statement terminator is used, unless it is required by the host language.

Identifiers

Identifiers are tokens used to provide names—names for objects such as schemata, tables, cursors, modules, procedures, form-of-use conversions, and assertions, as well as Authorization Identifiers (Authorization IDs, as the term has been used in this book), which provide names for users or, possibly, for sets of privileges associated with modules. The format of an identifier is this:

- It may optionally be preceded by a minus sign followed without a separator by a character set specification. If this specification is omitted, the current default applies, which will be one of the following:

  - That of the module if the identifier is contained in one.

  - That of the schema if the identifier is part of a CREATE SCHEMA sequence that is external to any module.

  - The current default for the session.

- It begins with a character set element. (This may be defined as a syllable or an ideogram as well as a character in the Western sense. For simplicity's sake, the term "character" as used in the remainder of this discussion will have this broad meaning unless otherwise indicated.)

- It is followed by a sequence of characters, digits, and/or underscores to total not more than 128. The underscores are traditionally used in place of spaces to separate words, because spaces and other SQL separators are disallowed in the bodies of regular identifiers.

- In a strict interpretation of Entry SQL92, identifiers can only consist of uppercase letters and numerals. Virtually all products disregard this, and, in our examples, we have as well so as to clearly distinguish identifiers from keywords, which are ALL CAPS by widespread convention.

If you do want to use spaces, you can use a delimited identifier. This is an identifier enclosed in double quotes ("). The double quotes distinguish it from string literals, which are enclosed in single quotes ('). Being written twice in succession represents either single or double quotes within the delimited identifier. In other words, within the identifier, a double quote would be "" and a single quote ''. Otherwise, these symbols will be interpreted as delimiters and probably produce a syntax error. Neither regular identifiers nor the delimited text of delimited identifiers may be identical to any SQL keywords (case ignored). The standard has, however, explicitly stated its intention to avoid having keywords end in underscores, so, if you wish to use a keyword, append an underscore to it (provided your implementation supports this; it is not required until Full SQL92 conformance). This identifier should be safe for all future SQL standards, keeping your code portable. Otherwise, the words you need to avoid as of SQL92 are listed at the end of this appendix.

Identifiers that provide names for objects may be qualified. Objects are arranged hierarchically, and identifiers for them need only be unique within the containing object (for example, columns within tables, domains and tables within schemata, and so on). Since there is usually a default at work, the containing objects often need not be specified. Any time a reference in a SQL statement is ambiguous, however, an object name identifier (object ID) may be qualified by the object IDs of its containing object(s), with the individual identifiers separated by periods (.), not separators. For example, a column name could be qualified as

```
table name.column name
```

or, for that matter

```
catalog name.schema name.table name.column name
```

The outermost level—the cluster name—should never need to be specified, as only one cluster is visible to a particular SQL session. The catalog and schema names can also be used to qualify the names of any objects that reside within schemata—for example, domains, assertions, character sets, collations, translations, and views. Declared local temporary tables are accessible only from within the module (or emulation thereof) within which they were created and are simply qualified with the keyword MODULE used as though it were a schema name.

If two identifiers are equal, including the default or explicit qualifiers, they indicate the same object or Authorization ID. Two regular identifiers are equal if they contain the same characters regardless of case. Two delimited identifiers are equal if they contain the same characters, converting single and double quotes as indicated above and taking case into account. A regular and a delimited identifier are equal if they contain the same characters, taking case into account, but first converting the regular (but not the delimited) identifier to all uppercase letters. In effect, a delimited identifier that contains lowercase letters can never equal a regular identifier, although it may equal another delimited one. Within the specifications regarding case outlined above, the definition of "equal" regarding character strings is that specified for comparison predicates (see Predicates in Part III).

SQL Keywords

ABSOLUTE, ACTION, ADA, ADD, ALL, ALLOCATE, ALTER, AND, ANY, ARE, AS, ASC, ASSERTION, AT, AUTHORIZATION, AVG, BEGIN, BETWEEN, BIT, BIT_LENGTH, BOTH, BY, C, CASCADE, CASCADED, CASE, CAST, CATALOG, CATALOG_NAME, CHAR, CHAR_LENGTH, CHARACTER, CHARACTER_LENGTH, CHARACTER_SET_CATALOG, CHARACTER_SET_NAME, CHARACTER_SET_SCHEMA, CHECK, CLASS_ORIGIN, CLOSE, COALESCE, COBOL, COLLATE, COLLATION, COLLATION_CATALOG, COLLATION_NAME, COLLATION_SCHEMA, COLUMN, COLUMN_NAME, COMMAND_FUNCTION, COMMIT, COMMITTED, CONDITION_NUMBER, CONNECT, CONNECTION, CONNECTION_NAME, CONSTRAINT, CONSTRAINT_CATALOG, CONSTRAINT_NAME, CONSTRAINT_SCHEMA, CONSTRAINTS, CONTINUE, CONVERT, CORRESPONDING, COUNT, CREATE, CROSS, CURRENT, CURRENT_DATE, CURRENT_TIME, CURRENT_TIMESTAMP, CURRENT_USER, CURSOR, CURSOR_NAME, DATA, DATE, DATETIME_INTERVAL_PRECISION, DATETIME_INTERVAL_CODE, DAY, DEALLOCATE, DEC, DECIMAL, DECLARE, DEFAULT, DEFERRABLE, DEFERRED, DELETE, DESC, DESCRIBE, DESCRIPTOR, DIAGNOSTICS, DISCONNECT, DISTINCT, DOMAIN, DOUBLE, DROP, DYNAMIC_FUNCTION, ELSE, END, END-EXEC, ESCAPE, EXCEPT, EXCEPTION, EXEC, EXECUTE, EXISTS, EXTERNAL, EXTRACT, FALSE, FETCH, FIRST, FLOAT, FOR, FOREIGN, FORTRAN, FOUND, FROM, FULL, GET, GLOBAL, GO, GOTO, GRANT, GROUP, HAVING, HOUR, IDENTITY, IMMEDIATE, IN, INDICATOR, INITIALLY, INNER, INPUT, INSENSITIVE, INSERT,

```
INT, INTEGER, INTERSECT, INTERVAL, INTO, IS, ISOLATION,
JOIN, KEY, LANGUAGE, LAST, LEADING, LEFT, LENGTH, LEVEL,
LIKE, LOCAL, LOWER, MATCH, MAX, MESSAGE_LENGTH,
MESSAGE_OCTET_LENGTH, MESSAGE_TEXT, MIN, MINUTE, MODULE,
MONTH, MORE, MUMPS, NAME, NAMES, NATIONAL, NATURAL, NCHAR,
NEXT, NO, NOT, NULL, NULLABLE, NULLIF, NUMBER, NUMERIC,
OCTET_LENGTH, OF, ON, ONLY, OPEN, OPTION, OR, ORDER, OUTER,
OUTPUT, OVERLAPS, PAD, PARTIAL, PASCAL, PLI, POSITION,
PRECISION, PREPARE, PRESERVE, PRIMARY, PRIOR, PRIVILEGES,
PROCEDURE, PUBLIC, READ, REAL, REFERENCES, RELATIVE,
REPEATABLE, RESTRICT, RETURNED_LENGTH, RETURNED_OCTET_LENGTH,
RETURNED_SQLSTATE, REVOKE, RIGHT, ROLLBACK, ROW_COUNT,
ROWS, SCALE, SCHEMA, SCHEMA_NAME, SCROLL, SECOND, SECTION,
SELECT, SERIALIZABLE, SERVER_NAME, SESSION, SESSION_USER,
SET, SIZE, SMALLINT, SOME, SPACE, SQL, SQLCODE, SQLERROR,
SQLSTATE, SUBCLASS_ORIGIN, SUBSTRING, SUM, SYSTEM_USER,
TABLE, TABLE_NAME, TEMPORARY, THEN, TIME, TIMESTAMP,
TIMEZONE_HOUR, TIMEZONE_MINUTE, TO, TRAILING, TRANSACTION,
TRANSLATE, TRANSLATION, TRIM, TRUE, TYPE, UNCOMMITTED,
UNION, UNIQUE, UNKNOWN, UNNAMED, UPDATE, UPPER, USAGE,
USER, USING, VALUE, VALUES, VARCHAR, VARYING, VIEW, WHEN,
WHENEVER, WHERE, WITH, WORK, WRITE, YEAR, ZONE
```

This list is a lot longer than the equivalent one in SQL89 and doesn't include all our new friends from SQL99. To help implementers and application developers avoid using terms that could turn up as SQL keywords in the next standard, ISO has provided a list of words that have the potential to become keywords. Naturally, the ISO is not committing itself in advance. Many of the words listed below may not become keywords, and there will certainly be other keywords not in this list. Nonetheless, the list is provided to offer what help it may. The words that are not keywords but are "on alert" are:

```
AFTER, ALIAS, ASYNC, BEFORE, BOOLEAN, BREADTH, COMPLETION,
CALL, CYCLE, DATA, DEPTH, DICTIONARY, EACH, ELSEIF, EQUALS,
GENERAL, IF, IGNORE, LEAVE, LESS, LIMIT, LOOP, MODIFY, NEW,
NONE, OBJECT, OFF, OID, OLD, OPERATION, OPERATORS, OTHERS,
PARAMETERS, PENDANT, PREORDER, PRIVATE, PROTECTED, RECURSIVE,
REF, REFERENCING, REPLACE, RESIGNAL, RETURN, RETURNS, ROLE,
ROUTINE, ROW, SAVEPOINT, SEARCH, SENSITIVE, SEQUENCE, SIGNAL,
SIMILAR, SQLEXCEPTION, SQLWARNING, STRUCTURE, TEST, THERE,
TRIGGER, TYPE, UNDER, VARIABLE, VIRTUAL, VISIBLE, WAIT,
WHILE, WITHOUT
```

In addition to uppercase and lowercase Latin letters and digits, SQL uses or reserves the following symbols:

```
<space> ::= (however defined for the character set)
| newline ::= (however defined for the character set)
| any of the following ::=
" % & ' ( ) * + , - .   / : ; < = > ? [ ] | <> >= <= || ..
```

Appendix E

Upgrade Path from SQL92 to Core SQL99

The appendix details the features of Core SQL99 that were not features of Entry SQL92. It supplements the more conceptual overview of Core given in Part IV, Chapter 2. That presentation focused on the features of Core that were fundamentally new. Much of Core, however, consists of enhancements to existing SQL functionality, and many of those enhancements had been part of the more advanced SQL92 conformance levels anyway. This appendix provides a guide to those enhancements.

Even though SQL92 sports three levels of conformance (Entry, Intermediate, and Full) SQL99 assumes only Entry. Hence, implementers can go straight from Entry SQL92 to Core SQL99, which is exactly what many of them are likely to do. At this point (2000), the functionality in SQL99 may seem more worth the trouble of implementing than the remainder of SQL92, though implementers are free to "cherry pick" the more advanced portions of SQL92 and have, in fact, been doing so for some time. In any case, because much of the functionality of the higher levels of SQL92 is also part of SQL99, the two projects are not mutually exclusive.

SQL99, in fact, has a different philosophy when it comes to conformance, in that such cherry picking is now encouraged, though in a structured rather than ad-hoc fashion. It offers a minimal set of functions called Core SQL, which is a superset of Entry SQL92. Any product that conforms to SQL99 at all must support Core. In addition, there are a variety of enhanced conformance packages, each of which builds on Core with a set of related features. These enhanced packages are listed in Part IV, Chapter 1. Implementers who support Core can choose which enhanced packages they would also like to support. They can support any, all, or none of these packages. Hence, they can cherry pick, but they do so in a standardized structure, rather than arbitrarily. That's the idea anyway. We explain all of this more thoroughly in Part IV, Chapter 1. This appendix specifies what, in addition to the material laid out in Part IV, Chapter 2, is necessary to get from Entry SQL92 to Core SQL99.

Core SQL99 Features

As we mentioned, these features assume Entry SQL92, but no more. The following are the features that must be added to Entry SQL92 to reach SQL99. Many of these are also features of Intermediate or Full SQL92 conformance. The changes fall into the following categories:

- General Rules
- INFORMATION_SCHEMA
- Data Definition
- External Routines
- Datatypes and Value Expressions
- Queries
- Data Manipulation

Let's look at each of these categories in detail.

General Rules

This section lists the most general changes between the standards.

SQL Flagger

Conforming products must provide a SQL flagger. This was also an advanced SQL92 requirement. A SQL flagger is a program that locates and marks non-standard syntax or standard syntax that may be handled in a non-standard way. It checks at some specified level of claimed SQL conformance, such as Entry SQL92 or

Core SQL99. Features that exceed the requirements of claimed conformance at the specified level are flagged as non-standard even if they do, in fact, conform to some other level of the standard. Core SQL99 requires support only for syntax flagging. This differs from the more advanced catalog flagging in that the latter uses the INFORMATION_SCHEMA and verifies whether the code executes as specified in the standard, whereas the former verifies only that the syntax is standard. With syntax-only flagging, the checking of functionality is limited.

Multiple Modules

Core-compliant products must support multiple modules. Multiple module support means that a single session can simultaneously invoke any number of modules, be they directly coded or emulated. This includes a requirement for dynamic linking. Hence, SQL will be able to dynamically link with and invoke remote programs. Keep in mind that modules also specify the semantics of Embedded or Dynamic SQL, so we are really talking about the remote invocation of multiple compilation units. For more on modules, see Appendix B.

The implication for application development is that you must avoid certain kinds of clashes between modules that may be dynamically linked. Specifically, you must make sure that dynamically generated object names are unique across all modules or embedded SQL emulations thereof. An easy way to achieve this is by using a prefix or suffix common to all objects, declared or allocated, in a given module. The objects you must be concerned with include allocated cursors, prepared statements, and descriptor areas.

More Liberal Identifier Conventions

Identifiers, such as table names, can take lowercase characters. In most products, such was always the case anyway. In this book, for example, we have assumed that identifiers can take lowercase characters, so as to distinguish more clearly between identifiers and keywords. But Core SQL99 requires this functionality. The previous identifier conventions are given in Appendix D.

Trailing underscores are permitted and encouraged in identifiers. A trailing underscore is expected to be safe for identifiers.

The idea is that no SQL keywords in present or future versions of the standard will so terminate, so identifiers that end this way will never clash with future reserved words.

More Liberal Syntax Conventions

Some syntax requirements have become more flexible, primarily to enhance compatibility with various products. These are the new requirements:

- You can optionally specify the noiseword AS before a correlation variable. Example: `FROM Salespeople AS s`, as an alternative to `FROM Salespeople s`.

- You can use the noiseword TABLE before the table specification in a GRANT statement. Example: `GRANT SELECT ON TABLE Salespeople`, as an alternative to `GRANT SELECT ON Salespeople`.

- You can use the noiseword FROM following FETCH in a FETCH statement. Example: `FETCH FROM daytotals`, as an alternative to `FETCH daytotals`.

- You can optionally omit the keyword WORK from the COMMIT WORK and ROLLBACK WORK statements. Example: `COMMIT`, as an alternative to `COMMIT WORK`.

INFORMATION_SCHEMA

The INFORMATION_SCHEMA, or system catalog tables, provide a common interface to query object definitions in a complying DBMS. The SQL92 INFORMATION_SCHEMA is not required for Entry-level conformance, but parts of it are required for Core. Those parts include the following tables: TABLES, VIEWS, COLUMNS, TABLE_CONSTRAINTS, REFERENTIAL_ CONSTRAINTS, CHECK_ CONSTRAINTS, CHARACTER_SETS, INFORMATION_SCHEMA_ CATALOG_NAME, and SQL_LANGUAGES.

DOCUMENTATION_SCHEMA is a second system table schema that is intended to describe what sort of SQL conformance the DBMS provides. This part of Core SQL99 is not part of SQL92 at any level of conformance. It consists of the following tables: SQL_FEATURES and SQL_SIZING. Here are the definitions of

these two tables (for an explanation of the syntax of the CREATE
SCHEMA statement, see CREATE SCHEMA in Part II):

```
CREATE TABLE SQL_FEATURES
     (FEATURE_ID INFORMATION_SCHEMA.CHARACTER_DATA,
      FEATURE_NAME INFORMATION_SCHEMA.CHARACTER_DATA
         CONSTRAINT SQL_FEATURES_FEATURE_NAME_NOT_NULL NOT
→ NULL,
         -- Zero for SUB_FEATURE_ID indicates a feature or a
→ package
         SUB_FEATURE_ID INFORMATION_SCHEMA.CHARACTER_DATA,
         -- Zero-length string for SUB_FEATURE_NAME indicates
         -- a feature or a package
         SUB_FEATURE_NAME INFORMATION_SCHEMA.CHARACTER_DATA
         FEATURE_SUBFEATURE_PACKAGE_CODE INFORMATION_SCHEMA.
→ CHARACTER_DATA

CONSTRAINT_SQL_FEATURES_FEATURE_SUBFEATURE_PACKAGE_CODE_CHECK
           CHECK ( FEATURE_SUBFEATURE_PACKAGE_CODE IN
                 ( 'FEATURE', 'SUBFEATURE', 'PACKAGE' ) ),
         CONSTRAINT SQL_FEATURES_SUB_FEATURE_NAME_NOT_NULL NOT
→ NULL,
      IS_SUPPORTED INFORMATION_SCHEMA.CHARACTER_DATA
         CONSTRAINT SQL_FEATURES_IS_SUPPORTED_NOT_NULL
            NOT NULL
         CONSTRAINT_SQL_FEATURES_IS_SUPPORTED_CHECK
            CHECK ( IS_SUPPORTED IN
                  ( 'YES', 'NO' ) ),
      IS_VERIFIED_BY INFORMATION_SCHEMA.CHARACTER_DATA,
      COMMENTS INFORMATION_SCHEMA.CHARACTER_DATA,
         CONSTRAINT SQL_FEATURES_PRIMARY_KEY
            PRIMARY KEY ( FEATURE_ID, SUB_FEATURE_ID ),
         CONSTRAINT SQL_FEATURES_CHECK_SUPPORTED_VERIFIED
           CHECK ( IS_SUPPORTED = 'YES'
               OR
                 IS_VERIFIED_BY IS NULL )
  );
CREATE TABLE SQL_SIZING
      (SIZING_ID INFORMATION_SCHEMA.CARDINAL_NUMBER,
       SIZING_NAME INFORMATION_SCHEMA.CHARACTER_DATA
         CONSTRAINT SQL_SIZING_SIZING_NAME_NOT_NULL
            NOT NULL,
       -- If SUPPORTED_VALUE in null, that means that
       -- the item being described is not applicable in the
```

```
-- implementation. If SUPPORTED_VALUE is 0 (zero), that
-- means that the item being described has no limit or
-- the limit cannot be determined.
SUPPORTED_VALUE INFORMATION_SCHEMA.CARDINAL_NUMBER,
COMMENTS INFORMATION_SCHEMA.CHARACTER_DATA,
    CONSTRAINT SQL_SIZING_PRIMARY_KEY
       PRIMARY KEY (SIZING_ID)
);
```

Data Definition

The Data Definition Language (DDL) supported syntax has changed only slightly with the addition of a few new statements and added features to a few others.

CREATE SCHEMA Statement

The CREATE SCHEMA statement has been added to DDL, but with only one schema per user. This includes the ability to specify circular references—two tables with foreign keys each referencing the other, a single table referencing itself, or some other form of circular reference—and the general capabilities specified for Intermediate SQL92 CREATE SCHEMA. For more information, see CREATE SCHEMA in Part II.

New Rules for Views

Restrictions on grouped views that existed in Entry SQL92 have been removed (since products are free to exceed the standard, this effectively means that functionality that was once optional is now required). A grouped view is a view that uses aggregate functions and the GROUP BY or HAVING clauses. For more on grouped views, see CREATE VIEW and SELECT in Part II. The restrictions now removed include the following:

- You could not use grouped views or queries specifying GROUP BY in subqueries that were part of expressions defined with comparison predicates.

- If a grouped view were referenced in the FROM clause of a query, that query could not itself use aggregate functions.

- A grouped view could not be used in a join. If a FROM clause referenced a grouped view, that view had to be the only table referenced in that clause.

Grouped views can be operated on just as other views in most respects, though they naturally are still not updatable.

The use of the UNION clause in views is supported. See SELECT in Part II.

Finally, views that contain subqueries are updatable in Core. For more on the updatability of views, see CREATE VIEW in Part II.

Additions to Existing DDL Statements

The following features have been added to existing DDL statements:

- ALTER TABLE ADD COLUMN (but not DROP COLUMN). This is described under ALTER TABLE in Part II.

- DROP TABLE ... RESTRICT. This is described under DROP TABLE in Part II.

- DROP VIEW ... RESTRICT. This is described under DROP VIEW in Part II.

- REVOKE ... RESTRICT, except for CASCADE option. This is described under REVOKE in Part II.

- PRIMARY KEY or UNIQUE implies NOT NULL, so that the NOT NULL constraint in addition to the PRIMARY KEY or the UNIQUE constraint is unnecessary. For UNIQUE especially, implementations may choose to disregard this as an extension, because there are arguments for allowing NULLs in UNIQUE columns and because allowing such is a feature of some enhanced SQL99 packages. For more information on these constraints, see CREATE TABLE in Part II, and Constraints in Part III.

- The columns in a FOREIGN KEY constraint do not have to be named in the same order as they were in the parent key it references. For more information on these columns, see CREATE TABLE in Part II, and Constraints in Part III.

- The columns in a FOREIGN KEY constraint need not be of the exact same datatype as the columns in the parent key they reference. They only have to be convertible as specified under

Cast Expressions in Part III. See also CREATE TABLE in Part II, and Constraints in Part III.

- Constraints are named, either explicitly or by default. See Constraints in Part III.

Changes to Cursors

Core supports holdable cursors. This means that the cursor can remain open between transactions. The syntax to achieve this is the keywords WITH HOLD at the end of the DECLARE or ALLO-CATE CURSOR statement. This was not part of SQL92 at any level. Here is an example:

```
DECLARE Salescursor
     WITH HOLD
     CURSOR FOR
     SELECT snum, sname, city, comm
          FROM Salespeople;
```

This cursor can remain open between transactions. However, even if it is opened and positioned on a row (i.e., it has been FETCHed at least once), it must be FETCHed again in the new transaction before any UPDATE or DELETE statements can be executed on it. If WITH HOLD is not specified, cursors are closed automatically whenever a transaction terminates.

For more information on cursors, see ALLOCATE CURSOR, DECLARE CURSOR, and OPEN in Part II. For more on transactions, see SET TRANSACTION in Part II.

Core also supports READ ONLY and UPDATABLE cursors. For more information on these, see DECLARE CURSOR in Part II.

External Routines

External routines are routines written in other languages but invoked from SQL. They are explained in Part IV, Chapter 2. The following restrictions on them apply for Core:

- The invoked routines cannot be overloaded. This means that there cannot be more than one routine with the same fully qualified name. Since implementations can exceed the standard, this actually means such functionality is not required, rather than being disallowed.

- The invoked routines need not be able to support an application-specified PATH. How the PATH is determined is implementation-defined.

Datatypes and Value Expressions

The biggest new features in this area are distinct user-defined datatypes (UDTs) and Large Objects (LOBs). Both are explained in Part IV, Chapter 2. There are also several minor improvements, described in this section.

LOB Support

To summarize, the features of LOBs that are part of Core consist of the Basic Object Support level, which is explained in Part IV, Chapter 2. These include the following:

- Both the BLOB (Binary Large Object) and CLOB (Character Large Object) datatypes.

- Support for the LENGTH and SUBSTRING functions on these datatypes.

- Concatenation of LOBs.

- Non-holdable locators for LOBs.

- The POSITION function for LOBs. POSITION for conventional strings is part of SQL92 and is described under Numeric Value Functions in Part III. Although POSITION operates on strings, including LOBs, its output is a number, so it is considered a numeric function.

UDT Support

This support includes everything indicated in Part IV, Chapter 2.

Datetime Features

Core includes the following datetime features:

- DATE, TIME, and TIMESTAMP datatypes.

- DATETIME literals.

- CURRENT_DATE, CURRENT_TIME, and CURRENT_TIMESTAMP. For more information on these, see Datetime Value Functions in Part III.

- CAST operations on DATETIME datatypes. For more information on these, see Cast Expressions in Part III.

- Comparisons of DATETIME values.

All of the above features are described in Datatypes in Part III, save where indicated. The following datetime features are *not* included:

- User-defined precision

- EXTRACT function

- INTERVAL datatype and associated operations

- DATETIME arithmetic

- OVERLAPS predicate

- TIMEZONE

VARCHAR Datatype

The VARCHAR (also known as CHARACTER VARYING or CHAR VARYING) datatype is supported with the implementation-defined possibility of an error if a zero-length character string arises. For more on VARCHAR, see Datatypes in Part III.

CAST Expressions

The following CAST expressions have been included:

- Implicit CAST operations of numeric and text datatypes

- Explicit CAST operations

CAST expressions are used to convert values from one datatype to another. For more information on CAST expressions, see Cast Expressions in Part III.

CASE (Conditional) Expressions

Core includes support for CASE expressions. These are explained in Case Expressions in Part III. Support includes the NULLIF and COALESCE variations.

String Value Functions

The following string value functions (see String Value Functions in Part III) are included:

- UPPER

- LOWER

- SUBSTRING (on CHAR and VARCHAR, not binary, datatypes)

- TRIM, with the implementation-defined possibility of an exception if the result is a zero-length string

The POSITION, CHAR_LENGTH, and OCTET_LENGTH Functions

POSITION, CHAR_LENGTH, and OCTET_LENGTH are functions that operate on strings, which in Core can include LOBs. Although they operate on strings, their results are numbers, so they are considered numeric functions and are explained in Numeric Value Functions in Part III.

Scalar Subqueries As Value Expressions

Scalar subqueries may be used anywhere that a value expression may, for example, among the output columns of a SELECT clause or as a value to be used in an UPDATE statement. Scalar subqueries are subqueries guaranteed to produce a single value. For more information, see Subqueries and Value Expressions in Part III.

New Uses of Default Values

The word DEFAULT in a row value constructor indicates a default value. You would use this, for example, in an INSERT statement to specify that the default for the column or domain was to be inserted. For more information, see CREATE DOMAIN and CREATE TABLE in Part II and Row and Table Value Constructors in Part III.

Similarly, you can use the keyword DEFAULT in an UPDATE statement to UPDATE to a default value.

Column definitions can now include the following (previously excluded) defaults:

- DATETIME value functions. For more on these, see Datetime Value Functions in Part III.

- USER value functions. For more on these, see Value Expressions in Part III.

Value Expressions in ORDER BY

Value expressions are allowed in the ORDER BY clause of queries (see SELECT in Part II and Value Expressions in Part III). Previously, only support for references to values directly taken from columns was required. The idea is that you can use a value expression in the SELECT clause and restate it in the ORDER BY clause, which will cause the output to be ordered by the value of that expression. The value expression used in ORDER BY must contain a column reference.

Value Expressions in the IS NULL Predicate

The IS NULL predicate can test any value expression, rather than just column references, for the presence of NULL values. For more on the IS NULL predicate, see Predicates in Part III.

Queries

Changes in the support of queries (SELECT statements) include the addition of some operators and the removal of certain restrictions, as indicated below.

Join Operators

Core supports the following join operators in a SELECT statement:

- INNER JOIN. Core does not require support for the keyword INNER, which, in this context, is a noiseword anyway.

- LEFT OUTER JOIN.

- RIGHT OUTER JOIN.

Core does not support the following join operators in a SELECT statement:

- FULL OUTER JOIN

- NATURAL JOIN

- CROSS JOIN

- UNION JOIN

For more on these join operators, see SELECT in Part II.

The EXCEPT Clause

In addition to the UNION clause used to combine queries, Core supports EXCEPT with both the ALL and DISTINCT arguments. For more on EXCEPT, see SELECT in Part II.

Core does not support the CORRESPONDING option or INTERSECT.

Qualified Asterisk

A qualified * is allowed in the SELECT clause of a query or sub-query. The use of this is explained under SELECT in Part II.

IS NULL Can Test Rows

The IS NULL predicate can be used to test entire rows given by row value constructors. The semantics of this for partially NULL rows are a bit complicated and are given in Predicates in Part III.

Subqueries May Use UNION and EXCEPT

Entry SQL92 did not require support for combining queries within subqueries. Core does. For more information on how this is done, see Subqueries in Part III.

New Rules for GROUP BY and ORDER BY

Restrictions on the GROUP BY clause have been loosened. Specifically, GROUP BY need not include all of the non-aggregated columns in the SELECT clause and both GROUP BY and ORDER BY can include columns that are not present in the SELECT clause at all.

Data Manipulation

Changes in the area of data manipulation include multiple row insertion and transaction management changes, as indicated below.

Multiple Row Insertion in INSERT

The VALUES clause of INSERT statements can insert multiple rows at once by using row value constructors. For more information, see INSERT in Part II, and Row and Table Value Constructors in Part III.

Transaction Management Changes

Core supports the SET TRANSACTION statement. However, the only isolation level required is SERIALIZABLE. READ WRITE and READ ONLY transactions are supported, as is the specification of a DIAGNOSTICS SIZE. For more on transactions, see SET TRANSACTION in Part II.

Appendix F

Error Codes

- SQLCODE
- SQLSTATE

This appendix describes the standard codes used for SQLSTATE and SQLCODE, which are status parameters or variables (depending on the context) that return information about the execution of the previous statement. (Note that SQLCODE is deprecated as of SQL92; see Appendix E.) These codes are stored in the diagnostics area after each statement, possibly supplemented by implementation-defined codes. The diagnostics area contains an implementation-defined number of error codes, all related to the immediately preceding statement. The first code in the diagnostics area will be the same as the one returned by SQLCODE or SQLSTATE. Subsequent codes are implementation-defined or correspond to multiple standard error messages produced by the same statement. Embedded and Dynamic SQL provide programmatic access to SQLCODE and SQLSTATE.

SQLCODE

The standard values of SQLCODE (SQLCOD in Fortran) are as follows:

- A value of 0 indicates successful completion.

- A value of 100 indicates that the statement produced no error but also had no effect, meaning it found no data to operate on. Examples would be a SELECT whose predicate was never satisfied, a FETCH from a cursor whose rows all had been fetched previously, a DELETE or UPDATE that found no row to change, and so on. This value will cause the NOT FOUND condition to become TRUE. This condition may be examined in a WHENEVER statement and may affect the control flow of the program. The SQLSTATE equivalent is '02'—no data.

- Any negative number indicates an error. In implementations, specific negative numbers map to specific errors, but there is no standardization here (this is why SQLCODE has been deprecated).

SQLSTATE

SQLSTATE is a five-character code with an implementation-defined character set consisting of digits and uppercase letters. It has two parts: the first two digits are the class, and the other three are the subclass. SQL92 provides standard classes and also reserves name space for implementation-defined classes. The standard classes can have standard or implementation-defined subclasses. If the class describes the error adequately, the subclass may be effectively omitted. "No subclass" is indicated with a subclass value of '000'. Standard classes begin with any of the following characters:

'0', '1', '2', '3', '4', 'A', 'B', 'C', 'D', 'E', 'F', 'G', 'H'

Subclasses within standard classes that begin with any of those characters are also standard. Other subclasses are implementation-defined. The following characters are reserved for implementation-defined classes:

'5', '6', '7', '8', '9' 'I', 'J', 'K', 'L', 'M', 'N', 'O', 'P', 'Q', 'R', 'S', 'T', 'U', 'V', 'W', 'X', 'Y', 'Z'

The standard classes and subclasses are described in Table F.1.

TABLE F.1: Standard Class and Subclass Values for SQLSTATE

Class	Condition	Subclass	Subcondition
00	successful completion	000	(no subclass)
01	warning	000	(no subclass)
		001	cursor operation conflict
		002	disconnect error
		003	null value eliminated in set function
		004	string data, right truncation
		005	insufficient item descriptor areas
		006	privilege not revoked
		007	privilege not granted
		008	implicit zero-bit padding
		009	search condition too long for information schema
		00A	query expression too long for information schema
02	no data	000	(no subclass)
07	Dynamic SQL error	000	(no subclass)
		001	using clause does not match dynamic parameters
		002	using clause does not match target specifications
		003	cursor specification cannot be executed
		004	using clause required for dynamic parameters

Continued on next page

TABLE F.1: Standard Class and Subclass Values for SQLSTATE (continued)

Class	Condition	Subclass	Subcondition
07	Dynamic SQL error	005	prepared statement not a cursor specification
		006	restricted data type attribute violation
		007	using clause required for result fields
		008	invalid descriptor count
		009	invalid descriptor index
08	connection exception	000	(no subclass)
		001	SQL-client unable to establish SQL-connection
		002	connection name in use
		003	connection does not exist
		004	SQL-server rejected establishment of SQL-connection
		006	connection failure
		007	transaction resolution unknown
0A	feature not supported	000	(no subclass)
		001	multiple server transactions
21	cardinality violation	000	(no subclass)
22	data exception	000	(no subclass)
		001	string data, right truncation
		002	null value, no indicator
		003	numeric value out of range

Continued on next page

TABLE F.1: Standard Class and Subclass Values for SQLSTATE (continued)

Class	Condition	Subclass	Subcondition
22	data exception	005	error in assignment
		007	invalid datetime format
		008	datetime field overflow
		009	invalid time zone displacement value
		011	substring error
		012	division by zero
		015	interval field overflow
		018	invalid character value for cast
		019	invalid escape character
		021	character not in repertoire
		022	indicator overflow
		023	invalid parameter value
		024	unterminated C string
		025	invalid escape sequence
		026	string data, length mismatch
		027	trim error
23	integrity constraint violation	000	(no subclass)
24	invalid cursor state	000	(no subclass)
25	invalid transaction state	000	(no subclass)
26	invalid SQL statement name	000	(no subclass)
27	triggered data change violation	000	(no subclass)
28	invalid authorization specification	000	(no subclass)

Continued on next page

TABLE F.1: Standard Class and Subclass Values for SQLSTATE (continued)

Class	Condition	Subclass	Subcondition
2A	syntax error or access rule violation in direct SQL statement	000	(no subclass)
2B	dependent privilege descriptors still exist	000	(no subclass)
2C	invalid character set name	000	(no subclass)
2D	invalid transaction termination	000	(no subclass)
2E	invalid connection name	000	(no subclass)
33	invalid SQL descriptor name	000	(no subclass)
34	invalid cursor name	000	(no subclass)
35	invalid condition number	000	(no subclass)
37	syntax error or access rule violation in Dynamic SQL statement	000	(no subclass)
3C	ambiguous cursor name	000	(no subclass)
3D	invalid catalog name	000	(no subclass)
3F	invalid schema name	000	(no subclass)
40	transaction rollback	000	(no subclass)
		001	serialization failure
		002	integrity constraint violation
		003	statement completion unknown
42	syntax error or access rule violation	000	(no subclass)
44	with check option violation	000	(no subclass)
HZ	remote database access	N/A	(See ISO/IEC 9579-2 for the definition of protocol subconditions and subclass code values.)

Appendix G

Glossary

Numerals

3VL   See *three-valued logic*.

4GL   See *fourth-generation language*.

A

aggregate functions   Functions that return single values from groups of values, for example, SUM, MIN, COUNT. In the official SQL92 standard, these are called *set functions*.

ANSI   The American National Standards Institute. Major definer of standards in the United States and major influence on the SQL standard.

atomic   Single-valued; cannot be meaningfully subdivided.

attribute   More formal name for *column*.

Authorization ID   The identifier of an issuer of SQL statements and of a body of privileges. May be a user or a module. The owner of a SQL schema and its contents.

B

base table   A table that contains data not derived from that in any other table (see also *derived table*).

binding style   Applications may either directly use groups of SQL procedures known as *modules*, which are called as subprograms from another language, or use SQL statements embedded in the source code of another language to emulate the effect of modules. Which of these approaches is chosen is called the *binding style*; the first binding style is called the *module language*, and the second is called *Embedded SQL*. For the purpose of determining the binding style, Dynamic SQL can be regarded as a variation on Embedded SQL.

bit string   Binary data. Most commonly represented as zeros and ones or in hexadecimal form (see *hexadecimal*).

BLOB   Binary Large Object. Essentially, a long bit string used for complex data, such as sound or graphics.

Boolean expression   Normally, an expression that can be TRUE or FALSE. In SQL, an expression that can be TRUE, FALSE, or UNKNOWN. Named for 19th-century English mathematician George Boole (see also *three-value logic*).

C

candidate row or tuple   A row subject to test by some predicate. A row that may be selected or updated depending on whether it passes the test.

cardinality   The number of columns in a row or table.

Cartesian product   A product of two or more sets that consists of all combinations of elements drawn one from each set. The underlying operation in SQL joins, wherein such combinations are derived and then tested against predicates. Named for Rene Descartes.

catalog   In the SQL92 standard, a group of schemas treated as an object. In some database products, the set of tables that define the structure of the database (see also *INFORMATION_SCHEMA*).

character repertoire   The characters that can be represented by a character set.

character set   A set of characters for character datatypes. Includes the characters to be represented (the character repertoire), the encodings used to represent them internally (the form-of-use), and the sorting order imposed on them (the collating sequence).

clause   A functional subunit of a statement. A portion of a statement that is complete enough for its effects on the statement to be understood.

client/server architecture   A configuration of computers on a network such that computing tasks are specialized—several computers (*clients*) interface to users while specialized operations are performed on another (typically smaller) group of one or more computers called *servers*. Clients to perform operations on data stored in servers typically use SQL. Internet and intranet systems can also be considered client/server architectures.

closure   The property that the fundamental structure in which the data is stored is the same structure that it retains in its final state (that is, queries operate on tables and produce tables) and the structure in which it can be described (the INFORMATION_SCHEMA).

cluster   In the SQL92 and later, a collection of catalogs. In some products, a cluster is an object created primarily for optimization purposes. Foreign keys and the parent keys they reference are stored together in a single structure so that joins execute more efficiently. Once created, these clusters are transparent to most SQL operations, save for their effect on performance.

collating sequence   An order imposed on a character set so that the characters can be sorted, that is, evaluated in terms of inequalities such as < and > =. Ideally, the collating sequence corresponds to something intelligible, such as alphabetical ordering.

collation   A database object that specifies a collating sequence.

column   Also called an *attribute* or a *field*. A set of corresponding values in a table's rows, all having the same datatypes and constraints. Represented as a vertical alignment when the table is pictured.

compilation unit   A body of executable code that is treated as a unit for the purposes of determining the scope of SQL statements and objects and of passing values between the DBMS and the application. Products may implement the standard by having SQL compilation units emulate the behavior of modules, although a single compilation unit may emulate several modules and vice versa.

composite key   A key—whether primary, unique, or foreign— consisting of more than one column. A concatenated key.

concatenated key   See *composite key*.

concurrency   Operations performed by different users that simultaneously access the same data.

constraint   A test that data cannot fail or it will be rejected. For more information, see Constraints in Part III.

cursor   An object used to store the output of a query for row-by-row processing by the application.

D

database   A structured body of information stored persistently. *Persistently* means that the data survives the termination of the session or application that generated it. There are several kinds of databases: relational, object-oriented, network, and hierarchical, for example. This book is primarily concerned with relational databases, since these are the industry standard and what SQL is designed for.

DBA (database administrator)   A database user who is in charge of installing, configuring, and running the DBMS. The equivalent of a system or network administrator, but for databases. Also in some systems, a privilege or role gives superuser authority for the purpose of performing the functions of the DBA.

DBMS   Database management system. A program that controls and encapsulates all access to data. These are sometimes now called *database servers*.

deadlock   A situation where none of two or more concurrent transactions can proceed because they have locks on the data that interfere with one another. Generally speaking, the DBMS will detect and resolve this automatically, but details will vary with each DBMS.

DEFINITION_SCHEMA   The set of base tables on which the INFORMATION_ SCHEMA is based. Not likely to actually exist. The DEFINITION_SCHEMA is supposed to be accessible only through the INFORMATION_ SCHEMA, and so long as the latter behaves as though a proper DEFINITION_SCHEMA were present, anything goes.

degree   The number of rows in a table.

denormalization   The opposite of *normalization*. Often, normalization breaks the data down into so many separate tables that it is difficult and inefficient to manage, so you denormalize to simplify the schema.

deprecated   Grudgingly supported. Supported by the current ISO standard to retain compatibility with earlier standards, but likely to be dropped in the future. Generally, a feature that is deprecated in one version of the standard will be omitted from the next version. For example, SQLCODE is deprecated in SQL92 and omitted from SQL99 (except in Annex E, Incompatibilities with ISO/IEC 9075:1992).

derived table   A table produced by extracting or deriving values from other tables. Technically, the output of every query is a derived table, but they may also be defined and treated as objects, in which case they are views, or they may be created within the FROM clauses of queries.

descriptor area   An allocated area of memory where descriptive information about the input or output parameters of dynamically generated statements is stored. The input or output of the statements may also be stored directly in the descriptor areas.

diagnostics area   An allocated area of memory where error messages are stored.

domain   An object that can be used as an alternative to a datatype in specifying a column. The domain will specify the datatype and may also define other things, such as a default value and one or more constraints. In theory, a domain denotes a logical category of values that are comparable, although this is not enforced in the standard.

dyadic   Taking two operands; for example, 2 + 2.

Dynamic SQL   SQL as used in applications that must be able to generate SQL code at runtime.

E

Embedded SQL   SQL code embedded into the source code of another language.

equijoin   A join that compares values in the joined column(s) and retrieves those row combinations that make the values equal.

F

field   An alternative name for *column*. Historically, the term is derived from the system of disk organization used in early databases. See also *record*.

flag   As used in this book, *flag* means some implementation-defined mark in the source code of an application that indicates whether a SQL statement conforms to the SQL92 standard at a specified level.

flagger   The program that puts the flags in the source code.

foreign key   A group of one or more columns in a table whose values must also be present in another group of one or more columns (the parent key) for the sake of the relational structure. The latter group of columns must be prohibited by a constraint from containing duplicate rows. This book uses the terms *foreign key* and *parent key*, rather than the standard *referencing key* and *referenced key*, for the sake of clarity.

form-of-use   The format of the encodings used internally to represent a character repertoire.

fourth-generation language (4GL)   A language that specifies the results of operations rather than procedures to achieve these results. In this sense, SQL is a fourth-generation language, but SQL is not a complete enough language in which to develop applications. As used in the database world, the term generally refers to nonprocedural application-development languages that use SQL to interface with the database. 4GLs are not standardized but vary from product to product.

G

generally underlying tables   All of the tables referenced in the FROM clause of a query, plus all the tables that those tables reference, all the way down to the base tables that contain the data, which are called the *leaf underlying tables*.

H

hexadecimal   A base-16 numbering system used as a more concise expression of binary data.

hierarchical database   A database wherein the data is structured in a hierarchy also called a *tree*. Very problematic for modeling many-to-many relationships. An older approach.

host language   A language used to develop an application that uses Embedded or Dynamic SQL or that calls procedures contained in a module.

host variable   A variable in the host language.

I

implementation-defined   Describes an area where the product implementing the standard is free to behave as it likes, but its behavior must be consistent and documented.

implementation-dependent   Describes an area where product implementing the standard is free to behave as it likes and need not document its behavior or ensure its consistency.

index   An object not specified in the standard but almost universally used, an index is an ordered list of single or grouped column values that stores the disk locations of the rows containing those values. Used to make processing more efficient and sometimes to ensure uniqueness (see *unique index*).

indicator parameter   A numeric parameter appended to another parameter whenever the latter might contain a SQL NULL. NULLs in the SQL sense are not used in most languages, so you use indicators to process them properly. Can also be used to insert NULLs or to indicate string truncation. Indicator parameters are used in the module language binding style.

indicator variable   A numeric variable appended to another variable whenever the latter might contain a SQL NULL. NULLs in the SQL sense are not used in most languages, so you use indicators to process them properly. Can also be used to insert NULLs or to indicate string truncation. Indicator variables are used in the Embedded SQL binding style.

INFORMATION_SCHEMA   A set of views that defines the objects in the database and provides fundamental information about them. Since it is a (theoretically derived) set of tables, the INFORMATION_ SCHEMA can be accessed with the same statements you use to access other tables. It cannot, however, be directly updated. The system changes its content automatically to reflect current conditions.

interval   A period of time between two dates or times. When capitalized, refers to the corresponding SQL datatype.

ISO   The International Organization for Standardization. Publisher of SQL92, SQL99, and many other standards.

isolation level   The extent to which a transaction is affected by the actions of other transactions on the same data.

J

join   A combination of two or more tables achieved by finding every combination of rows possible, taking one row from each table joined (a Cartesian product). Normally, only combinations that meet certain criteria are selected, and most often the key criterion is a match between the values in the columns of one of the tables and the values of the other(s) (such a join is called an *equi-join*). The tables joined need not be distinct (see *self-join*).

L

leading blanks Blank spaces, however that character is defined for a given character set, at the beginning of a text string.

leading significant digits The leftmost digits of a number.

leaf underlying tables Views are tables that are based on data in other tables, which may also be views. Eventually, however, views must directly or indirectly reference some set of base tables that actually do contain data (circular referencing in views is prohibited). If you think of any view as the root of a tree and think of the objects it references as its branch nodes, you will see that you must eventually reach the leaf nodes, which correspond exactly to the leaf underlying tables. You also could call them the *underlying base tables*. On the same principle, one may speak of the leaf underlying tables of any derived table, such as the derived tables created by explicit joins or by subqueries.

literal A value expression that represents itself, rather than a variable, parameter, value function, column reference, or other value expression that indicates a value indirectly. In SQL92, literals are often preceded by datatype specifications (see Datatypes in Part III).

lock A mechanism that prevents concurrent operations from interfering with each other.

M

metadata Data that describes the data. In other words, the content of the INFORMATION_SCHEMA.

middleware A software module that lies between the user and the database or the server. What is middleware can depend on the context. A Web server is itself a kind of server, of course, but it may also function as middleware to a database server. Some products are designed to be middleware between Web servers and database servers.

module A set of SQL procedures that is called by another program. In SQL 92 and after, a module may possess an Authorization ID and thus have privileges.

module language   The paradigm used in the standard to describe the semantics of SQL. Either Static or Dynamic SQL emulates the behavior of modules of SQL procedures called as subprograms by a program written in another language. These modules need not be actually implemented as such. Implementations have the option of allowing application developers to directly create modules. If this is done, the modules should conform to the syntactic conventions that the standard specifies, which are collectively referred to as the module language.

monadic   Taking one operand. For example, TRIM(' hello '), which removes the leading and trailing blanks from the contained string.

multicolumn key   See *composite key*.

N

network database   A database founded on a graph structure, where items of data point to other items. An older approach that evolved from the hierarchical database structure, but it has pretty much been suspended by the relational model.

noiseword   Also called *syntactic sugar*, this is a word in the SQL syntax that has no effect on the functioning of the statement and is simply provided to make the statement more intelligible to humans.

normal form   Any of a number of stages in the process of normalization.

normalization   The process of analyzing the data to be represented and breaking it down into separate tables in accordance with the principles of relational structure.

NULL   A marker used in SQL to indicate that a value is missing or unknown. Differs from zeros, blanks, and other neutral or default values in that it produces a Boolean value of UNKNOWN when used in most comparisons (see *three-valued logic*).

nullable   May possibly contain NULLs.

O

object   As used in SQL, an entity in the database having a persistent identity, for example, tables, domains, schemata, collations, and assertions. This usage does not correspond to the definition of object specified by object-oriented programming.

object-oriented   An approach to computer programming that is integrated with SQL in the SQL99 standard. In this approach, a computer program and its data are modeled as a group of autonomous objects that respond to messages sent by one object to another. The internal structure and processes of each object are, in principle, invisible to other objects, although products and philosophies vary in the extent to which they enforce this.

octet   A sequence of eight bits. Strikingly similar to what many call a byte.

OODB   Object-oriented database system. A DBMS based on the object-oriented model. The idea is to extend the capabilities of object-oriented languages like C++ and Java by adding persistent data, which, to be consistent with those languages, should be in the form of objects. SQL99 provides an approach to integrating OODBs with relational DBMSs.

outer reference   A reference in a correlated subquery to a value in some containing query. It forces the correlated subquery to be performed separately for each distinct referenced value and thus to produce different results for different rows of the containing query.

P

parent key   The primary or unique key referenced by a foreign key. This book uses the terms *parent key* and *foreign key*, rather than the standard *referenced key* and *referencing key*, for clarity.

permanent base table   A base table whose data is retained between SQL sessions.

persistent base table   See *permanent base table*.

positioned deletion   A DELETE statement performed on a cursor using a WHERE CURRENT OF clause.

positioned update   An UPDATE statement performed on a cursor using a WHERE CURRENT OF clause.

possibly nondeterministic query   A query whose results could vary depending on factors that are up to the implementation's discretion.

possibly nullable   May possibly contain NULLs. (Synonymous with *nullable*.)

precompiler   A program that examines and processes source code before it is compiled. Used in Embedded SQL to process the SQL statements in the source code.

predicate   An expression that may have a Boolean value of TRUE, FALSE, or UNKNOWN. Predicates are used in certain statements to test values and determine whether the effects of the statement should be applied to a particular use.

preprocessor   See *precompiler*.

primary key   The group of one or more columns used to uniquely identify each row of a base table. Also, the constraint used to enforce that these columns are not nullable and are unique.

Q

query   A statement that extracts information from the database, most often selecting the information based on a predicate. A SELECT statement.

R

RDBMS   Relational database management system. A DBMS (see *DBMS*) that has a relational structure (see *relational database*). In fact, all of the major ones do, and these are the ones to which SQL is applicable, so in this book, RDBMS and DBMS are effectively synonymous.

record   A unit of disk storage usually corresponding to a row of a base table and often used as a synonym for *row*.

referential integrity   A state that a system has when all foreign key references are valid, that is to say, when all foreign key values are present in their parent keys.

relation   A more formal term for table (see *table*).

relational database   A database (see *database*) composed of relations and conforming to a set of principles (called "Codd's 12 Rules" after E. F. Codd, the father of relational database theory) governing how such relations are supposed to behave. There are many database systems that use tables but don't conform to all of the principles. These are often called *semirelational* systems.

row   A sequence of values in a table or view, one value for each column.

S

scalar expression   A scalar value or a value expression involving multiple scalar values.

scalar value   A value that is sortable. This means it can be meaningfully compared to other values of the same or related datatypes in terms of inequalities (< and >). Datatypes whose values are scalar include all numeric types, which are sorted numerically, character string types, which are sorted according to the collation in use, and datetime types, which are sorted according to orientation in time. In theory, a relational database contains only scalar values, but many contemporary databases and SQL99 include BLOBs, which may not be meaningfully sortable, for things like multimedia data.

schema   A named group of related objects, under the control of a single Authorization ID.

schemata   The plural of *schema*. Some of the literature uses the less-formal *schemas*.

scope   The visibility of an object or statement to various processes. Applies to descriptor areas, temporary tables, and prepared statements. Can be *global*, which makes the object or statement visible to all processes within the session, or *local*, which restricts the visibility to the defining module or compilation unit.

searched deletion   A DELETE clause that affects all rows satisfying some predicate.

searched update   An UPDATE clause that affects all rows satisfying some predicate.

self-join   A join of a table to itself. A join is performed between two tables, but there is no requirement that they be distinct. A self-join is performed as a join of two identical tables.

semirelational   A system that represents data in the form of tables but does not conform to all the principles governing relational databases, for example, the principle that the data should be accessible only through a high-level query language like SQL.

separator   A delineator in SQL statements that indicates divisions between parts of statements. Blank spaces and newlines are considered equivalent separators, although these may be implemented differently on different implementations or in different character repertoires. Comments, which are explanatory text beginning with two consecutive minus signs and ending with a newline, are also separators. Any number of subsequent contiguous separators have the same effect as a single separator.

server   See *client/server architecture*.

session   The set of operations performed by a user during a connection. Begins with an explicit or implicit CONNECT statement, and terminates with an explicit or implicit DISCONNECT.

set functions   See *aggregate functions*.

simply underlying tables   The tables directly referenced in the FROM clause of a query including views, or the results of explicit joins or subqueries, but not the tables referenced by the views, joins, or subqueries.

source code   Code written in a programming language that needs to be converted to an executable form.

statement terminator   A special symbol that marks the end of a statement. In Interactive SQL and the module language, the terminator is the semicolon (;). In Embedded SQL, it depends on the host language, and in Dynamic SQL, it is omitted.

status parameters or variables   Parameters or variables that pass information about the execution of the preceding statement. These are, specifically, SQLCODE and SQLSTATE.

string   A sequence of characters or bits.

subquery   A query used within another statement to produce a set of values that are used by the rest of the statement.

T

table   The fundamental data structure of relational databases. A set of values that can be partitioned into rows and columns such that there is one, possibly NULL, value at each intersection of a column and row, and all of the values in a column are of the same datatype. The columns are named, and the rows are identified with unique identifier column values called *primary keys*, unless the table is derived from another table (see also *derived table, primary key*).

target specification   A variable or parameter that is to be assigned a value by a SQL statement. May include an indicator variable or indicator parameter, respectively.

temporary base table   A base table whose data is automatically destroyed at the end of every session or at the end of every transaction.

three-valued logic (3VL)   A variation of Boolean logic used in SQL where expressions may be TRUE, FALSE, or UNKNOWN. UNKNOWN occurs when NULLs are compared to other values or to each other.

trailing blanks   Blank spaces, however those are defined for the character repertoire, filling the rightmost positions in a character string.

transaction   A set of successive statements that succeed or fail as a group so that all effects of the group are retained or all are disregarded.

triadic   Taking three operators; for example, SUBSTRING ('Astarte' FROM 2 FOR 4).

truncation   The disregarding of the rightmost characters, bits, or digits of a data item.

tuple   A more formal term for *row*.

U

underlying query   A query contained in the definition of a cursor or view.

underlying tables   All of the tables referenced in a query, plus all of the tables any of those tables reference, and so on, all the way to the leaf underlying tables that actually contain the data. Synonym for *generally underlying tables*. This term is used most often in reference to queries contained in cursors or views.

unique identifier   Any unique value that identifies an entity; for example, social security numbers. In SQL, the important unique identifiers are object names and primary keys.

unique index   An index that forces values to be unique (see *index*) by allowing only one entry per distinct value.

unique key   A group of one or more columns that should be unique for logical reasons rather than for the needs of the relational structure. Also, the constraint used to enforce such uniqueness, which differs from the primary key constraint in that, in some versions of the standard, it permits NULL values to be entered.

UNKNOWN (Boolean value)   A Boolean value that emerges in SQL from the referencing of NULLs (see *three-valued logic*).

V

viewed tables   See *views*.

views   Tables whose content is derived from other tables with the use of a query. Derived tables with definitions that are persistent in the database.

Note to the Reader: Throughout this index **boldfaced** page numbers indicate primary discussions of a topic.

procedures
in external routines, 273
in module language, **301–304**
in SQL99, 250
programmatic extensions in SQL99,
250–251
PSM (Persistent Stored Modules)
conformance level, 246–247

Q

qualified identifiers, 309
quantified comparison predicates,
220–223
queries, 8, 345
in Core SQL99, **324–325**
as named objects, 249
recursive, **249–250**
subqueries, **234–236**
question marks (?) for parameters,
303

R

RDMSs (relational database
management systems), 345
READ COMMITTED option, 148
read-only cursors, 18
READ ONLY option, 148–149
read-only transactions, 21, 148–149
READ UNCOMMITTED option, 148
READ WRITE option, 148–149
REAL datatype, 191, 204
records, 346. *See also* rows
recursive queries, **249–250**
Reference datatype, **248**
REFERENCES constraint, **176–177**
in CREATE TABLE, 61
in GRANT, 104–106
referential integrity, 6
defined, 346
refinements to, **32–33**
referential triggered actions,
180–182
regular expressions, **250**
relational database management
systems (RDMSs), 345
relational databases, **2–3**, 346
designing, **6–8**
joining tables in, **8–9**
rules and principles in, **4–5**

relations
defined, 346
in relational databases, 4
RELATIVE option, 98
REPEAT statement, 253
REPEATABLE READ option, 148
repertoires for character sets, 50,
335
RESTRICT option
in ALTER TABLE, 43–44
in DROP DOMAIN, 87
in DROP SCHEMA, 88
in DROP TABLE, 89
in DROP VIEW, 90
in REVOKE, 117
RETURNS clause, **276**
REVOKE statement, **114–118**
RIGHT joins, 17, 127, **130**
ROLLBACK statement, 21, **119**
rolled back transactions, 21
row subqueries, 235
row value constructors, **31–32**,
229–231
with MATCH, 225
with OVERLAPS, 227–228
quantified comparison predicates
for, 221
with UNIQUE, 224
rows, 346
deleting, **78–80**
inserting, **107–109**
ordering, **73–74**
in relational databases, 4
retrieving. *See* SELECT statement
Rows datatype in SQL99, 248

S

scalar expressions, 346
scalar subqueries, 235, 323
scalar values, 346
scale of EXACT NUMERIC, 189–190
schema definition statements, **15**
schema names, 57
for constraints, 48
in module language, **301**
schemas, 9, 346
current, **146**
defining, **56–58**
deleting assertions from, **84–85**
destroying, **88**
scope, 347

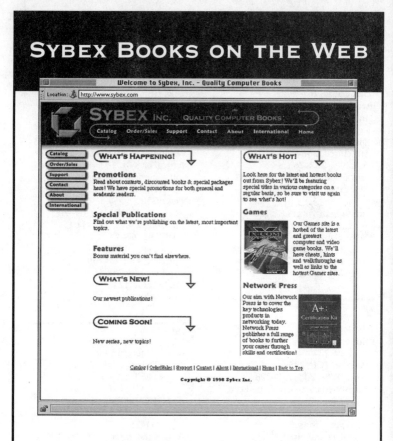

Contents Grouped by Subject (continued)

This section groups the statements and common elements according to their logical function, which will make it easier to find the statement you need to perform a specific task. Once you find the desired statement or element, you can search for it alphabetically in the reference itself.

Setting Up the Session Parameters

CONNECT   Starts a SQL session.

DISCONNECT   Ends a SQL session.

SET CONSTRAINTS MODE   Controls when constraints* are checked.

SET NAMES   Sets name defaults.

SET SCHEMA   Specifies the current schema.*

SET SESSION AUTHORIZATION   Specifies the current session user.

SET TIME ZONE   Specifies the current time zone.

SET TRANSACTION   Prevents or allows changing of data.

Static Coded Applications

CLOSE   Empties a cursor* of data.

DECLARE CURSOR   Creates a cursor.*

OPEN   Readies a cursor* for use.

FETCH   Retrieves rows from cursors.*

Appendix A   Mapping SQL to Other Languages.*

Appendix B   Specification of the Module Language.*